DRESS REGULATIONS FOR THE ARMY 1900

DRESS REGULATIONS
FOR THE ARMY
1900

A reprint of the official War Office publication
*Dress Regulations for the Officers of the Army
(including the Militia)*
originally issued in 1900

DAVID & CHARLES REPRINTS

7153   4709   8

This book was
originally published by
Her Majesty's Stationery Office
in 1900

Reprinted by David & Charles (Publishers) Limited in 1970

Printed in Great Britain by
Latimer Trend & Company Limited Whitstable
for David & Charles (Publishers) Limited
South Devon House Newton Abbot
Devon

38407 / Dress / 141 DRESS REGULATIONS

FOR

THE OFFICERS OF THE ARMY.

(INCLUDING THE MILITIA.)

WAR OFFICE,

1900.

LONDON:
PRINTED FOR HER MAJESTY'S STATIONERY OFFICE,
BY HARRISON AND SONS, ST. MARTIN'S LANE,
PRINTERS IN ORDINARY TO HER MAJESTY.

And to be purchased, either directly or through any Bookseller, from
EYRE & SPOTTISWOODE, EAST HARDING STREET, FLEET STREET, E.C.; or
JOHN MENZIES & Co., 12, HANOVER STREET, EDINBURGH, and
90, WEST NILE STREET, GLASGOW; or
HODGES, FIGGIS, & Co., Limited, 104, GRAFTON STREET, DUBLIN.

Price { Four Shillings and Sixpence, plain.
{ Five Shillings and Sixpence, interleaved.

HER MAJESTY has been graciously pleased to approve the following revised $\frac{61002}{6972}$ "Dress Regulations for the Officers of the Army," and to command that they be strictly observed on all occasions.

General Officers Commanding, and Commanding Officers of units will be held responsible that no deviations from the authorised patterns in the uniform of Officers are permitted in their respective commands.

It is to be clearly understood that no Commanding Officer has any authority to order Officers under his command to provide themselves with any articles or any pattern of articles of Dress or Equipment other than those authorised by Regulation. Commanding Officers will be held personally responsible for the payment of any expense which may be entailed on Officers by their having to replace, or to restore to the authorised pattern, articles which may be found by General Officers to be not in conformity therewith.

Wolseley F.M.

Commander-in-Chief.

WAR OFFICE,
    9th July, 1900.

TABLE OF CONTENTS.

DRESS REGULATIONS

FOR THE OFFICERS OF THE ARMY,

(INCLUDING THE MILITIA),

1900.

GENERAL INSTRUCTIONS.	Pattern.		No. of Plate.
	No.	Sealed.	
1. **Aiguillette.**—The Staff aiguillette is the distinguishing mark of officers serving on the Head Quarter, General and Personal Staff. It is worn by those officers only when performing staff duties, as laid down in the Queen's Regulations, paragraph 1980. For description of aiguillette and method of wearing it, see paragraph 162. The description of aiguillette for Field Marshals, Personal Staff of the Queen and Royal Family, and Household Cavalry is included in the description of their respective uniforms.	311	3.3.97	13
2. **Badges of Rank**—The rank of officers is shown by badges as under :—	500	25.8.98	1

2. **Badges of Rank**—The rank of officers is shown by badges as under :—

Field-Marshal—Crossed batons on a wreath of laurel, with a crown above.
General—Crossed sword and baton, with star and crown above.
Lieutenant-General—Crossed sword and baton, with crown above.
Major-General—Crossed sword and baton, with star above.
Brigadier-General—Crossed sword and baton.
Colonel—Crown and two stars below.
Lieutenant-Colonel—Crown and one star below.
Major—Crown.
Captain—Two stars.
Lieutenant—One star.
Second Lieutenant—No badge.*

Badges of rank, except when otherwise ordered, will be worn on all shoulder cords and shoulder straps. They will be in silver embroidery on shoulder cords, and gold-laced shoulder straps, and gilt or gilding metal on plain cloth shoulder straps. In Rifle Regiments they will be in bronze. The crossed sword is 2 inches full and the baton $\frac{1}{4}$ inch shorter. The crowns when laid on shoulder cords or straps are 1 inch broad and $\frac{7}{8}$ inch in height ; the stars are 1 inch between opposite points.

The batons forming part of the Field Marshal's badges will be in embroidery and crimson velvet.

General Officers' badges are worn in pairs, point of sword to the front and edge of blade outwards or towards the arm.

Regimental Officers having Brevet Rank wear the badges of their army rank ; Departmental Officers having honorary rank, the badges of that rank ; and Departmental Officers not having honorary rank, the badges of the combatant grade with which they rank.

3. **Badges, Special**—A detailed description of all badges is given in Appendix I. No badges of a special character are allowed to be worn, except those authorized by these Regulations.

Collar badges will be fixed with the centre of the badge 2 inches from the opening of the collar.

4. **Boots**—

Mounted Officers—(1.) When on mounted duties.—Except where otherwise specified, knee boots will be worn. The knee boots will be cut with a V at the top in front of the knee ; the height will depend upon the length of the leg and the relative height of the calf. The boot, which is sloped at the back, should reach in front to about 4 inches from the top of the knee and at the back just to the top of the calf. The leg of the boot should be jacked sufficiently to prevent it sinking. A spur rest 2 inches above the top edge of the heel to keep the spur horizontal. (2.) When dismounted.—Wellington boots with boxes for spurs.

Dismounted Officers—Wellington boots in review order and in the evening. Shooting boots in marching and drill order.

	501	6.11.96	
	502	6.11.96	
	502	6.11.96	

5. **Braid, Buttons, &c.**—Unless otherwise specified, loops, frogs, and buttons on the front of tunics, &c., will be at equal distances.

The sizes for the buttons are given in Appendix III.

---

* With this exception, the uniform of 2nd Lieutenants is the same as that for Lieutenants.

B

		Pattern.		No. of Plate.
		No.	Sealed.	
54 Officers 89	**6. Cape Protector**—Brown hog hide leather, $7\frac{1}{2}$ inches by $9\frac{1}{2}$ inches, rounded corners, no straps or buckles. A leather loop $\frac{3}{4}$ inch by $1\frac{1}{4}$ inches sewn on $\frac{1}{2}$ inch from centre of front edge for strap. The cape is attached to the protector by the centre cloak strap.			
	7. Cocked-Hats—Cocked-hats will be of black silk. Dimensions for medium size :—	1	23.8.98	2
	The left side $6\frac{1}{4}$ inches high, the right side $5\frac{3}{4}$ inches ; each corner $4\frac{3}{8}$ inches long.			3
	On the right side, a black silk cockade with a loop fastened by a button ; at each corner, a bullion tassel, consisting (except where otherwise stated) of nine gold bullions and eleven crimson bullions under them, $1\frac{3}{4}$ inches long, exclusive of the head ; midway between the loop and tassel, front and back, a band of $1\frac{3}{4}$-inch black braid of oak-leaf pattern.	2	29.11.98	
	8. Collars and Neckties—The collars of tunics, frock-coats, and jackets will, unless otherwise stated, be cut square at the top in front, and fastened with two hooks and eyes ; a black silk tab sewn on inside. The height is not to exceed 2 inches.*			
A.O. 83 1896 61002 Infantry 149	Collars, white linen, are worn in undress uniform in the 7th Hussars and in the Oxfordshire Light Infantry. With white or khaki frocks they are optional, but all officers of a unit must be dressed alike. The collar is not to show more than $\frac{1}{8}$ inch above the uniform. With mess waistcoats open in front, or kamarbands, collars and black neckties (white in the Oxfordshire Light Infantry) are worn.			
	9. Depth of Skirts—The skirts of tunics for officers 5 feet 9 inches in height will be :— For Field Marshals, General Officers and Colonels on the Staff, Royal Artillery, Royal Engineers, Foot Guards, Infantry Regiments, Army Service Corps, Royal Army Medical Corps and Departments generally—10 inches. For Staff, Cavalry, and Rifle Regiments—9 inches. The skirts of frock coats will be 17 inches deep for all Officers 5 feet 9 inches in height. The proportionate variation for each inch of difference in height is about $\frac{1}{4}$ inch in the skirts of frock coats and $\frac{1}{8}$ inch in the skirts of tunics.			
A.O. 111 1896	**10. Field Caps**—Folding, blue cloth unless otherwise stated, about $4\frac{1}{2}$ inches high, and not less than $3\frac{3}{4}$ inches across the top, crown shaped similar to the glengarry, folding peak in front, flaps at the sides to let down, lower flaps to fasten under the chin when unfolded, when folded they fasten in the front of the cap with two gorget (*or 20-line*) buttons. Crown,	26	2.3.94	9
A.C.D. Patrns. 9174	buttons, and piping of regimental or departmental pattern. Badge, unless otherwise stated, $1\frac{5}{8}$ inches in height, on the left side, $3\frac{1}{2}$ inches from the front, and 1 inch from the top of the cap—measured from the centre of the badge. (See Appendix I.) All mounted Officers may wear a chin-strap.			9
	11. Forage Caps— *Staff pattern.*—Blue cloth—Officers of Rifle Regiments, Rifle green cloth—with three cloth welts, $3\frac{1}{4}$ inches total depth, diameter across the top $8\frac{1}{4}$ inches for a cap fitting $21\frac{3}{4}$ inches in circumference, the top to be $\frac{1}{8}$ inch larger or smaller in diameter for every $\frac{1}{4}$ inch the cap may vary in size of head above or below the before-mentioned standard, *e.g.*, a cap $22\frac{1}{4}$ inches in circumference, diameter across the top $8\frac{1}{2}$ inches ; cap 21 inches in circumference, diameter $7\frac{7}{8}$ inches. The sides to be made in four pieces, and to be $1\frac{1}{2}$ inches deep between the welts ; a cloth band $1\frac{3}{4}$ inches wide placed between the two lower welts. For colour of band, see services in which worn. For badge, *see* Appendix I. The cap set up on a band of stiff leather, or other material, $1\frac{3}{4}$ inches deep.			8
61002 Staff 19	Chin-strap for all officers to be made of black patent leather $\frac{3}{8}$ inch wide, buttoned on to two gorget buttons placed immediately behind the corners of the peak. The peak of the cap will be of the following pattern :—			
	For Field Marshals and General Officers.—Patent leather, and embroidered all round with oak leaves in gold $\frac{3}{4}$ inch wide.	28	14.7.98	8
	For Field Officers.—The same as for General Officers, but embroidered on the front edge only.	31	14.7.98	8
	For other Officers.—Patent leather without embroidery. The peak to droop at an angle of 45 degrees, and to be 2 inches deep in the middle when worn with embroidery, and $1\frac{3}{4}$ inches when plain.	32	5.7.98	8
	Round Forage Caps.—Round forage caps with peaks will, unless otherwise stated, be 3 inches high ; without peaks $2\frac{5}{8}$ inches.	33	13.11.96	8
	12. Frocks, Jackets, and Tunics—Frocks—tartan,‡ serge, or khaki—should be made so that warm clothing can be worn underneath them in cold weather, and so that the freedom of fit essential to a working and service dress may be ensured. All frocks, tunics, and jackets will be single-breasted unless otherwise specified.			9
	13. Gloves—Gloves, except as under, or where otherwise stated, will be of white doeskin or buckskin.			
	Brown dogskin or brown buckskin gloves will be worn as directed in the Queen's Regulations and Orders for the Army.	506 507	25.4.88 5.5.90	
61002 6616 61002 6790 61002 6708	Of the alternative patterns, buckskin is recommended as more durable and as being the more easily cleaned. All the officers of a unit must wear the same pattern.	508 509	29.4.98 23.8.98	

* Garments now in wear need not be altered prior to 31st December, 1904.
‡ Tartan is a term for material which is between a serge and a tweed.

	Pattern.		No. of Plate.
	No.	Sealed.	

14. **Great-Coats and Capes**—Great-coats will be made according to the following description :—
Milled cloth, double-breasted, to reach within a foot of the ground. Stand and fall collar 4½ inches deep, with a fly to cover the band of the cape when buttoned on. Loose round cuffs, 6 inches deep. 2 pockets with flaps at the waist in front, 2 openings behind at the side-seams, with pointed flaps 11 inches long at the points; a pocket inside the left breast. A slit 6 inches deep in the left side for hilt of sword to pass through. An opening behind, 19 inches long, with a fly. 2 rows of buttons down the front, 6 in each row, the top buttons 6 inches apart, the bottom ones 4 inches from centre to centre; 3 buttons on each skirt-flap, 4 small, silk-covered buttons at the opening behind, and 5 flat buttons under the fly at the collar. A cloth back-strap, attached to the top button of the skirt-flap, to confine the coat at the waist, a button-hole in the centre of the strap; 2 hooks and eyes to the collar. Shoulder-straps on the coat, of the same material as the garment; a small button of the pattern authorized for the respective services at the top. Cape of the same cloth as the coat, and long enough to cover the knuckles; 4 small buttons in front; to fasten at the neck with a leather strap, runner and buckle. For description of web belt and slings for carriage of coat, see Appendix VIII (3).   *(Pattern No. 100, Sealed 13.2.99)*

In the case of the Mounted Officers for whom the above of pattern coat is authorized, the following modifications will be made :—The opening of the coat behind will be long enough to reach to the cantle of the saddle, and a gusset will be introduced commencing at the top of the slit and extending downwards to about 24 inches, with about 19 inches' width at the bottom. A tab with button-hole near the bottom of the gusset to close it when the coat is worn on foot. A small pocket with a flap at the back of the left sleeve. On the inside of each skirt a cloth band with button to secure the skirts over the knees when the coat is worn on mounted duties. The four buttons at the opening behind are omitted. The coat to reach to the ankles when worn on foot.

15. **Haversacks.**—Black for Rifles; white or khaki for all other services. One large pocket. At the back of the pocket, two smaller pockets, and a loop for a knife and fork. Flap fastened with a small button of Regimental or Departmental pattern. White or khaki web strap with white metal fittings; for Rifles, black strap with black metal fittings.   *(Pattern No. 300, Sealed 22.6.98)*

16. **Helmet, Universal Home Pattern** (Colonial Helmet, see paragraph 1187)—
(*a*) Cork, covered with blue cloth in four seams, two on each side; peaks front and back, stiffened and covered with cloth with a seam at each side; the front peak bound with metal $\frac{3}{16}$ inch wide, the back peak with patent leather $\frac{1}{8}$ inch wide. Above the peaks and going round the helmet a cloth band $\frac{3}{4}$ inch wide, and stitched top and bottom. Back peak to centre of crown 10½ inches; front peak to centre of crown 10¼ inches; side to centre of crown 8 inches. Curb-chain chin strap, the links $\frac{5}{8}$ inch wide and the strap lined with patent leather, backed with black velvet. Rose fastenings at the sides; convex bar, $\frac{1}{4}$ inch wide, down the centre of the back, and to the bottom of the back peak. The bar is in one piece, and is fastened to the helmet by means of two studs and a flattened prolongation of the bar under the back peak. At the top of the helmet, a spike mounted on a cross-piece base.   *(Pattern No. 3, Sealed 7.12.98, Plate 5)*

The dimensions of the spike are—

Height of spike from place of insertion in the top rose of the cross-piece base ... ...   } $2\frac{3}{4}$ inches.

Total height of spike and base... ... ... $3\frac{1}{4}$ inches.

Diameter of spike at point of contact with the top rose of base ... $\frac{7}{8}$ inch.

The cross-piece base is of metal; there is a rose at the top into which the spike is screwed, and a smaller rose on each of the four terminations of the base. A hook at the back of the base, to which the chin strap is attached when not required to be worn under the chin. The width of the base from the point of the front termination to the point of the rear termination, measured in a straight line underneath, 4¾ inches, that from side to side 3¼ inches. The base is attached to the helmet by four screws and nuts. For ventilation, the base is perforated with four holes. A collet is inserted in the crown of the helmet.

(*b*) In Field and Garrison Artillery, in the Army Service Corps, the Royal Army Medical Corps, and the Army Veterinary Department, a ball in a leaf cup is substituted for the spike. Height of ball and cup, 1¾ inches.   *(Plate 5)*

(*c*) In Light Infantry, the helmet is covered with dark green cloth.

(*d*) A description of the plates worn with this pattern of helmet is included in the Dress of the Services for which it is regulation. See also Appendix I.

17. **Leggings.**—Brown or black leather as worn by the men, 8½ inches high for an officer 5 feet 8 inches in height; a variation not exceeding 1 inch for officers above 5 feet 10 inches or under 5 feet 6 inches. A leather strap, $\frac{5}{8}$ inch wide, is sewn all round the top, terminating with brass buckle and thong. Whipcord laces and 4 eyelets.   *(Pattern No. 529, Sealed 20.12.98)*

18. **Metal for Ornaments, Badges, Devices, Furniture, &c.**—For standard quality of gold lace see Appendix III. The yellow metal for officers' badges, ornaments, devices, and furniture generally can be either of gilding metal or of gilding metal water-gilt.

61002
———
6787

61002
———
6632

		Pattern.		No. of Plate.
		No.	Sealed.	

Ref.		Pattern No.	Sealed	Plate
61002 / Infy / 10	Contractors usually supply the latter, but gilding metal is recommended as always presenting the same appearance, as the water-gilt wears off in cleaning. Gilding metal is also cheaper. Water gilding increases the cost from 10°/$_{\circ}$ to 30°/$_{\circ}$ according to the nature of the article. "Gilding" metal, *i.e.*, metal suitable for gilding purposes, is composed of 8 parts copper to 1 of zinc. *Note.*—The terms gilt or silver imply metal, unless embroidery is stated.			
61002 / 6844	19. **Mourning band**—Crape $3\frac{1}{4}$ inches wide, worn above the left elbow.			
61002 / 5515	20. **Revolver**—A revolver forms part of an Officer's equipment. No pattern has been sealed, but the weapon must carry Government ammunition. Officers are recommended to supply themselves with revolvers of service pattern. See Appendix IV.			
	21. **Sabretaches**—Staff Officers—Russia leather sabretaches with three slings, according to sealed pattern. For description see Appendix V.	301	11.5.95	
	Officers of Household Cavalry, Dragoon Guards, Dragoons and Lancers, Mounted Officers of Royal Engineers, Foot Guards, Royal Army Medical Corps, and Departments,—black leather sabretaches of similar pattern, with three slings, $\frac{3}{4}$ inch wide, of patterns to match their sword-slings. Metal ornaments of regimental pattern, or of departmental pattern, will be worn on the flaps.	302	11.5.95	
61002 / 4798 / A.O. 180 / 1894	Mounted Officers of Infantry wear sabretaches of the pattern above described, but (except in the Rifles) without metal ornaments. For description see Appendix V.	302	11.5.95	
	22. **Saddlery**—The patterns of saddlery approved for— 1.—Field Marshal and General Officer. 2.—Officers of Mounted Services, under the rank of General Officer, except Royal Artillery. 3.—Royal Artillery. 4.—Colonel on the Staff, Mounted Officer of Infantry, &c., are described in Appendix VI. With regard to (1) and (4), Officers are permitted to use ordinary hunting saddles in lieu of those described, but they are recommended to provide themselves with the latter, as the articles laid down to be carried on the saddle, in marching order, cannot be satisfactorily carried on the hunting saddle; this, however, is a *recommendation*, and not an instruction.			
61002 / 6110	For Active Service, Staff Officers and Mounted Officers of Infantry should provide themselves with numnahs of regulation pattern, and with a corn sack, 12-lb., described in List of Changes, paragraph 8337. Numnahs of regulation shape, or leather numnahs cut to the shape of the saddle are permissive in peace time, but the Officers of each unit must turn out alike.			
61002 / 6515 / ... / 6825	23. **Sashes**—Sashes are worn by Field Marshals, General Officers, Colonels on the Staff, and Equerries to members of the Royal Family, round the waist, the tassels hanging from the left side. By other Officers, including A.D.C.'s and Equerries to the Queen, sashes are worn diagonally over the left shoulder under the left shoulder-strap and over the sword belt: the ends are crossed through a runner at the waist. Sashes will be of such length that the ends of the tassels shall just reach the bottom of the skirt of the tunic.	510 511 512 513	2.6.99 2.9.95 2.9.95 12.4.78	
	24. **Shoulder-cords or Shoulder-straps**—Shoulder-cords or shoulder straps, except where otherwise provided, are worn on tunics, mess-jackets, frock-coats, patrol-jackets, frocks, cloaks, and greatcoats. A description is included in that of the articles on which they are worn.			62 63
	25. **Spurs**—(1.) With knee boots. Jack spurs with straps, buckles, and chains. (2.) With Wellington boots. Box spurs.			
61002 / 5232 / 61002 / Cavalry / 11	Steel spurs will be worn, except on State occasions, in the evening when review order is worn, and in Mess Order, when brass box spurs with dumb rowels will be worn. For exceptions see under the services concerned.	503 504 505	} 31.3.96	
A.O. 4 / and 111 / 1896	26. **Straps**—Whenever spurs are worn with trousers, straps are to be worn also. Foot chains are worn in the 3rd Dragoon Guards.			
	27. **Swords**—Swords, unless otherwise described, will be made according to the specification given in Appendix VII.			
	28. **Sword Belts, Dress and Undress**—As described for the respective Services in which they are worn.			64
61002 / 6890	The universal pattern "Sam Browne" with two braces, revolver case, ammunition pouch, frog and brown leather scabbard is worn in all branches of the Service. For description see Appendices VII and VIII. Sword belts, other than the "Sam Browne" belt, will be worn as follows:—			
61002 / 6515 / 61002 / Art. / 16 / 61002 / 6943	Over the tunic (or doublet) by the Personal Staff of the Sovereign and Royal Family, and by Officers of all arms except by Field-Marshals, General Officers, Colonels on the Staff, Equerries to the Royal Family, Officers of Cavalry of the Line, Mounted Officers of Royal Artillery, and Rifle Regiments. Over the blue frock-coat and under patrol jackets and frocks. The web belt, described in Appendix VIII (2), will be worn by Officers of all branches of the Service who wear the sword belt under the tunic, patrol jacket, or frock. Slings will be made with studs and holes, so that they can be removed from the belt if required.			

	Pattern.		No. of Plate.
	No.	Sealed.	

29. Trousers and Pantaloons—For Mounted Officers, trousers or overalls should be cut straight, and from 1½ to 2 inches longer than ordinary trousers. They should be strapped firmly down to the boot and fit closely above the spurs.

For Dismounted Officers, Full Dress trousers may be cut straight down the leg, but care must be taken that Undress trousers are cut with sufficient room in the knee and thigh to allow free movement of the leg when marching.

Pantaloons should be cut loose in the thigh and tight at the knee. Ample length from the hip to the knee is essential so that the wearer can have the necessary freedom in mounting and dismounting. They should have buckskin strapping at the knee, and if, made for hard wear, seat strapping also. The pockets of trousers and pantaloons should be cut across.

A waist strap and buckle should be fitted.

30. Waterproof Cloaks—For all ranks, in accordance with the patterns for mounted and dismounted Services respectively, deposited at the War Office. Length of the cloak to vary according to height of wearer.

61002 / 5769

31. Whistles—There is no sealed pattern, but all the Officers of a unit should carry the same pattern. They will be attached to a silk lanyard of the colour of the frock, except in Light Infantry, in which the lanyard will be dark green.

For rows 30:

| | 101 | 5.8.90 | |
| | 102 | 5.8.90 | |

SEALED PATTERNS.

32. Sealed patterns of garments, buttons, lace, embroidery, badges of rank, special badges, devices, horse furniture and appointments, are deposited at the War Office for reference and guidance.

In providing themselves with uniform and equipment, in case of any doubt arising as to the correct pattern, Officers should make sure (if possible, by personal inspection) that articles according to sealed pattern are being supplied them.

SUPPLY OF MATERIALS FOR OFFICERS' UNIFORMS BY THE ROYAL ARMY CLOTHING DEPARTMENT ON REPAYMENT.

38407 / Dress / 143

33. For the convenience of Officers, articles of clothing and necessaries, and materials of Army Pattern can be supplied to them from the Royal Army Clothing Department on repayment. Special quality for Officers cannot be supplied, but the materials supplied for the garments of warrant officers are in many cases suitable for wear by Officers. A list of materials which can be supplied is given in Appendix XI, and patterns can be seen at the War Office.

The Rules under which these issues can be made will be found in the Clothing Regulations.

SUPPLY OF ARMS AND ARTICLES OF EQUIPMENT FROM ARMY ORDNANCE DEPARTMENT.

A.O. 44 / 1898 / 38407 / Dress / 161

34. Officers are permitted to draw from the Army Ordnance Department on repayment any Arms, Accoutrements, or Saddlery of Service Patterns which form part of their Regulation Equipment, and which they may require for their personal use.

	Pattern.		No. of Plate.
	No.	Sealed.	

DECORATIONS AND MEDALS.

68 / Gen. No. / 1358A. / 61002 / 6278

35. Military decorations and medals are to be worn over the sash and under the pouch-belt on the left breast of the garment which is the full dress of the unit or individual. They are to be worn in a horizontal line, suspended from a single bar (of which the buckle is not to be seen) or stitched to the garment, and placed between the first and second buttons from the bottom of the collar of the garment; in Hussar regiments, immediately below the top bar of lace on the left breast of the tunic when that garment is worn. The riband is not to exceed 1 inch in length, unless the number of clasps require it to be longer. The buckles attached to the ribands of the third class of the Orders of the Bath and of St. Michael and St. George should be seen. When the decorations and medals cannot, on account of the number, be suspended from the bar so as to be fully seen, they are to overlap. The width of a military medal riband is 1¼ inches.

68 / Central Africa / 222

	Pattern.		No. of Plate.
	No.	Sealed.	

Military medals will be worn in the order of the dates of the campaigns for which they have been conferred ; the first decoration or medal obtained being placed farthest from the left shoulder.

Medals awarded by the Royal Humane Society for bravery in saving life will be worn, when authorized, on the right breast.

61002 / 6945 — Stars of Foreign Orders will be worn on the right or left breast according to the regulation laid down by the Sovereign by whom they are conferred.

On all occasions when the Sovereign, or the representative of the Sovereign, is present, on the parade in celebration of the birthday of the Sovereign, and on State occasions, including levees, drawing-rooms, and balls, Officers of the Army who are Knights Grand Cross or Knights Grand Commanders of any British Orders, except the Order of the Garter and Order of the Thistle, will, when in uniform, wear the broad ribands of the Orders to which they belong, over the right shoulder and under the sash or belt. The ribands of the Order of the Garter and Order of the Thistle are worn over the left shoulder. Knights Commanders and Commanders will wear the ribands of the Orders to which they belong

61002 / 6967 — inside the collar of the tunic, the badge being suspended 2 inches below the lower edge of the collar. The ribands of Orders will not be worn by Officers attending military funerals in review order.

Stars of Orders will be worn on occasions as above and in review order, but will not be worn with undress uniform or mess dress.

On the occasions specified above, Officers of the Army, who may be members and honorary associates of the Order of the Hospital of St. John of Jerusalem in England, will wear the badge of the Order.

In foreign countries, Officers of the Army will wear their stars when foreign Officers wear theirs.

Ribands only of medals and decorations will be worn with undress, mess-dress, or khaki uniform, and with white uniform except when it is worn in Review Order. These ribands will be ½ inch in length, and will be sewn on to the cloth of the coat or jacket, or, with white or khaki, worn on a bar, without intervals. They should not be made to overlap, and when there is not sufficient room to wear the ribands in one row, they should be worn in two rows, the lower being arranged directly under the upper. When there is not room for them

61002 / 6801 — on the mess jacket with roll collar they should extend on to the lappel below the collar badge. The riband of a Knight Grand Cross, Knight Grand Commander, Knight Commander, or Commander of an Order is not to be worn, the riband of the Companionship or Membership of the Order being in these cases substituted. Miniature orders or medals will not be worn in uniform.

Stars of Orders and miniature decorations and medals will be worn in evening dress (plain clothes) in the presence of members of the Royal Family, or of Viceroys and Governors-General, and on public and official occasions. On such occasions, Officers who are Knights

... / 6987 — Grand Cross or Knights Grand Commander of Orders will wear the broad ribands of the Orders to which they belong. Knights Commanders and Commanders will wear the riband and badge of the Orders to which they belong inside the collar of the coat, the badge being suspended 2 inches below the lower edge of the collar of the shirt.

61002 / 6583 — When a decoration is worn round the neck, the miniature will not be worn.

These Regulations extend to retired Officers, provided that under the Regulations they are allowed to wear uniform.

36. Decorations and medals and the ribands appertaining thereto will be worn in the following order :—

61002 / 6278 —
Order of the Garter.
Order of the Thistle.
Order of St. Patrick.
Order of the Bath.
Order of the Star of India.
Order of St. Michael and St. George.
Order of the Indian Empire.
Royal Victorian Order.
Victoria Cross.
Distinguished Service Order.
Queen's Jubilee Commemoration Medal.
Albert Medal.
British War Medals.
Medal for Distinguished Conduct in the Field.*

... / 6801 —
Order of St. John of Jerusalem.
Medal for Meritorious Service.
Long Service and Good Conduct Medal.
Volunteer Officers' Decoration.
Foreign Decorations.
Foreign War Medals.

* This medal is to be worn immediately after the medal for the campaign for which it was awarded.

	Pattern.		No. of Plate.
	No.	Sealed.	

FIELD-MARSHAL.
GENERAL, LIEUTENANT-GENERAL, MAJOR-GENERAL, BRIGADIER-GENERAL. COLONEL ON THE STAFF. SUBSTANTIVE COLONEL. COLONEL NOT ON THE CADRE OF A UNIT.

FIELD-MARSHAL.

FULL DRESS.

	No.	Sealed.	Plate
37. Cocked Hat—As described in paragraph 7, with loop of four gold bullions, the inner rows twisted ; gold purl netted button ; tassels, gold worked head, six gold bullions, with five crimson bullions under them.	1	23.8.98	2 & 3
38. Plume—White swan feathers, drooping outwards, 10 inches long, with red feathers under them long enough to reach the ends of the white ones ; feathered stem 3 inches long.	27	17.12.75	2
39. Tunic—Scarlet cloth, with blue cloth collar and cuffs. The collar embroidered in gold. The cuffs round, 3 inches deep, with gold embroidery $2\frac{1}{4}$ inches deep round the top ; a scarlet flap on each sleeve, $6\frac{1}{2}$ inches deep and 2 inches wide between the points, embroidered in gold. A similar flap on each skirt behind, $\frac{1}{2}$ inch shorter than the length of the skirt and 3 inches wide at the bottom point ; 8 buttons down the front ; 3 on each flap ; 2 at the waist behind. The front, collar, cuffs, and flaps edged with white cloth, $\frac{3}{16}$ inch wide. Gold shoulder cords of plaited gold wire basket cord $\frac{3}{16}$ inch in diameter, small gold gimp down the centre, strap of the shoulder-cord $2\frac{1}{4}$ inches wide, terminating in a 4-inch wing. An aiguillette of gold wire cord, $\frac{1}{4}$ inch in diameter, with gilt embossed tags will be worn on the right shoulder.	103 104 105 514	23.8.98 21.6.80 21.6.80 21.1.98	12 62
40. Embroidery—Oak-leaf pattern, in dead and bright gold.			12
41. Lace—Gold, oak-leaf pattern.	701	13.12.1900	72
42. Buttons—See Appendix I.			
43. Pantaloons—White leather. } To be worn at Drawing-Rooms, and on other State occasions.			
44. Boots—Jacked. }			
45. Pantaloons—Blue cloth with scarlet stripes $2\frac{1}{2}$ inches wide and welted at the edges, down the side seams. } To be worn on semi-State occasions, and on ordinary occasions when mounted.	501	6.11.96	
46. Boots—Knee. }			
47. Trousers—Blue cloth, with $2\frac{1}{2}$-inch lace down the side seams. } To be worn at levées and on occasions of semi-State if dismounted.			
48. Boots—Wellington. }	502	6.11.96	
49. Spurs*—As described in paragraph 25.			
50. Sash—Gold and crimson silk net, $2\frac{1}{4}$ inches wide ; two crimson stripes $\frac{3}{8}$ inch wide, the rest gold ; round loose gold bullion fringe tassels, 9 inches long, round heads. The sash fastened with buckles, round the waist, the tassels hanging from the left side.	510	2.6.99	
51. Sword—Mameluke hilt, with device of crossed batons encircled with oak-leaves ; ivory grip ; scimitar blade—As described in Appendix VII.	303	27.7.96	66
52. Scabbard*—Steel, ridged, with cross lockets and rings—As described in Appendix VII.	304	4.5.98	66
53. Sword Belt—Web, $1\frac{3}{4}$ inches wide, with leather furniture and metal dees for slings. Web shoulder suspender. For description, see Appendix VIII. (2).	305	1.6.98	
54. Sword Slings—Russia leather 1 inch wide, gold oak-leaf embroidery.	306	21.6.80	64
55. Sword Knot—Gold and crimson cord and acorn.	307	23.8.98	64

UNDRESS.

	No.	Sealed.	Plate
56. Forage Cap—As described in paragraph 11. Band of scarlet cloth. For Badge, see Appendix I.	28	14.7.98	8
57. Field Cap—As described in paragraph 10, but with scarlet cloth top. Gold French braid welts on cap, and at front and back seams. For Badge, see Appendix I.	29	13.7.96	9
58. Frock Coat—Blue cloth. double-breasted, with blue velvet collar and cuffs ; the cuffs round, 3 inches deep. Plain flaps at the plaits behind, $1\frac{1}{2}$ inches wide, and, for an officer 5 feet 9 inches in height, 11 inches long, two rows of buttons down the front, eight in each row, the rows 8 inches apart at the top and 4 inches at the waist ; two buttons at the waist behind, and one at the bottom of each skirt flap. The skirts lined with black. Shoulder cords as for tunic.	106	15.9.91	12
59. Frock—Blue angola, tartan or serge according to climate, full in chest, cut with broad back, slits at sides, five regulation buttons down the front. Two breast patch pockets outside, $6\frac{3}{4}$ inches wide, 8 inches deep from the top of the flap, the top edge of pocket in line with the second button, with three-pointed flap, small regulation button and hole, loose plait on rear side of pocket, two similar outside patch pockets below, with three-pointed flap. Two inside breast pockets up and down with hole and button, two inside skirt pockets, with hole and button. Black alpaca lining. Shoulder straps of same material as the frock, fastened with a small regulation button. Stand and fall collar, fastened with one hook and eye. On the collar sewn on to each side in front and meeting at the	108 109	18.7.96 16.8.98	12

Left margin references:
38407
Dress
106
61002
6093
61002
Staff
7
61002
Staff
7
61002
Staff
39
61002
5410
A. O.
148
1896
61002
Staff
26

---

* Brass spurs and scabbards may continue in wear until worn out.

	Pattern.		No. of Plate.
	No.	Sealed.	

<table>
<tr><td>

61002 / 6470

fastening, gorget patches pointed at the outer end. The gorget patches to be of scarlet cloth 4½ inches long, and showing a $\frac{3}{16}$-inch blue light above and below the patch, a loop of gold oak-leaf embroidery along the centre, with a button 1 inch from the point. Sleeves with pointed cuffs, 6 inches high, with 2¼-inch slit, two small buttons and button holes.

</td><td>109</td><td>16.8.98</td><td>12</td></tr>
</table>

60. Trousers—Blue cloth, with scarlet stripes, as on the pantaloons.

61. Sword Slings for Web Belt—As for full dress, except that plain brown leather will be substituted for Russia leather, no embroidery, plain square buckles. | 308 | 9.2.94 | 64

61002 / 6890

A. O. / 148 / 1896

Belts—"Sam Browne."
Scabbard—Brown leather. } See Appendices VII and VIII.

62. Sword Knot—Brown leather, as described in Appendix VIII. Other articles as in Full Dress. | 309 | 24.11.97 | 44

Great Coat and Cape.

63. Blue milled cloth, of the pattern described in paragraph 14, lined with scarlet rattinet; blue velvet collar. Shoulder-straps of the same material as the garment; a small button at the top. | 100 | 13.2.99 |

Mess Dress.

61002 / 6093

64. Mess Jacket—Scarlet cloth, edged all round, including the collar, with 1 inch oak-leaf lace forming barrels at the bottom of the back seams. Blue cloth collar and cuffs, the collar square in front, with a loop of gold braid at the bottom to fasten across the neck. A tracing of $\frac{3}{8}$-inch gold chain gimp along the bottom of the collar. Fastened with hooks and eyes, a row of studs in front on the left side. The cuffs pointed and edged with 1-inch oak-leaf lace, the lace extending to 6 inches from the bottom of the cuff in front and 2⅜ inches behind. Shoulder-straps of blue cloth, edged with ½-inch oak-leaf lace, except at the base. A small button at the top. Scarlet silk lining. | 110 | 13.11.90 | 14

65. Mess Waistcoat—Blue cloth, to close at the neck. Edged with ½-inch *full* oak-leaf lace at the top of the collar, down the front and along the bottom to the side seams; at $\frac{1}{8}$-inch from the gold lace, a tracing of gold Russia braid. The braid forms eyes 2¾ inches from each end of the collar, down the front and at the bottom to the side seams. The pockets edged with eyes in gold Russia braid with a crow's foot at each end. A row of studs and hooks and eyes down the front. | 111 | 16.7.90 | 14

66. Trousers, Boots, and Spurs—As in Full Dress.

Horse Furniture.

67. Saddle—As described in Appendix VI., or "Hunting Saddle," see paragraph 22; blue girths. | 600 | 24.9 97 |

68. Stirrups—Review Order—Gilt, or gilding metal, square-set, with oval bottoms; the sides engraved with oak-leaves; the top to cover the eye, and to have crossed batons and crown in relief.

Marching and Drill Order—As described in Appendix VI.

69. Holsters—Review Order—Brown leather, with gilt caps to the pipes, chased with a double row of pointed leaves; covers of blue cloth, and cloth flounces, laced all round with two stripes of 1½-inch lace, ¼ inch apart; on each flounce crossed batons of crimson velvet and gold with a crown in gold above on a laurel wreath embroidered in silver.

70. Wallets—Marching and Drill Order—Brown leather.

71. Bridle and Breast Plate—Brown leather.

72. Saddle-Cloth—Blue cloth, 3 feet 2 inches long at the bottom, and 2 feet 2 inches deep, laced all round with two stripes of 1½-inch lace, ¼ inch apart; at each hind corner, crossed batons of crimson velvet and gold with a crown in gold above on a laurel wreath embroidered in silver. | 600 / 602 | 24.9.97 / 8.9.96 |

73. Head Stall and Bridoon Rein—Review Order only—Gold lace, an inch wide, lined with red Morocco leather; gilt or gilding metal collar chain.

GENERAL, LIEUTENANT-GENERAL, MAJOR-GENERAL, BRIGADIER-GENERAL.

Full Dress.

74. Cocked Hat—As described in paragraphs 7 and 37. | 1 | 23.8.98 | 2 & 3

75. Plume—White swan feathers, drooping outwards, 10 inches long, with red feathers under them long enough to reach the ends of the white ones; feathered stem 3 inches long. | 27 | 17.12.75 | 2

76. Tunic—Scarlet cloth, with blue cloth collar and cuffs. The collar embroidered in gold. The cuffs round, 3 inches deep, with gold embroidery 2¼ inches deep round the top; a scarlet flap on each sleeve, 6½ inches deep and 22 inches wide between the points, embroidered in gold. A similar flap on each skirt behind, ½ inch shorter than the length of the skirt and 23 inches wide at the bottom point; eight buttons down the | 103 / 104 / 105 | 23.8.98 / 21.6.80 / 21.6.80 | 12 / 12 / 12

		Pattern.		No. of Plate.
		No.	Sealed.	

front; three on each flap; two at the waist behind. The front, collar, cuffs and flaps edged with white cloth, $\frac{3}{16}$ inch wide. Gold shoulder-cords of plaited gold wire basket cord, $\frac{3}{16}$ inch in diameter, small gold gimp down the centre, strap of the shoulder-cord $2\frac{1}{4}$ inches wide, terminating in a small 4-inch wing. Eyelet hole at the end next to the collar for small gilt button. The underside of the cord is lined with scarlet cloth, and has a gilt or gilding metal fastening below. — Pattern No. 514, Sealed 21.1.98, Plate 62

77. **Embroidery**—Oak-leaf pattern, in dead and bright gold. — 103–105, Plate 12

78. **Lace**—Gold, oak-leaf pattern. — 701, 13.2.1900, Plate 72

79. **Buttons**—See Appendix I.

80. **Trousers**—Blue cloth, with $2\frac{1}{2}$-inch lace down the side seams.

81. **Pantaloons**—Blue cloth, with scarlet cloth stripes, $2\frac{1}{2}$ inches wide and welted at the edges down the side seams.

82. **Boots and Spurs***—As described in paragraphs 4 and 25.

$\frac{61002}{6817}$ 83. **Sash**—Gold and crimson silk net, $2\frac{1}{4}$ inches wide; two crimson stripes $\frac{3}{8}$ inch wide, the rest gold; round tassels of gold fringe, 9 inches long. Web or leather lining with loops for sword slings, fastened with buckles, when worn with the frock coat, if the web sword belt is not worn. — 510, 2.6.99

84. **Sword**—Mameluke hilt, with device of sword and baton crossed, encircled with oak leaves; ivory grip; scimitar blade—as described in Appendix VII. — 303, 27.7.96, Plate 66

$\frac{A.\,O.\,4}{1896}$ 85. **Scabbard**†—Steel, ridged, with cross lockets and rings—as described in Appendix VII. — 304, 4.5.98, Plate 66

86. **Sword Belt**—Web, as for Field-Marshal, see Appendix VIII (2). — 305, 1.6.98

87. **Sword Slings**—Russia leather, 1 inch wide, with gold oak-leaf embroidery. Billets fitted with studs and holes. — 306, 21.6.80, Plate 64

88. **Sword Knot**—Gold and crimson cord and acorn. — 307, 23.8.98, Plate 64

UNDRESS.

$\frac{61002}{\text{Staff}}$
$\frac{29}{61002}$
$\frac{}{5410}$

89. **Forage Cap**—As for Field Marshal. For badge, see Appendix I. — 28, 14.7.98, Plate 8

90. **Field Cap**—As described in paragraph 10, but with scarlet top, gold French braid welts on cap and flaps, and at front and back seams. For badge, see Appendix I. — 29, 13.7.96, Plate 9

91. **Frock Coat**—Blue cloth, double-breasted, with blue velvet collar and cuffs; the cuffs round, 3 inches deep. Plain flaps at the plaits behind, $1\frac{1}{2}$ inches wide, and, for an Officer 5 feet 9 inches in height, 11 inches long; two rows of buttons down the front, eight in each row, the rows 8 inches apart at the top and 4 inches at the waist; two buttons at the waist behind, and one at the bottom of each skirt-flap; the skirts lined with black. Shoulder-cords as for tunic. — 106, 15.9.91, Plate 12

92. **Frock**—As for Field-Marshal. — 108, 18.7.96, Plate 12

93. **Trousers**—Blue cloth, with scarlet stripes, $2\frac{1}{2}$ inches wide and welted at the edges, down the side seams.

$\frac{61002}{6515}$ 94. **Sword**—The sword laid down for the arm of the Service to which the Officer formerly belonged.‡

95. **Sword Slings for Web Belt**—As for full dress, except that plain brown leather will be substituted for Russia leather, no embroidery, plain square buckles. — 308, 9.2.94, Plate 64

$\frac{61002}{6890}$ 96. **Belts**—"Sam Browne" **Scabbard**—Brown leather } See Appendices VII and VIII.

$\frac{A.\,O.}{148}$
$\frac{}{1896}$ 97. **Sword Knot**—Brown leather, as described in Appendix VIII. — 309, 24.11.97, Plate 64
Other articles as in Full Dress.

GREAT COAT AND CAPE.

98. Blue milled cloth, of the pattern described in paragraph 14, lined with scarlet rattinett; blue velvet collar. Shoulder-straps of the same material as the garment, a small button at the top. — 100, 13.2.99

MESS DRESS.

99. As described for Field-Marshal. The badges of rank are smaller than those described in paragraph 2, and the hilt of the sword is in gold embroidery. — Plate 14

HORSE FURNITURE.

100. **Saddle**—As described in Appendix VI; or Hunting, see paragraph 22. — 600, 24.9.97

101. **Saddlecloth**—Blue cloth, 3 feet 2 inches long at the bottom, and 2 feet 2 inches deep laced all round with two stripes of $1\frac{1}{2}$-inch lace, $\frac{1}{4}$ inch apart; at each hind corner badges according to rank, see paragraph 2. The crown, star and baton, and hilt of sword will be in gold embroidery, the blade of sword will be in silver embroidery.

---

* Brass spurs may continue in wear until worn out.
† The brass scabbard may continue in wear until worn out.
‡ General Officers who have disposed of these swords may continue to wear the scimitar pattern in all orders of dress.

	Pattern.		No. of Plate.
	No.	Sealed.	

102. **Wallets**—Brown leather, see Appendix VI. For Review Order, covers of blue cloth, and cloth flounces, laced all round with two stripes of 1½-inch lace, ¼ inch apart; on each flounce, badges according to rank. Crown, star and baton, and hilt of sword in gold embroidery, blade of sword in silver embroidery.   600 / 24.9.97 ; 615 / 3.3.98

103. **Bridle and Breast Plate**—Brown leather, as described in Appendix VI.   602 / 8.9.96

61002 / 6783

OFFICERS COMMANDING VOLUNTEER INFANTRY BRIGADES.

V / Bdes. / 932

104. Uniform and horse furniture as for a Brigadier-General, except that Officers Commanding regiments or Regimental Districts, who are *ex officio* Brigadiers of Volunteer Brigades, will wear their regimental uniform. Officers Commanding Volunteer Infantry Brigades who retire from the service on completion of not less than 5 years' service in that appointment, may wear the uniform of a Brigadier-General on the retired list.

105. Officers holding rank, honorary or otherwise, higher than that of Brigadier-General will wear the badges of the higher rank.

COLONEL ON THE STAFF. SUBSTANTIVE COLONEL. COLONEL NOT ON THE CADRE OF A UNIT.

FULL DRESS.

106. **Cocked Hat**—As described in paragraph 7, with loop of ¾-inch lace, and netted gold purl head.   { 1 / 23.8.98 ; 2 / 29.11.98   2 & 3

107. **Plume**—White swan feathers, drooping outwards, 8 inches long, with red feathers under them, long enough to reach the ends of the white ones; feathered stem, 3 inches long.   30 / 17.12.75   2

61002 / 5543 — A.O. / 26 / 1897

108. **Tunic**—Scarlet cloth, with blue cloth collar and cuffs. The collar laced round the top and bottom with ⅝-inch lace; the cuffs round, 3 inches deep, with two bars of ⅝-inch lace round the top, showing ⅛ inch of blue cloth between the bars. A scarlet flap on each sleeve, 6 inches long, and 2½ inches wide at the points, edged with ⅝-inch lace, and a similar flap reaching to ½ inch from the bottom of the skirt on each skirt behind, the flaps ½ inch wide at the top, 1½ inches at the centre point and 2¼ inches at the bottom. A bar of ⅝-inch lace from the centre of the waist to the bottom of the skirt; eight buttons down the front; three on each flap, the top buttons on the flaps behind being at the waist. The front, collar, cuffs, flaps and bar of lace on the skirts edged with white cloth 3/16 inch wide. The tunic lined with white, round the waist a band of white leather 2 inches wide fastened with two hooks and eyes. Twisted round gold shoulder cords, universal pattern, lined with scarlet; a small button at the top.   112 / 3.3.97 / 13 ; 515 / 17.8.95 / 63

A.O. 26 / 1897

109. **Lace**—Gold, staff pattern.   701 / 13.2.1900 / 72

110. **Buttons**—See Appendix I.

111. **Trousers**—Blue cloth, with 1¾-inch lace down the side seams.

61002 / 6583

112. **Pantaloons**—Blue cloth, with scarlet cloth stripes, 1¾ inches wide down the side seams.

113. **Boots and Spurs**—As described in paragraphs 4 and 25.

61002 / 6515

114. **Sash**—As for General Officer.   510 / 2.6.99

115. **Sword**—As for the arm of the Service to which the Officer formerly belonged.*

6540

116. **Scabbard**—Steel.

61002 / 6348

117. **Sword Belt**—Web, as for General Officer, see Appendix VIII (2).   305 / 1.6.98 / 64

118. **Sword Slings**—Russia leather, an inch wide; two stripes of gold embroidery. Lion head buckles.   310 / 26.11.97 / 64

119. **Sword Knot**—Gold and crimson cord and acorn.   307 / 23.8.98 / 64

120. **Sabretache**—As described in paragraph 21.   301 / 11.5.95

UNDRESS.

61002 / Staff / 39

121. **Forage Cap**—As described in paragraph 11. Band of blue cloth. For badge, see Appendix I.   31 / 14.7.98 / 8

61002 / 5410

122. **Field Cap**—As for General Officer. For badge, see Appendix I.   29 / 13.7.96 / 9

A.O. 26 / 1897

123. **Frock Coat**—Blue cloth, double-breasted, with collar and cuffs of the same material as the coat; the cuffs round, 3 inches deep, a flap and three small buttons on each sleeve.† Plain flaps at the plaits behind, 1½ inches wide, and, for an Officer 5 feet 9 inches in height, 11 inches long; two rows of buttons down the front, eight in each row, the rows 8 inches apart at the top and 4 inches at the waist; two buttons at the waist behind and one at the bottom of each skirt flap, the skirts lined with black. Buttons and shoulder cords, as for the tunic.   107 / 27.3.97 / 12

61002 / 6540

* Officers already in possession of the sword described in paragraph 27 may continue to wear it.

† The buttons are to be plugged through the flap *only* to render it more easily removeable for conversion to frock coat for General Officer.

		Pattern No.	Pattern Sealed.	No. of Plate.
A.O. 148 / 1896; 61002 / 6470; 61002 / Staff 8	**124. Frock**—Blue angola, tartan, or serge according to climate, full in chest, cut with broad back, slits at sides, five regulation buttons down the front. Two breast patch pockets outside, $6\frac{3}{4}$ inches wide, 8 inches deep, the top edge of pocket in line with the second button, with three-pointed flap, small regulation button and hole, loose plait on rear side of pocket, two similar outside patch pockets below, with three-pointed flap. Two inside breast pockets up and down with hole and button, two inside skirt pockets, with hole and button. Black alpaca lining. Shoulder straps of same material as the frock, fastened with a small regulation button. Stand-up collar from $1\frac{1}{4}$ to $1\frac{3}{4}$ inches high. On the collar sewn on to each side in front and meeting at the fastening, gorget patches pointed at the outer end. The gorget patches to be of scarlet cloth, $4\frac{1}{2}$ inches long, showing a $\frac{3}{16}$-inch blue light above and below the patch, a loop of crimson silk cord $\frac{3}{20}$ inch in diameter along the centre, with a button 1 inch from the end. Sleeves with pointed cuffs, 6 inches high, with $2\frac{1}{4}$-inch slit, two small buttons and button holes.	108	18.7.96	12 13
	125. Trousers—Blue cloth, with scarlet stripes $1\frac{3}{4}$ inches wide down the side seams.			
	126. Sword Slings for Web Belt—Same as for Full Dress, except that plain brown leather will be substituted for Russia leather; plain square buckles.	308	9.2.94	64
	127. Belts—"Sam Browne." See Appendices VII and VIII.			
	128. Scabbard—Brown leather. See Appendices VII and VIII.			
	129. Sword Knot—Brown leather, as described in Appendix VIII. Other articles as in Full Dress.	309	24.11.97	64
	GREAT COAT AND CAPE.			
	130. Blue milled cloth, of the pattern described in paragraph 14, lined with scarlet rattinett; blue velvet collar. Shoulder straps of the same material as the garment; a small button at the top.	100	13.2.99	
	MESS DRESS.			
61002 / 5845	**131. Mess Jacket**—Scarlet cloth, edged all round, including the collar, with $\frac{5}{8}$-inch lace forming barrels at the bottom of the back seams. Blue cloth collar and cuffs; a line of gold braid along the bottom of the collar with an eye in the centre; the cuffs pointed, $6\frac{1}{4}$ inches deep at the point of the lace and $3\frac{1}{4}$ inches deep at the back, with 2 bars of $\frac{5}{8}$-inch lace, $\frac{1}{4}$ inch apart, on the cuffs. A row of studs in front on the left side. Scarlet silk lining. Inside breast pocket, up and down. Hooks and eyes in front, and a loop of gold braid at the bottom of the collar, to fasten across the neck. Shoulder straps of blue cloth, edged (except at the base) with $\frac{1}{2}$-inch lace; small button at the top.	113	23.4.97	14
61002 / 6037	**132. Mess Waistcoat**—Blue cloth closed at the neck; gold Russia braid edging round the top, down the front, and along the bottom to the side seams; at half an inch from the edging, gold Russia braid forming eyes at the front of the collar down the front of the waistcoat and along the bottom to the side seams. The pockets edged with eyes in gold Russia braid, with a crow's foot at each end. A row of studs and hooks and eyes down the front.	114	1.10.97	14
	133. Trousers, Boots, and Spurs—As for Full Dress.			
	HORSE FURNITURE.			
	134. Saddle—As described in Appendix VI; or Hunting, see paragraph 22.	600	24.9.97	
	135. Bridle and Breast Plate, Wallets—Brown leather, see Appendix VI.	601 607	24.9.97 14.9.96	
A.C. 26 / 1897	OFFICERS UNDER THE RANK OF COLONEL, NOT ON THE CADRE OF A UNIT, EXCLUSIVE OF GARRISON STAFF. SUBSTANTIVE LIEUTENANT-COLONELS EXTRA-REGIMENTALLY EMPLOYED.			
	136. Uniform and horse furniture as for Colonel on the Staff, with the following exceptions:—			
	137. Forage Cap—As described in paragraph 11. Band of blue cloth.	33	13.11.96	
	138. Tunic—One bar of lace only on the collar and cuffs.	112	3.3.97	13
	139. Frock—As for Colonel on the Staff, but without gorget patches.			
	140. Sash—Gold, as for Infantry of the Line.			
	141. Sword Belt (Full Dress)—Russia leather, $1\frac{1}{2}$ inches wide, with slings an inch wide; two stripes of gold embroidery on belt and slings; a hook to hook up the sword. Gilt lion-head buckles.	310	26.11.97	64
	142. Sword Belt (Undress)—Same as for Full Dress, except that plain brown leather will be substituted for Russia leather; no embroidery; and there will be plain square buckles on the slings.	308	9.2.94	64
	143. Mess Jacket—One bar only of $\frac{5}{8}$-inch lace on the cuffs.			

	Pattern.		No. of Plate.
	No.	Sealed.	

61002
Staff
72

CAMP OR GARRISON QUARTERMASTER NOT ON THE CADRE OF A UNIT.

144. Cocked Hat—As described in paragraph 7.
145. Plume—White swan feathers drooping outwards, 6 inches long, with red feathers under them long enough to reach the ends of the white ones ; feathered stem 3 inches long.
146. Forage Cap—As described in paragraph 11.   Band of blue cloth.
147. Field Cap—Blue cloth, as described in paragraph 10.   Gold French braid along the top and flaps, and down the front and back seams.
148. Tunic—Scarlet cloth of the same pattern as for Officers of the Infantry of the Line, with blue cloth collar and cuffs.
149. Lace ⎫
150. Buttons ⎬ Staff pattern.
151. Trousers—Blue cloth, with 1¾ inch lace down the side seams.
152. Pantaloons—Blue cloth, with 1¾ inch scarlet cloth stripes down the side seams.
153. Sword Belt ⎫
154. Shoulder Belt ⎬ Black, as for Quartermasters of Infantry of the Line.
155. Pouch ⎭
156. Sashes are not worn except by Officers commissioned as Adjutant and Quartermaster, when the sash will be worn instead of the pouch belt.
157. The other articles of uniform as for Officers of the Infantry of the Line.

GREAT COAT AND CAPE.

158. As for Colonel on the Staff.   See paragraph 130.

HORSE FURNITURE.

159. As described in Appendix VI.
160. Officers transferred from a unit may continue to wear the uniform of that unit.   No article described above may be worn with regimental or departmental uniform.

Pattern Nos. and Sealed dates (aligned to rows above):

Item	No.	Sealed	Plate
144	2	29.11.98	2 / 3
147	26	2.3.94	
148	153	16.10.95	
156	358		
158	100	13.2.99	

HEAD-QUARTERS, GENERAL AND PERSONAL STAFF.*

EXCLUDING THE PERSONAL STAFF OF THE QUEEN AND ROYAL FAMILY AND VICE-REGAL STAFF.†

STAFF OFFICERS NOT ON THE CADRES OF UNITS.

	Pattern.		No. of Plate.
	No.	Sealed.	

161. Officers of the Head-Quarters Staff, and of the General and Personal Staff as detailed in paragraph 177, wear the uniform of their rank with the following additions or exceptions :—

With the tunic and frock-coat an aiguillette of the following pattern :—

(A.O. 26 / 1897) **162. Aiguillette§**—Cord ¼-inch gold and red Orris basket, with plait and cord loop in front and same at back, the plaits ending in plain cord with gilt metal tags. The plaits and cords, front and back, are joined together by a short scarlet cloth strap, in which is worked a button hole. The aiguillette is attached to the shoulder of the tunic or frock coat by a button placed under the outer end of the shoulder cord. The long cord is looped up on the top or front cord, the front cord and the short and long plaits are fastened together, and a small gold braid loop is fixed thereon to attach to the top button of the tunic and frock coat,—on the latter on the side on which the aiguillette is worn. The arm is passed between the front plait and cord, and the back or long plait and cord. — **Pattern No. 311, Sealed 3.3.97, Plate 13**

(61002 / Staff / 10) The aiguillette is worn on the right shoulder by all Officers of the Head-Quarters Staff of the Army, and by the Personal Staff of the Governor-General of Canada and Colonial Governors, and on the left shoulder by other Staff Officers entitled to wear it.

(61002 / 6583 / ... / Staff / 39) **163. Forage Cap**—
As described in paragraph 11. Band of scarlet cloth. — **Pattern Nos. 28.31.32, Sealed 14.7.98, Plate 8**

(61002 / 6277) **164. Field Cap**—As described in paragraph 57.

165. Gorget Patches‡—To be worn on the frock by :—

(61002 / Staff / 8) (1) GENERAL OFFICERS ON THE HEAD-QUARTER STAFF.
Scarlet cloth 4½ inches in length, pointed at the outer end, showing a $\frac{3}{16}$-inch blue light above and below the patch. In the centre, a loop of gold chain gimp $1\frac{3}{40}$ inch wide and ⅛ inch deep. A gorget button 1 inch from the point. — **Pattern No. 249, Sealed 30.6.98, Plate 12**

(2) OFFICERS BELOW THE RANK OF GENERAL OFFICER.
As for General Officer, but with gimp of crimson silk instead of gold. — **Pattern No. 250, Sealed 28.11.99, Plate 13**

STAFF OFFICERS ON THE CADRES OF UNITS.

166. Regimental uniform with the following additions or exceptions :—

167. Aiguillette§—As described above. — **Pattern No. 311, Sealed 3.3.97, Plate 13**

(61002 / Staff / 47) **168. Head-dress**—Full dress.
With the tunic :—
Officers of Household Cavalry, Dragoon Guards and Dragoons, Hussars, Lancers of the Line, Royal Horse Artillery, Foot Guards ; Fusilier, Highland or Rifle Regiments of the Line ;—the regimental full dress head-dress. Other officers—cocked hat as for Colonel on the Staff.
With the frock coat :—
Cocked hat as for Colonel on the Staff. — **Pattern No. 2, Sealed 23.8.98, Plate 2 & 3**

169. Plume—Officers of the Head-Quarters or General Staff, as for Colonel on the Staff. — **Pattern No. 30, Sealed 17.12.75, Plate 2**
For officers below the rank of Colonel, the plume will be 6 inches in length.
Officers on the Personal Staff, as for A.D.C. to the Queen. See paragraph 181. — **Pattern No. 34, Sealed 17.12.75, Plate 2**

170. Head-dress—Undress { Forage cap, as described in paragraph 11. Band of scarlet cloth. — **Pattern Nos. 31 & 32, Sealed 14.7.98, Plate 8**
{ Field cap, as described in paragraph 57. — **Pattern No. 29, Sealed 13.7.96, Plate 9**

171. Frock Coat—As for Colonel on the Staff. — **Pattern No. 107, Sealed 27.3.97, Plate 12**

172. Frock—(Except for Officers belonging to Rifle Regiments). If not in possession of a blue frock, Officers will provide themselves with one as for Colonel on the Staff, but fitted with gorget patches as described in paragraph 165 (2). — **Pattern No. 108, Sealed 18.7.96, Plate 13**
Officers belonging to units which wear collars of the colour of their facings, must replace these collars by blue ones with the Staff gorget patches laid down in paragraph 165 (2), or will provide themselves with Staff frocks. — **Plate 13**
Staff Officers belonging to Rifle Regiments will wear their regimental frocks with the Staff gorget patch as laid down in paragraph 165 (2). — **Plate 13**

173. Sword Belt—For wear with the frock coat—Full dress or undress, according to the Order of Dress in which the frock coat is worn—*Vide* Queen's Regulations. Regimental pattern.
Officers whose regimental uniform does not include a sword belt, must provide themselves with a belt to match their sword slings. The belt will be 1½ inches in width. The waistplate will be as for Officers under the rank of Colonel on the Staff not on the cadres of units, except for officers of Rifle Regiments who will wear a snake clasp, in silver. For description of waist plate, see Appendix I.

(61002 / Staff / 53) **174.** No sash or shoulder belt will be worn with the frock coat.

175. Officers of Household Cavalry do not wear the cuirass.

HORSE FURNITURE.

176. Regimental pattern.

LIST OF APPOINTMENTS REFERRED TO IN PARAGRAPH 161.

177. Deputy Adjutant-General, Assistant Adjutant-General, Deputy Assistant Adjutant-General, Assistant Military Secretary, Aide-de-Camp, Brigade Major, Garrison Adjutant.

178. Sabretache.—The sabretache is not worn by Officers serving on the Head-Quarters Staff.

(61002 / 6583)
* Old Pattern Staff Uniform may be worn until 31st December, 1901, by Officers having it in their possession.
† For the uniform worn by the Vice-Regal Staff in India, see Army Regulations, India, Vol. VII.
‡ The patches described for wear on the khaki frock will be retained on that frock by Officers serving on the General Staff.
§ Officers of the Household Cavalry do not wear this aiguillette, but continue to wear on the right shoulder the aiguillette belonging to the uniform of their unit. — **Plate 15**

	Pattern.		No. of Plate.
	No.	Sealed.	

OFFICERS ON THE STAFF OF VOLUNTEER BRIGADES.

Brigade Major.

<table>
<tr><td>61002
6628</td><td>

179. Uniform of their rank with the addition of the distinctions worn by Officers holding similar appointments in the Regular Forces—but with silver substituted for gold on the aiguillette, forage cap and gorget patch, as prescribed in the Volunteer Regulations.
</td></tr>
</table>

AIDE-DE-CAMP TO THE QUEEN.

Full Dress.

		No.	Sealed.	No. of Plate.
	180. Cocked Hat—As described in paragraph 7, with loop of gold plaited gimp; half ball netted button.	1 & 2	23.8.98 29.11.98	2 & 3
	181. Plume—Red and white upright swan feathers, 5 inches long.	34	17.12.75	2
61002 6575 ... 61002 6583 ... 6626	**182. Tunic**—Scarlet cloth, with blue cloth collar and cuffs, the skirt 12 inches deep for an Officer 5 feet 9 inches in height, with a proportionate variation for any difference in height. On each side in front, eight straight loops of scarlet mohair cord,* 4 inches long, five of them above the waist on the left side with buttons, the rest without. A gold embroidered frog-drop loop on each side of the collar. Round cuffs, 3 inches deep. A scarlet flap on each sleeve, with three embroidered loops and buttons, each loop 1¾ inches long exclusive of the drop. A scarlet flap on each back skirt, 10 inches long and 2 inches wide, with two loops and buttons similar to those on the sleeve; two buttons at the waist behind. A gold aiguillette, the cord ¼ inch in thickness, gilt metal tags, on the right shoulder, and a gold cord loop, with a small button, on the left. The collar, cuffs, flaps and back skirts edged with white cloth, ¼ inch wide, and the skirts lined with white. A pocket inside the left breast and inside each skirt behind. Hooks and eyes in front. Shoulder-cords with badges of rank are *not* worn.	115	21.12.97	14
	183. Lace—Gold, oak-leaf pattern.			
	184. Buttons—See Appendix I.			

	185. Trousers,
	    Pantaloons, } As for Colonel on the Staff.
	    Boots,			

	186. Spurs—Brass.	504	31.3.96	
	187. Sash—Gold and crimson silk net; plaited runner and fringe, tassels of gold and crimson silk.			
	188. Sword—Mameluke gilt hilt, with device of the Royal Cypher and Crown; ivory grip. scimitar blade. See Appendix VII.	313		
	189. Scabbard—Steel, with gilt or gilding metal mountings.	313		
	190. Sword Belt—Russia leather, 1½ inches wide, with slings an inch wide; three stripes of gold embroidery on belt and slings; leather sword piece; a hook to hook up the sword; flat billets and gilt studs.	312	2.6.99	64
	191. Waist Plate—See Appendix I.			
	192. Sword Knot—Gold and crimson lace strap, with gold acorn.	355	23.8.98	64

Undress.

		No.	Sealed.	No. of Plate.
61002 6476	**193. Forage Cap,** } As for Officers on the Head-Quarter, General or Personal Staff. **Frock,**			8
61002 6583 ... 6626	**194. Frock Coat†**—Blue cloth, single-breasted, eight loops of blue silk twist on each side of the breast; a similar loop, 5 inches long, with a small button, at each side of the collar. Plain cuffs, with two holes and buttons to each. A flap on each skirt behind, with a button at the bottom. A gold aiguillette, as for the tunic, on the right shoulder, and a gold cord, with a small button, on the left; two buttons at the waist behind. The skirts lined with black. A pocket inside each skirt behind. Shoulder-straps with badges of rank are *not* worn.	116		

	195. Field Cap,
	    Trousers,
	    Pantaloons, } As for Colonel on the Staff.
	    Boots,
	    Spurs,			

61002 6825	**196.** Sash, sword, sword-belt, and sword-knot as in Full Dress.			

Great Coat and Cape.

		No.	Sealed.	No. of Plate.
	197. Blue milled cloth, of the pattern described in paragraph 14, lined with scarlet rattinett; blue velvet collar.	100	13.2.99	

<table>
<tr><td>61002
6575</td><td>* The loops of mohair cord are not to be pierced through the cloth, but carried to the front edge and turned in, so that the garment may be available for further use on promotion.
† This frock coat is not required for the ordinary routine duties of an Aide-de-Camp to the Sovereign.</td></tr>
</table>

	Pattern.		No. of Plate.
	No.	Sealed.	

HORSE FURNITURE.

198. Saddle—As described in Appendix VI ; or Hunting saddle, with plain stirrups and blue girths, see paragraph 22.   — 600 | 24.9.97

199. Wallets—Brown leather, see Appendix VI. In full dress, blue cloth covers as for General Officers, but without badges of rank.   — | 24.9.97

200. Bridle and Breast Plate—Brown leather, see Appendix VI.   — 607 | 14.9.96

GENERAL REGULATIONS.

201. Aides-de-Camp to the Queen, if on full pay of the Royal Artillery, are to wear *blue* tunics with blue cord loops, scarlet collar and cuffs, and blue flaps. Scarlet piping on the flaps.

202. The uniform and horse furniture of Aides-de-Camp to the Queen appointed from the Militia and Yeomanry are the same as for those appointed from the Regular Forces. For Yeomanry Aides-de-Camp the embroidery, lace, &c., are of silver, instead of gold (except the sash which is as described in paragraph 187).

203. The aiguillette will not be worn with regimental uniform by Officers appointed from the Regular Forces, Militia, or Yeomanry, nor by those appointed from the Volunteers, when doing duty with their corps. This regulation does not apply to Personal Aides-de-Camp to the Sovereign.

204. The uniform and horse furniture of Volunteer Officers who may be appointed Aides-de-Camp to the Queen will either be of regimental pattern, with silver aiguillette, or the uniform and horse furniture prescribed for Aides-de-Camp to Her Majesty appointed from the Regular Forces, with the exception that silver will be substituted for gold in the aiguillette, embroidery, lace, buttons, cocked hat, sword knot, sword belt and slings, waist plate and horse furniture. The sash will be of gold and crimson silk net, with plaited runner and fringe, tassels of gold and crimson silk.

EQUERRY TO THE QUEEN.

205. The uniform and horse furniture of the Queen's Equerries are the same as those described for Her Majesty's Aides-de-Camp, except that the full dress tunic is as described below, and an undress tunic is also worn.

206. Full-dress Tunic—Scarlet cloth, with blue cloth collar and cuffs, the skirt 12 inches deep for an Officer 5 feet 9 inches in height, with a proportionate variation for any difference in height. On each side in front, eight embroidered frog-drop loops, 4 inches long exclusive of the drops, five of them above the waist on the left side with buttons, the rest without. A similar loop on each side of the collar. Round cuffs, 3 inches deep. A scarlet flap on each sleeve, with four embroidered loops and buttons, each loop 1¾ inches long exclusive of the drop. A scarlet flap on each back skirt, 10 inches long and 2 inches wide, with two loops and buttons similar to those on the sleeve ; two buttons at the waist behind. A gold aiguillette, the cord ¼ inch in thickness, gilt metal tags, on the right shoulder, and a gold cord loop, with a small button, on the left. The collar, cuffs, flaps, and back skirts edged with white cloth, ¼ inch wide, and the skirts lined with white. A pocket inside the left breast and inside each skirt behind. Hooks and eyes in front. Shoulder cords with badges of rank are *not* worn.   — 115 | 21.12.97

207. Undress Tunic—The same as the dress tunic, except that instead of the frog-drop loops there are straight loops of scarlet mohair cord, and on the collar a straight blue cord loop with a gorget button at each end.   — 115 | 21.12.97

208. Equerries, if General Officers, may wear the uniform of their rank with aiguillette on the right shoulder.

HONORARY PHYSICIANS AND HONORARY SURGEONS TO THE QUEEN.

209. Uniform of the Royal Army Medical Corps, and horse furniture according to rank, but on State occasions, as a mark of the distinction conferred on them, they will wear instead of the pouch-belt and pouch, a gold sash 2½ inches wide, with two ¼-inch black lines ¾ inch apart, gold and black tassel 9 inches long.   — 513 | 12.4.78

EQUERRY TO THE PRINCE OF WALES.

210. The uniform and horse furniture are the same as those of the Queen's Equerries, with the following exceptions :—

211. There is a Prince of Wales's Plume on the sword hilt and on the buttons, instead of the Royal Cypher.

212. The sash is worn round the waist over the sword-belt, and is made of gold web 2½ inches wide, with seven crimson stripes ⅛ inch wide, gold and crimson tassels with round heads, fastened at the side with gilt wire buckles. The two shoulder cords are of the same pattern,

S
Sligo
Arty.
300

61002
6583

	Pattern.		No. of Plate.
	No.	Sealed.	

EQUERRIES TO THE ROYAL FAMILY.

213. The uniform and horse furniture are the same as those of the Queen's Equerries, with the following exceptions:—

214. **Tunic**—The same as the full dress tunic of Queen's Equerries, but without loops of embroidery, or cord on the breast, and with eight buttons down the front; three loops and buttons on each skirt flap, instead of two; the front edged with white cloth.

(Pattern No. 115, Sealed 21.12.97)

215. **Lace**—Gold, staff pattern.

216. **Buttons**—Burnished, with a crown in the centre.

217. **Frock Coat**—Without loops on the breast or collar; the cord of the aiguillette is $\frac{8}{40}$ inch in thickness.

218. **Sword**—Special device on the hilt.

219. **Sword Belt**—Only two stripes of embroidery on belt and slings.

220. **Sash**—The sash is worn round the waist.

61002
6825

61002
6224

AIDE-DE-CAMP TO THE LIEUTENANT-GENERAL AND GENERAL GOVERNOR OF IRELAND.

61002
5999

221. The uniform and horse furniture are the same as those of an Aide-de-Camp to the Queen, except that instead of the frog-drop loops on the tunic, a device of shamrocks in gold embroidery is worn, and that the frock-coat is of the pattern described below :—

222. **Frock Coat**—Blue cloth, double breasted. Roll collar; the front and collar edged with $\frac{3}{4}$-inch black mohair braid. An Austrian knot of black Russia braid on each sleeve, reaching to 6 inches from the bottom of the cuff; 5 loops of black Russia braid on each side of the breast fastening with black olivets; 2 olivets at the waist behind. The skirts lined with black. Shoulder-straps of the same material as the garment, edged with $\frac{1}{2}$-inch black mohair braid, except at the base; black netted button at the top.

223. **False Waistcoat**—Scarlet cloth, without collar, edged with gold Russia braid, and fastening with hooks and eyes. A pocket on each side.

CAVALRY.

HOUSEHOLD CAVALRY.

FULL DRESS.

	Pattern.		No. of Plate.
	No.	Sealed.	

224. Helmet—German silver, with gilt ornaments.

225. Plume—White horsehair, in the 1st and 2nd Life Guards; red horsehair, in the Royal Horse Guards. — Plate 4

226. Tunic—First Life Guards—Scarlet cloth, with blue velvet collar and cuffs, and blue cloth edging. — Plate 15

[margin: 38407 / Dress / 131]
Second Life Guards—Scarlet cloth, with blue velvet collar, cuffs, and edging, with stitched edges.

[margin: 38407 / Dress / 131]
Royal Horse Guards—Blue cloth, with scarlet cloth collar, cuffs, and edging.

On the collar, an embroidered device on each side, 5½ to 6 inches long and 2 inches wide. Gauntlet cuffs, embroidered like the collar, with button in centre of embroidery and three loops of similar embroidery on each back-skirt. 9 buttons in front and 2 at the waist behind. The skirt rounded in front, and lined with blue cassimere in the 1st Life Guards; with scarlet Italian cloth in the 2nd Life Guards; and with scarlet cassimere in the Royal Horse Guards. An aiguillette of gold cord, with gilt engraved tags, on the right shoulder; and a plaited gold cord on each shoulder.

The Field Officers are further distinguished by a stripe of embroidery, ½ inch wide, round the top of the collar and cuffs.

227. Embroidery—Gold, oak and laurel leaf pattern.

228. Lace—Gold, oak-leaf pattern in 1st and 2nd Life Guards; regimental pattern in the Royal Horse Guards. — No. 701, Sealed 13.2.1900, Plate 72

229. Buttons—See Appendix I.

230. Pantaloons—White leather.

231. Trousers—Blue cloth, with gold lace down the side seams; two stripes, each 1¼ inches wide, with scarlet welt in the centre, for the 1st Life Guards; one stripe, 2½ inches wide, with blue cord in the centre, for the 2nd Life Guards; one stripe, 2¼ inches wide, for the Royal Horse Guards.

232. Boots and Spurs—Jacked boots and steel spurs, with chains and buckles. Wellington boots with gilt metal spurs.

233. Gauntlets—White leather.

234. Sword—Half-basket steel hilt, with brass ornaments; black fish-skin grip, 5 to 5¾ inches long, to suit the size of the hand; straight cut and thrust blade, 39 inches long, and fully an inch wide at the shoulder. Extreme length of the sword, 45 inches.

235. Scabbard—Steel, with plain brass mountings.

236. Sword-Belt—Gold lace, 1¾ inches wide, with slings an inch wide lined with blue Morocco leather for Life Guards, and scarlet Morocco leather for Royal Horse Guards. Billets and gilt studs. — Plate 64

237. Sword-Knot—White leather strap in 1st Life Guards; embroidered crimson leather strap in 2nd Life Guards and Royal Horse Guards; gold and crimson tassel. — Plate 64

238. Shoulder-Belt—Gold lace, 2½ inches wide, lined with scarlet Morocco leather and edged with blue velvet for Life Guards, and scarlet Morocco leather for Royal Horse Guards; gilt mountings; a red stripe in the centre in the Royal Horse Guards.

On the centre of the belt, attached by three gold braid loops, a flask cord, scarlet in the 1st Life Guards and Royal Horse Guards, and blue in the 2nd Life Guards.

239. Pouch—Black patent leather, with gilt mountings.

240. Cuirass—Front and back of polished steel, ornamented with brass studs; bound with brass ½ inch wide in the Royal Horse Guards; Morocco leather lining, and velvet edging of the same colour as the facings; gilt scales of regimental patterns, lined with Morocco leather; straps and buckles of regimental patterns.

UNDRESS.

[margin: 38407 / Dress / 131]
241. Forage Cap—Blue cloth, with scarlet cloth band, and scarlet welt round the crown; gold embroidered peak and chin-strap of regimental patterns. In the 2nd Life Guards a gold French braid figure on the top. — Plate 8

[margin: 61002]
242. Field Cap—As described in paragraph 10, but trimmed as follows:—

[margin: 5736 ...]
1st Life Guards—Scarlet top, with gold French braid round the top, on the flaps, and down the front and back seams. — No. 35, Sealed 23.1.97, Plate 9

[margin: 5632 ...]
2nd Life Guards—As for the 1st Life Guards, but with scarlet welts instead of gold braid. — No. 36, Sealed 9.12.96

[margin: 6156]
Royal Horse Guards—As for 1st Life Guards. For badge, see Appendix I. — No. 37, Sealed 13.8.97

243. Frock Coat—Blue cloth, single-breasted. Stand-up collar, ornamented with figured braiding; and figured braiding on each sleeve, extending to 12 inches from the bottom of the cuff. 6 loops of ¾-inch black braid down the front on each side, with 2 olivets on each loop, the top loops reaching to the shoulder seams, those at the waist 4 inches long; ¾-inch braid on the outer seams of sleeves and back seams, with eyes and fringe at the waist, and tassels on the back skirts. Hooks and eyes in front. The skirt lined with black silk. Shoulder-straps of the same material as the garment, edged with ½-inch black mohair braid, except at the base; black netted button at the top. — Plate 15

		Pattern.		No. of Plate.
		No.	Sealed.	

244. Frock—1st Life Guards—Blue. Collar and shoulder straps of the same colour and material as the rest of the jacket, with small regimental button at top of shoulder-straps. Six small regimental buttons down the front. A patch pocket with box pleat and shaped flap and button on each breast, and two other pockets below the waist. Slits at the sides 4 inches deep. No cuffs. Two small buttons at the wrists.   **259**   **23.12.90**

    2nd Life Guards—As for 1st Life Guards, but with five regimental buttons down the front.   **259**   **23.12.90**

    Royal Horse Guards—Blue. Full in the chest; shoulder-straps, collars, and cuffs of the same colour and material as the rest of the jacket. Shoulder-straps with small regimental button at the top. Three small regimental buttons down the front. Four pleats at the waist behind and two pleats at each side in front. A band round the waist to button in front. A patch pocket with flap and small button on each breast; a patch pocket with flap on each side below the band Wrist-bands 1½ inches deep, with an opening at the back extending to 3 inches. The wrist-band fastened with small regimental button. A box pleat in front at the top of the band.   **260**

61002
Cav.
18

61002
6685
Cav.
20

245. Frock*—Blue angola, tartan, or serge, full in chest, cut with side bodies, slits at sides, five small regimental buttons down the front. Two breast patch pockets outside, 6¼ inches wide, 8½ inches deep from the top of the flap, the top edge of pocket in line with the second button, with three-pointed flap, small regimental button and hole, loose plait on rear side of pocket, two outside patch pockets below, with three-pointed flap. Two inside breast pockets up and down with hole and button. Two inside skirt pockets, with hole and button. Shoulder straps of the same colour and material as the rest of the garment, shaped for shoulder chains fastened with a small regimental button. Steel shoulder chains with badges of rank. Black lining. Collar of the colour of the regimental facings. Sleeves with pointed cuffs, 6 inches high in front and 2¼ inches behind, with slit and two small buttons and button holes.   **126**   **26.3.98**

246. Trousers—Blue cloth, with scarlet cloth stripes, of regimental patterns, down the side seams, viz. :—

38407
Dress
131

    1st and 2nd Life Guards—Two stripes, welted, 1st Life Guards, 1½ inches, 2nd Life Guards, 1¼ inches wide and ½ inch apart; a scarlet welt between the stripes.

    Royal Horse Guards—Single stripe, 2½ inches wide.

247. Pantaloons—Blue cloth, with stripes as on trousers.

248. Knee Boots and Spurs—As described in paragraphs 4 and 25.

249. Sword-Belt—White leather, 2 inches wide, with slings an inch wide. Billets and gilt studs. See also paragraph 28.   **64**

61002
6943

250. Belts, "Sam Browne."

61002
6890

    Scabbard—Brown leather.   } See Appendices VII and VIII.
    Sword Knot—Brown leather.   }

251. Sword Knot—White leather.

252. Shoulder-Belt—White leather, 2½ inches wide, with gilt mountings, and a silk flask cord on the centre as on the dress belt, but smaller.   **64**

    Other articles as in Full Dress.

CLOAK.

253. 1st Life Guards—Scarlet cloth, with blue cloth collar and cape, rose and chain fastening, and scarlet serge lining.

    2nd Life Guards—Scarlet cloth, with blue cloth cape, rose and chain fastening, scarlet collar, and scarlet shalloon lining.

    Royal Horse Guards—Blue cloth, with scarlet cloth collar, and scarlet rattinet lining.

    Shoulder-straps of the same material as the garment, with a small button of regimental pattern at the top.

MESS DRESS.

254. Mess Jacket—1st and 2nd Life Guards—Scarlet cloth, with blue velvet collar, cuffs, and edging, lined drab silk. Royal Horse Guards—Blue cloth, with scarlet cloth collar, cuffs, and edging.   **16**

38407
Dress
131

    Gold lace an inch wide all round the jacket, within the edging (2nd Life Guards—an edging of velvet within the lace), and round the top of the cuffs, which are pointed and 5 inches deep. The 1st and 2nd Life Guards have a row of gilt studs down the front. Gold shoulder-cords of plaited chain gimp 1¼ inches wide.

    Field Officers are further distinguished by gold gimp round the collar and cuffs in the Life Guards, and ½-inch lace in the Royal Horse Guards at the bottom of the collar and top of the cuffs.

38407
Dress
131

255. Mess Waistcoat—1st Life Guards—Blue cloth closed at the neck, edged all round with 1-inch lace, gilt studs down the front, pockets curved, no welts or lace.   **16**

    2nd Life Guards—Light blue cloth, open in front, ¾-inch lace round the edges and across the top of the pockets. Gilt studs down the front.   **16**

...
135
61002
Cav.
71

    Royal Horse Guards—Scarlet cloth, closed at the neck, fastened with hooks and eyes. Edged all round, including the collar, with 1-inch gold lace, two pockets trimmed with similar lace.   **16**

A.C.D.
Cav.
866

256. Trousers, Boots and Spurs—As in full dress.

---

* To be provided when this pattern is issued to N.C.O.'s and men.

	Pattern.		No. of Plate.
	No.	Sealed.	

REGIMENTAL STAFF OFFICERS.

257. The Adjutant and Riding-Master wear the uniform of their rank.

258. The Medical Officers, the Veterinary Officer, and the Quarter-master wear the same uniform as other Officers of corresponding rank, with the following exceptions :—

259. Cocked-Hat (instead of the Helmet for Medical Officers and Veterinary Officers).—As described in paragraph 7 ; the Medical Officer's, with gold lace loop, tassels, and plume of black cock's-tail feathers ; the Veterinary Officer's plume is of red swan feathers. The cuirass is not worn.

260. Shoulder-Belt and Instrument Case for Veterinary Officer— White patent leather belt and instrument case of departmental patterns. The Veterinary Officer will wear in Levée and Review Order, a dress pouch and pouch-belt of regimental pattern.

HORSE FURNITURE—1ST LIFE GUARDS.

261. Shabracque—Blue cloth, 41 inches long at the bottom and 28 inches deep, with the fore and hind corners pointed ; 3 stripes of gold lace all round, showing ½ inch of scarlet cloth between the stripes, the centre stripe 2½ inches wide, the others ⅝ inch. On each hind corner, a crown, scrolls bearing the word "Dettingen," "Peninsula," "Waterloo," "Egypt, 1882," and "Tel-el-Kebir" ; and reversed cypher L.G. embroidered in gold ; a Garter star below. Holster covers of blue cloth, 23 inches deep and 15 inches wide, laced to match the shabracque, with crown and regimental cypher, with "1" above, embroidered in gold ; black bear-skin caps. Doe-skin seat. White web surcingle.

262. Saddle—High mounting saddle, with brass cantle, shoe cases, and white web girths. White leather cover with full dress.

263. Stirrups—Large, square-set, steel ; with plain brown stirrup-leathers.

264. Slides and Tips—Brass, with steel studs.

265. Holsters—Brown leather, with black plain leather straps.

266. Bridle—Plain black leather, with brass whole buckles. Chain head-piece and front, brass plates with steel stars in the centres, and a boss at each end. Plain black leather head collar. Steel bit, with bar and water chain ; Russian hooks and steel loops for cheeks of bridle ; brass bosses, with Royal Crest and regimental cypher. Plain ring bridoon, with gold lace reins for full dress.

267. Breast-Plate—Plain black leather, with brass whole buckles, and boss.

268. Chain—Steel.

269. Undress Shabracque—Black bear-skin, plain brown leather surcingle.

HORSE FURNITURE—2ND LIFE GUARDS.

270. Shabracque—Blue cloth, 48 inches long at the bottom and 32 inches deep, with the fore and hind corners rounded ; a scarlet cloth border 4¾ inches wide, 1¼ inch from the edge of the shabracque : a stripe of gold lace 2⅔ inches wide, ¾ inch from the outer edge of the scarlet border. On each hind corner, the Royal Crest, scrolls with the words "Dettingen," "Peninsula," "Waterloo," "Egypt, 1882," and "Tel-el-Kebir" ; and a laurel wreath embroidered in gold ; within the wreath, a Garter star and "2" below. On each fore corner as on each hind corner, except that the number 2 is omitted. Brown leather surcingle.

271. Saddle—High mounting saddle, with brass cantle, fan-tails, shoe-cases and white web girths.

272. Stirrups—Oval pattern, steel, with plain brown stirrup leathers.

273. Slides—Brass, with steel centres.

274. Holsters—Brown leather, with holster and cloak strap in one.

275. Bridle—Plain black leather, with brass buckles. Brass scale head-piece, with silver studs, white buff front for full dress. Black leather collar, steel bit with bar, and brass bosses bearing the Royal Crest, encircled with the words "Peninsula" and "Waterloo." Ring bridoon, with gold lace head and reins, for full dress.

276. Breast-Plate—Black patent leather, with silver Garter star, for full dress ; plain black leather, with brass boss as on bit, for undress.

277. Chain—Steel.

278. Undress Shabracque—Black bear-skin.

38407
Dress
135

HORSE FURNITURE—ROYAL HORSE GUARDS.

61002
4810

279. Shabracque—Scarlet cloth, 50 inches long at bottom and 35 inches deep, with the fore corners rounded and the hind corners pointed ; 2 stripes of gold lace all round, showing ¼ inch of blue cloth between the stripes, the outer lace ¾ inch, the inner an inch wide. On each fore and hind corner, a crown, scrolls with the words "Dettingen," "Peninsula," "Waterloo," "Egypt, 1882," "Tel-el-Kebir" ; and laurel leaves embroidered in gold, with a Garter star below. Black patent leather surcingle.

280. Saddle—High mounting saddle, with Prince's metal cantle, fan-tails, brass nails with regimental cypher, and white web girths.

281. Stirrups—Large, square-set, steel, with plain brown stirrup leathers.

282. Slides—Brass.

283. Holsters—Brown leather, with brown leather straps.

For the 1st Life Guards entry (259): No. 1 and 2, Sealed 23.8.98 and 29.11.98, No. of Plate 2 & 3.

	Pattern.		No. of Plate.
	No.	Sealed.	

284. Bridle—Plain black leather. Head-chain, 2 rows of brass plates with cut steel studs, and a large plate at each end with similar studs. Plain leather front, with a brass shield. For undress, a similar bridle, but with plain leather head-piece and front. Plain leather collar. Steel bit, with twisted beard, bent bar, and brass bosses with cut steel centres. Plain ring bridoon.

285. Breast-Plate—Plain black leather, with boss as on bit.

286. Chain—Steel.

287. Undress Shabracque—Black lambskin.

61002
Cavalry
147

CAVALRY OF THE LINE.

Officers Commanding Cavalry Brigades and Officers serving on their Staff.

288. Uniform of their rank or regiment, with shoulder straps and shoulder chains for the frock as for regimental Cavalry Officers. See paragraph 315.

DRAGOON GUARDS AND DRAGOONS.

Full Dress.

289. Helmet—Gilt or gilding metal, bound round the edge. At the top a crosspiece base and a plume socket, 4 inches high from point of insertion in base. A laurel wreath above the front peak, and an oak-leaf band up the back. Plain burnished chain, 1 inch wide, mounted on black patent leather, lined with velvet and fastened on each side with a rose ornament. Furniture, gilt or gilding metal.   [No. 6 | 23.8.98 | Plate 3]

61002
5202
61002
6398

A diamond-cut silver star in front; on the star in gilt or gilding metal, the garter pierced with the motto, "Honi soit qui mal y pense," or an elliptical ring with the designation of the regiment. Within the garter or ring the regimental device or number. (For detailed description see Appendix I.) In the 6th Dragoon Guards the star has plain rays.

290. Helmet for 1st and 6th Dragoons—Of the same pattern as for Dragoon Guards, but of white metal, with gilt or gilding metal ornaments.   [No. 6 | 23.8.98]

291. Plume—Horsehair, of the colour stated below for each regiment. The plume rises 2 inches from point of insertion in socket, and falls as far as the bottom of the helmet. A rose at the top screwed on to the stem of the plume. Steel stem with screw and fly-nut.   [No. 38 | | Plate 4]

Regiment.		Colour of Plume.
1st Dragoon Guards		Red.
2nd "		Black.
3rd "		Black and Red.
4th "		White.
5th "		Red and White.
6th "		White.
7th "		Black and White.
1st Dragoons		Black.
6th "		White.

292. Cap for 2nd Dragoons—Black bearskin, a grenade, fitted with a spring on the left side as a plume socket. Plain burnished chain, lined with patent leather, backed with velvet. For Officers not exceeding 5 ft. 6 in. in height, 9½ in. high.   [No. 7 | 23.8.98 | Plate 4]

    5 ft. 6 in.   "   5 " 9 "   "   10 " "
    5 " 9 "   "   6 " 0 "   "   10½ " "
    6 " 0 " and upwards   11 " "
For device on grenade see Appendix I.

293. Plume—White hackle feather, 10 inches high, to the top of the plume.   [No. 18 | 23.8.98 | Plate 4]

294. Tunic (except for the 6th Dragoon Guards—Carabineers)—Scarlet cloth; with collar and cuffs of the colour of the regimental facings, in the 1st (King's), 3rd (Prince of Wales's), 4th (Royal Irish), 5th (Princess Charlotte of Wales's), and 7th Dragoon Guards, of velvet; in the 2nd Dragoon Guards (Queen's Bays) and the 1st (Royal), 2nd (Royal Scots Greys), and 6th (Inniskilling), Dragoons, of cloth. The collar ornamented with ¾-inch lace (1-inch for 2nd Dragoon Guards (Queen's Bays), and 1st (Royal) Dragoons), all round for Field Officers, but round the top only for Captains and Lieutenants. The cuffs 2 inches deep at the point and 1¼ inches at the back, edged with round-back gold cord, forming, for Field Officers, a triple Austrian knot, traced round with gold Russia braid, and extending to 11¾ inches from the bottom of the cuffs; for Captains, a double Austrian knot similarly traced, 9¾ inches deep, and for Lieutenants, a single Austrian knot, 7¾ inches deep. Eight buttons in front, and two at the waist behind; a three-pointed scarlet flap on each skirt behind, with three buttons, and edged with round-back gold cord, traced inside and out with gold Russia braid. The front edged with the same material and colour as the facings, and the skirts lined with white. Plaited gold shoulder cord, lined with scarlet; a small button at the top.   [No. 117 | | Plate 17]

61002
Cav.
107

[No. 517 | 23.8.98 | Plate 62]

	Pattern.		No. of Plate.
	No.	Sealed.	
295. Tunic, for 6th Dragoon Guards—Blue cloth, edged all round, including the top and bottom of the collar, with round-back gold cord. Collar and pointed cuffs of white cloth. The collar laced within the cord, like that for other Dragoon Guard regiments. The cuffs trimmed for Field Officers with 1½-inch lace round the top and figured braiding extending to 11½ inches from the bottom of the cuff, for Captains, with an Austrian knot of round-back gold cord and a tracing of braid in the form of eyes, 8½ inches deep, and for Lieutenants, with a similar knot and a tracing of plain braid, 7½ inches deep. Eight buttons in front, and two at the waist behind. A three-pointed blue cloth flap on each skirt behind, with three buttons, and edged with round-back gold cord. Plaited flat gold shoulder cord, lined with blue; a small button at the top.	118 / See 157		62
296. Lace—Gold, of regimental patterns.	704 to 712, 716		72, 73, 74, 76
297. Buttons—See Appendix I.			
298. Trousers—Blue cloth, with 1¾-inch lace down the side seams. In the 2nd Dragoon Guards and 6th Dragoon Guards (the latter wear a double stripe) the stripes are of white cloth instead of gold lace. Foot chains instead of foot-straps are worn in the 3rd Dragoon Guards.			
299. Pantaloons—Blue cloth, with cloth stripes of the same colour as those worn by the men.			
300. Boots and Spurs—As described in paragraphs 4 and 25, except that in the 2nd Dragoon Guards steel spurs are always worn.			
301. Sword—Cavalry pattern, as described in Appendix VII.	314	11.9.93	67
302. Scabbard—Steel, as described in Appendix VII.	314	11.9 96	67
303. Sword Belt—Web, 1½ inches wide, with leather furniture and metal dees for slings. Shoulder suspender attached by hooks to dees, see Appendix VIII.	305	1.6.98	64
304. Sword Slings—Gold lace 1 inch wide, morocco leather lining, and edging of the same colour as the facings.	315	15.9.91	64
305. Girdle—Gold lace, not exceeding 2¼ inches wide (2½ inches in the 7th Dragoon Guards), morocco leather lining, edging of the colour of the facings.			
306. Waist Plate—Gilt rectangular plate, with burnished rim. For device, see Appendix I.			
307. Sword Knot—White leather strap with gold acorn. In the 3rd and 6th Dragoon Guards, 1st Dragoons, gold cord and acorn. In the 7th Dragoon Guards, gold and black cord and acorn. In the 2nd Dragoons, gold cord with gold thistle. In the 6th Dragoons, gold and crimson cord and acorn.	316 / 317 / 318	23.8.98 / 23.8.98 / 23.8.98	64
308. Shoulder Belt—Gold lace, not less than 2¼ inches or more than 2½ inches in width (2 inches in the 6th Dragoon Guards), with the same lining and edging as the sword slings; gilt buckle, tip, and slide of regimental pattern. In the 6th Dragoon Guards and 6th Dragoons the buckle, tip, and slide, and breast ornament are of silver.	319	15.9.91	
309. Pouch—Black leather, with gold embroidered edging round the top; solid silver flap, 7½ inches long and 2¾ inches deep, engraved round the edges. Silver loops and stud.	320	15.9.91	
310. Gauntlets—White leather.	516	23.8 98	
311. Sabretache—As described in paragraph 21, except that regiments having special regimental patterns are allowed to retain them.	302	11.5.95	
UNDRESS.			
312. Forage Cap—Blue cloth; with 1¾-inch gold lace; gold purl button, braided figure on the crown except in the 2nd Dragoons; black patent leather chin-strap.	39 / 40	2.6.99 / 10.9.91	8
313. Field Cap—As described in paragraph 10, but with yellow body, except for the 2nd and 6th Dragoon Guards. in which regiments it is white. Gold French braid welts on cap and flaps, and at front and back seams. Regimental badge on left side, see Appendix I.	41 / 42	5.4.98 / 5.4.98	9
314. Frock Coat—Blue cloth, single-breasted. The collar edged all round with ¾-inch black braid, and with figuring in narrow braid. A braided figure on each sleeve, extending to 10 inches from the bottom of the cuff. 6 loops of inch braid across the breast, with 4 rows of olivets. Hooks and eyes down the front. The sleeves, the front, and the skirts edged with inch braid, and the back seams and skirts trimmed with inch braid, traced round with narrow braid, and with olivets and tassels. The skirts lined with black. Shoulder straps of the same material as the garment, edged with ½-inch black mohair braid, except at the base; black netted button at the top.	119	23.8.98	19
315. Frock—Red angola, tartan, or serge, full in chest, cut with side bodies, slits at sides, five small regimental buttons down the front. Two breast patch pockets outside, 6¼ inches wide, 8½ inches deep from the top of the flap, the top edge of pocket in line with the second button, with three-pointed flap, small regimental button and hole, loose plait on rear side of pocket, two outside patch pockets below, with three-pointed flap. Two inside breast pockets up and down with hole and button, two inside skirt pockets, with hole and button. Shoulder straps of the same colour and material as the garment, shaped for shoulder chains, fastened with a small regimental button. Steel shoulder chains with badges of rank. See Appendix X. Italian cloth or thin serge lining. Collar of the colour of the regimental facings. Sleeves with pointed cuffs, 6 inches high in front and 2¼ inches behind, with slit and two small buttons and button holes.	120	26.3.98	19 / 63

Margin reference codes (left margin):

61002 / Cavalry / 11

61002 / 5084

61002 / 6335

61002 / 6568 / ... / Cavalry / 52

61002 / 6591 / ... / 6620 / ... / 6663

61002 / 6765

61002 / 6817

61002 / Cav. / 1

61002 / 6673

61002 / Cav. / 20

61002 / Cav / 37

	Pattern.		No. of Plate.
	No.	Sealed.	

$\frac{61002}{6943}$ **316. Sword Belt**—White leather, 1½ inches wide, with slings an inch wide, gilt mountings ; waist plate as in Appendix I. See also paragraph 28.   *(321 — 3.9.91 — 64)*

$\frac{61002}{6783}$ **317. Sword Knot**—White leather strap and gold acorn, white acorn in the 2nd and 7th Dragoon Guards and the 1st and 6th Dragoons.   *(64)*

$\frac{61002}{6890}$ **318. Belts**—"Sam Browne"—
     Scabbard—Brown leather } See Appendices VII and VIII.
     Sword Knot—Brown leather }

319. Shoulder Belt—White leather, 2½ inches wide, with brass buckle, tip, and slide. The Undress shoulder belt is not worn in the 6th Dragoon Guards.   *(322)*
     Other articles as in Full Dress.

CLOAK AND CAPE.

$\frac{61002}{6568}$
$\frac{...}{67\varepsilon3}$ **320.** Blue cloth, of the same pattern as for rank and file ; to reach to the ankles when worn on foot. White shalloon lining in the 2nd, 3rd, and 6th Dragoon Guards and 1st and 6th Dragoons ; scarlet in other regiments. Collar of cloak of white cloth in the 6th Dragoon Guards, red in the 1st Dragoons, black velvet in the 7th Dragoon Guards, and blue cloth in the other regiments. Red lining to the collar in the 1st Dragoon Guards and 2nd Dragoons. Buttons of regimental patterns. Shoulder straps of the same material as the garment ; a small button at the top.   *(121 — 11.5.92)* *(122 — 11.5.92)*

MESS DRESS.

321. Mess Jacket—Blue cloth in the 6th Dragoon Guards, scarlet in the other regiments ; edged all round, including the collar, with inch gold lace (1½ inches for Field Officers) of the same pattern as that on the tunic. The gold lace forms a pear-shaped eye at the bottom of each back seam, except in the 6th Dragoon Guards, in which regiment it forms dummies. Hooks and eyes down the front. Collar and cuffs of the regimental facings ; the cuffs pointed with inch lace round the top, 5½ inches deep at the point and 1¾ inches at the back seam. Two buttons on the sleeve behind. Shoulder cords as for tunic, plaited flat lace in the 7th Dragoon Guards.   *(123 — 11.12.61 — 26)*

$\frac{61002}{6783}$ **322. Mess Waistcoat**—According to regimental patterns.
     Other articles as in Full Dress.

REGIMENTAL STAFF OFFICERS.

323. The Adjutant, Riding-Master, and Quartermaster wear the same uniform as the other Officers of their rank.

HORSE FURNITURE.

324. Saddle
     Bridle } Cavalry pattern, as described in Appendix VI.   *(605 — 24.9.97)* *(607 — 14.9.96)* *(601)*
     Breast Plate
     Surcingle

$\frac{61002}{6565}$ **325. Horse Plume**—Dragoons only, horse hair, 18 inches long. 1st Dragoons, black ; 2nd Dragoons, black and red ; 6th Dragoons, white. Brass ball and socket.

326. Head Rope
     Lance Bucket } Universal pattern.   *(608 — 8.7.96)*

$\frac{54}{\text{Officers}}$
$\frac{}{58}$ **327. Lambskin***—Front and rear portions of black Ukraine lambskin, connected by a central piece, forming the seat, of black bag hide. Two holes in front portion, giving access to wallets, and covered by a flap. Lambskin points edged with cloth of the colour of the facings, red in the 1st and 2nd Dragoons. The whole lined with moleskin.   *(535 — 10.12.98)*

     Extreme length .... 3 ft. 5 in.
     Extreme width of front .... 2 ft. 11 in.
     Width of rear portion immediately behind leather .... 2 ft. 1 in.
     Width of leather seat at middle .... 2 ft. 1½ in.

HUSSARS.

FULL DRESS.

328. Busby—Black sable fur ; outside measurement, 6¼ inches high in front, and 7¾ inches at the back ; ½ inch smaller round the top than the bottom. A gold gimp oval cockade, 2 inches deep and 1½ inches wide, in the centre in front, the top on a level with the top of the busby. A spring socket behind the cockade. A cloth bag covering the top of the busby, and falling down the right side to the bottom ; a line of gold braid along the seam of the bag, and down the centre, with a gold gimp button at the bottom ; for colour, see paragraph 345. A hook at the top on the right, to hook up the chain.   *(8 — 12.11.87 — 4)*

$\frac{61002}{6620}$ The cockade is not worn in the 14th Hussars.

$\frac{61002}{\text{Infy.}}$
$\frac{}{228}$ **329. Plume**—Ostrich feather, 15 inches high from the top of the busby to the top of the plume ; encircled by a ring. Vulture feather bottom in a corded gilt ball socket with four upright leaves. For colour of plume, see paragraph 345.   *(43 — 4)*

---

* Hitherto called *Sheepskin*.

		No.	Sealed.	No. of Plate.
			Pattern.	

61002 / Cav. / 97
330. Busby Chain— Dead and bright gilt corded chain ; lined with black morocco leather, white in the 13th Hussars, yellow in the 14th Hussars and crimson in the 15th Hussars, the leather backed with velvet. — No. 8, Sealed 12.11.87, Plate 4

61002 / 6568
331. Busby Line— Gold purl cord, with sliders and olive ends ; encircling the busby diagonally three times, passing through a ring under the bag, then round the body, and looped on the breast. A swivel hook on the end of the line. In the 11th Hussars the line is plaited. — No. 8, Sealed 12.11.87

332. Tunic— Blue cloth, edged all round with gold chain gimp. The collar edged along the top with ¾-inch lace. On each side of the breast six loops of gold chain gimp, with caps and drops fastening with gold-worked olivets. On each back-seam a double line of the same gimp, forming three eyes at the top, passing under a netted cap at the waist, and ending in an Austrian knot reaching to the bottom of the skirt, with a tracing of gold braid all round the gimp. An Austrian knot of gold chain gimp on each sleeve, reaching to 8 inches from the bottom of the cuff. The skirt rounded off in front, closed behind, and lined with black. Shoulder cords of plaited gold chain gimp, lined with blue ; a small button at the top. — No. 124, Plate 18; No. 518, Sealed 23.8.98, Plate 62

Field Officers have figured braiding below the lace on the collar, and figured braiding on the sleeve, round the Austrian knot, extending to 11 inches from the bottom of the cuff.

Captains have a row of braided eyes on the collar, below the lace, and a tracing of braided eyes round the knot on the sleeve, 9 inches deep.

Lieutenants have a tracing of plain braid only below the lace on the collar and round the knot on the sleeve, 8 inches deep.

The 3rd Hussars wear scarlet, and the 13th Hussars buff cloth collars.

333. Lace— Regimental pattern, see also paragraph 345.

334. Trousers— Blue cloth (crimson cloth in 11th Hussars), with two stripes of ¾-inch lace, ¼ inch apart, down each side seam. In the 13th Hussars white cloth stripes are worn. — No. 713-730, Plate 74, 75, 76, 77, 78

335. Pantaloons— Blue cloth (crimson cloth in 11th Hussars) with two ¾-inch cloth stripes, ⅛ inch apart, of the same colour as those worn by the men.

38407 / Dress / 107
For Levées and in the evening when in Full Dress :—
Blue cloth (scarlet Berlin diagonal cloth in the 10th Hussars, and crimson cloth in the 11th Hussars), with a stripe of ¾-inch gold lace down each side seam, traced with gold Russia braid, showing a blue light of ⅛ inch.

336. Boots and Spurs— As described in paragraphs 4 and 25 ; a gold gimp oval boss, 2 inches long and 1¼ inches wide, is introduced at the bottom of the V cut.

Hessian Boots— Round the top gold gimp lace ⅜ inch wide, terminating in an oval boss in front, 2 inches long and 1¼ inches wide. The height of the boots at the back to reach just above the centre of the calf of the leg, the slope behind to be 1½ inches lower than the top of the peak which forms the V cut in front ; patent boxes worked into the heels.

Brass Spurs— With Hessian boots straight-neck brass spurs are to be worn. Length of neck 1⅝ inches, exclusive of the rowel.

A O 111 / 1896
337. Sword— Cavalry pattern, see Appendix VII.

338. Scabbard— Steel, see Appendix VII. — No. 314, Sealed 11.9.96, Plate 67

61002 / 6660
339. Sword Belt— Web, as described in paragraph 303. — No. 314, Sealed 11.9.96, Plate 67

340. Slings, Sword, and Sabretache— Sword slings, gold lace, 1 inch *full* wide, sabretache slings, ¾-inch wide, morocco leather lining and edging, of the colour of the sabretache. For stripe in centre, see paragraph 345. Lion head buckles. — No. 305, Sealed 1.6.98, Plate 64; No. 323

61002 / 6765
341. Sword Knot— Gold and crimson cord and acorn. No crimson in the 13th and 14th Hussars. — No. 324, Sealed 23.8.98, Plate 64

61002 / 6663
342. Shoulder Belt— In the 10th Hussars, black patent leather, with metal chain ornament ; in the other regiments, gold lace, the width not to exceed 2 inches ; morocco leather lining and edging of the same colour as the sabretache. Regimental pattern buckle, tip and slide ; ornamented in the 7th, 8th, 10th, 15th, and 18th Hussars ; in the other regiments the buckle, tip, and slide are of silver, and silver engraved breast ornaments with chain and pickers are worn. — No. 325, 327

In the 13th Hussars honours are worn on the shoulder-belt. — No. 326, Sealed 10.10.88

343. Pouch— As described in paragraph 345. — No. 325, 327, 328, Sealed 17.1.65

61002 / 6568
344. Sabretache— Cloth face, crimson in the 11th and 20th Hussars, buff in the 13th, and scarlet in the other regiments ; with lace of authorized regimental pattern ; yellow lining in the 14th Hussars. Embroidered regimental device in the centre. Dimensions not to exceed 7¾ inches at the top, 10½ inches at the bottom, and 12 inches in length. Morocco leather pocket of the same colour as the cloth face. Three slings ¾ inch wide. In the 11th Hussars the crest and motto of H.R.H. the late Prince Consort are worn over the regimental device. See paragraph 345. — No. 329; No. 320

345. REGIMENTAL PATTERNS :—

	Busby Bag.	Plume.	Pouch.
3rd Hussars	Garter Blue	White ….	{ Black leather, silver flap, and gilt or gilding metal ornaments.
4th „	Yellow ….	Scarlet ….	{
7th „	Scarlet ….	White ….	} Scarlet cloth, embroidered in gold.
8th „	Scarlet ….	Red and White	}

	Busby Bag.	Plume.	Pouch.
10th Hussars	Scarlet	.... Black and White	Black patent leather of special pattern, gilt metal leaves for loops.
11th "	Crimson	.... Crimson and White	Crimson leather, gilt or gilding metal flap, and silver ornaments.
13th "	Buff	.... White	Black leather, silver flap, and gilt or gilding metal ornaments.
14th "	Yellow	.... White	(as 13th)
15th "	Scarlet	.... Scarlet	Scarlet cloth, embroidered in gold.
18th "	Blue	.... Scarlet and White	Scarlet leather, embroidered in gold.
19th "	White	.... White	Black leather, silver flap, and gilt or gilding metal ornaments.
20th "	Crimson	.... Yellow	(as 19th)

N.B.—The second colour is that of the vulture feather bottom.

The undermentioned regiments have a silk stripe $\frac{1}{4}$ inch *full* in the centre of the shoulder belt, a stripe $\frac{1}{8}$ inch *full* in the centre of the lace round the sabretache ; and $\frac{1}{8}$-inch stripe in the centre of the sword slings, of the colours specified for each : –3rd, 4th, 15th Hussars, scarlet ; 13th, buff ; 14th gold ; 19th white ; 20th, crimson.

Margin		Pattern No.	Sealed.	No. of Plate.
	UNDRESS.			
	346. Forage Cap—Crimson cloth in the 11th Hussars, scarlet in the 15th, and blue in the other regiments ; with band of $1\frac{3}{4}$-inch gold lace ; gold purl button and braided figure on the crown, and a line of gold braid round the crown seam.	44	4.9.91	8
61002 / Cav. / 1; 61002 / Cav. / 117	**347. Field Cap**—As described in paragraph 10, except that the cap is crimson in the 11th, and scarlet in the other regiments. In the 13th Hussars the body and crown of the cap are white, and the flaps blue. Gold French braid welts on caps and flaps, and at front and back seams. Regimental badge on left side. See Appendix I.	45 46 42	5.4.98 5.4.98 5.4.98	9
61002 / Cav. / 97	**348. Patrol Jacket**—Blue cloth, 28 inches long from the bottom of the collar behind for an Officer 5 feet 9 inches in height, with a proportionate variation for any difference in height, rounded in front and edged with astrachan fur all round. Collar and cuffs of astrachan fur. Trimmed with mohair braid according to regimental pattern. Hooks and eyes in front ; pocket inside left breast. Shoulder straps of the same material as the garment, edged with $\frac{1}{2}$-inch black mohair braid, except at the base ; black netted button at the top. In the 13th Hussars a special pattern short jacket is worn.			20 21 22 23 24 25
61002 / 6685; 61002 / Cav. / 20	**349. Frock**—Blue angola, tartan, or serge, full in chest, cut with side bodies, slits at sides, five small regimental buttons down the front. Two breast patch pockets outside, $6\frac{1}{4}$ inches wide, $8\frac{1}{2}$ inches deep from the top of the flap, the top edge of pocket in line with the second button, with three-pointed flap, small regimental button and hole, loose plait on rear side of pocket, two outside patch pockets below, with three-pointed flap. Two inside breast pockets up and down with hole and button. Two inside skirt pockets, with hole and button. Shoulder straps of the same colour and material as the rest of the garment, shaped for shoulder chains, fastened with a small regimental button. Steel shoulder chains with badges of rank. See Appendix X. Italian cloth or thin serge lining. Collar of the colour of the regimental facings. Sleeves with pointed cuffs, 6 inches high in front and $2\frac{1}{4}$ inches behind, with slit and two small buttons and button holes.	126	26.3.98	19 63
	350. Slings—Sword and sabretache. **Sword Knot**— } Same as in Full Dress, except that plain buff leather will be substituted for gold lace and gold cord.	331	23.8.98	64
	In 10th Hussars, of crimson morocco leather, edged with gold wire, with scroll of the same material down the centre.	332	23.8.98	
61002 / 6890	**351. Belts**—"Sam Browne" **Scabbard**—Brown leather **Sword Knot**—Brown leather } See Appendices VII and VIII.			
	352. Sabretache—As described in Appendix V, except that regiments having special regimental patterns are allowed to retain them. In the 10th Hussars the Prince of Wales's plume, in silver, is worn on the sabretache. Other articles as in Full Dress.	302	11.5.95	
	CLOAK AND CAPE.			
61002 / 6783; ... / Cav. / 97	**353.** Blue cloth, of the same pattern as for Officers of Dragoon Guards and Dragoons, with white lining in the 8th and 13th Hussars, crimson lining in the 11th Hussars, yellow in the 14th Hussars, and scarlet in the other regiments.	121 122	11.5.92 11.5.92	
	MESS DRESS.			
	354. Mess Jacket—Blue cloth, with olivets and lace, or cord, and shoulder cords, according to regimental patterns. The 3rd Hussars wear scarlet, and the 13th Hussars buff collars.			
	355. Mess Waistcoat—According to regimental patterns. Other articles as in Full Dress.			

REGIMENTAL STAFF OFFICERS.

356. The Adjutant, Riding-Master and Quartermaster wear the same uniform as the other Officers of their rank

	Pattern.		No. of Plate.
	No.	Sealed.	

HORSE FURNITURE.

357. Horse Plume.—Horsehair, 18 inches long, of the colours given below, viz. :—

3rd Hussars	....	White.
4th ,,	....	Scarlet.
7th ,,	....	White.
8th ,,	....	Red and White.
10th ,,	....	Black and White.
11th ,,	....	Crimson and White.
13th ,,	....	White.
14th ,,	....	White.
15th ,,	....	Scarlet.
18th ,,	....	Scarlet and White.
19th ,,	,...	White.
20th ,,	....	Crimson.

Brass ball and socket.

61002 / 6568

358. Lambskin—As for Dragoon Guards and Dragoons, or **Leopard Skin**, but edged with cloth of the colour of the busby bag. In the 3rd Hussars the edging is scarlet. The lambskin is not worn in India.

Pattern No. 535, 536, 537 — Sealed 10.12.98

61002 / Cav. / 8

359. Bosses of regimental pattern. Other articles of Cavalry pattern, see Appendix VI. The 10th Hussars are permitted to wear, in review order only, a bridle and breastplate, ornamented with shells. The 15th Hussars wear crossed flags, pointing downwards, on the leopard skin.

Plate 71

LANCERS.

FULL DRESS.

61002 / 5832

360. Cap [except for 9th Lancers]—Lancer pattern ; 6½ inches high in front, 7 inches at the sides, and 8½ inches at the back ; 7 inches square at the top. Skull covered with black patent leather, the upper part and top with cloth of the same colour as the facings. Gold gimp and orris cord across the top and down the angles. On the left side, in front, a gold bullion rosette, with Royal cypher, embroidered on blue velvet in the 12th and 17th Lancers, on green in the 5th, on scarlet in the 16th, and the Imperial cypher on French grey in the 21st ; at the back of the rosette, a spring socket for the plume stem. A band of inch lace round the waist, with two bands of gold braid below, the upper ½ inch wide ; the lower ¼ inch ; and a similar double band of braid round the bottom of the cap, the ½-inch braid being the lower ; the lace and the several bands of braid to be ⅛ inch apart. A gilt or gilding metal plate in front, with silver badge of regimental pattern. Black patent leather peak, embroidered with three stripes of gold purl. Plain burnished chain, ¾ inch wide, mounted on black patent leather lined with velvet, attached to lions' heads at the sides. Rings and hook on a metal leaf at the back of the waist, for the cap line and chain.

Pattern No. 9, 11, 12, 13 — Sealed 11.7.56 — Plate 5

361. Cap, for 9th Lancers—Of the size and shape described above. The skull and top covered with black patent leather ; the upper part only with blue cloth. Strips of metal covering the angles, with metal ornaments at the corners of the top. On the left side, in front, a metal rosette, with a button in the centre, and a spring socket for the plume stem behind the rosette. A band of metal, an inch wide, round the waist. A ring and hook at the back for the cap-line and chain. Black patent leather peak, with a binding of metal, ¼ inch wide. Gilt or gilding metal cord chain ¾ inch wide, mounted on black patent leather, lined with velvet, attached to lions' heads at the sides.

Pattern No. 10 — Sealed 11.7.56 — Plate 5

362. Cap Line—Gold gimp and orris cord, with slide and olive ends, encircling the cap once, passing round the body, and looped on the left breast.

Pattern No. 47 — Sealed 11 7.56

61002 / 6550

363. Plume—Drooping swan feathers, length 14 inches in front and 7 inches behind from the bend of the feathers :—

Plate 5

For 5th Lancers	....	Green.
,, 9th ,,	....	Black and White.
,, 12th ,,	....	Scarlet.
,, 16th ,,	....	Black.
,, 17th ,,	....	White.
,, 21st ,,	....	White.

Pattern No. 48, 49, 50, 51 — Sealed 29.3.75, 29.3.75, 29.3.75

Gilt plume socket with five leaves.

38407 / Dress / 157

364. Tunic—Blue cloth [scarlet in the 16th Lancers], double-breasted, with front, collar, and cuffs of the regimental facings ; the cuffs pointed, the collar and cuffs ornamented with inch lace round the top, the point of the cuff extending to 8½ inches from the bottom. Two rows of buttons in front, seven in each row, the rows 8 inches apart at the top, and 4 inches at the waist, where the buttons are flat to go under the girdle ; two buttons at the waist behind. A three-pointed flap on back of each skirt, edged with square gold cord, three buttons on each flap. A welt of the regimental facings in the sleeve and back

Pattern No. 127 — Sealed 11.12.61 — Plate 18

	Pattern		No. of Plate.
	No.	Sealed.	

seams, down the front, and round the skirts, which are lined with white in the 16th, with black in the other regiments. Gold wire shoulder cords, lined with scarlet in the 16th Lancers; blue in other regiments. Small button at the top. | 519 | 23.8.98 | 62

Field Officers are further distinguished by lace round the bottom of the collar, and by a second line of lace round the cuff.

365. Lace—Of regimental patterns. | 715-731 | | { 75, 76, 77, 78

366. Buttons—As described in Appendix I.

367. Trousers—Blue cloth, with two stripes of ¾-inch lace, ¼ inch apart, down each side seam; in the 17th Lancers the stripe is of white cloth instead of gold lace.

368. Pantaloons—Blue cloth, with cloth stripes of the same colour as those worn by the men.

61002 / 6549   **369. Girdle**—Gold lace, 2½ inches wide, with two crimson silk stripes; fastened with a small strap and buckle on the inside and outside with gold Russia braid loops and gold olivets; the loops in three rows, three loops in each row. The girdle to be 3½ inches larger than the actual waist measurement to allow for lap. | 127 / 731 | 11.12.61 / 23.10.99 | 18

370. Boots and Spurs—As described in paragraphs 4 and 25, except that steel spurs are worn in all orders of dress in the 17th Lancers.

371. Sword
Scabbard } Cavalry pattern, see Appendix VII. | 314 | 11.9.96 | 67

61002 / 6660   **372. Sword Belt**—Web, as described in paragraph 303. | 305 | 1.6.98 | 64

373. Slings, Sword and Sabretache—Sword slings, gold lace, 1 inch *full*, with ⅛-inch, silk stripe, sabretache slings, ¾-inch, with 1/16-inch silk stripe in the centre; no stripe in the 9th Lancers; morocco leather lining and edging; fastened to rings, buckles and leather straps. The silk stripes, lining, and edging of the colour of the regimental facings. Oval wire buckles. | 333 | |

374. Sword Knot—As for Hussars, see paragraph 341. | 324 | 23.8.98 | 64

61002 / 6660   **375. Shoulder Belt**—Gold lace, 2 inches wide, with ¼-inch *full* silk stripe, morocco leather lining and edging as for sword belt; silver breast-ornament, with pickers and chains, buckle, tip, and slide of regimental pattern. | 334 | |

There is no silk stripe in the 9th Lancers, and the ornaments are of gilt or gilding metal. In the 21st Lancers the shoulder belt is as for Hussars.

376. Pouch—Scarlet leather in the 5th, 9th, 12th, and 16th Lancers, blue leather in the 17th, with gold embroidery round the top. Solid metal flap, 7½ inches long and 2¾ inches deep. For devices, see Appendix I. Silver loops and stud. | 335 | |

61002 / 5832   In the 21st Lancers the pouch is of black leather, with silver flap and gilt or gilding metal ornaments.

377. Sabretache—As described in Appendix V., except that regiments having regimental patterns are allowed to retain them. | 302 | 11.5.95 |

378. Gauntlets—White leather. | 516 | 23.8.98 |

UNDRESS.

379. Forage Cap—Blue cloth (scarlet in the 12th Lancers), with band of 1¾-inch lace, gold purl button on the top, and gold braid crossing the crown at right angles, and ending under the band. | 52 | 2.6.99 | 8

61002 / Cavalry / I. / ... / 169   **380. Field Cap**—As described in paragraph 10, but the body of the cap is of scarlet cloth, except in the 17th Lancers, in which regiment it is white, and in the 21st, in which it is French grey. Gold French braid welts on cap and flaps, and at front and back seams. Regimental badge on left side, see Appendix I. | 53 / 42 | 5.4.98 / 5.4.98 | 9 / 9

61002 / 5776   **381. Patrol Jacket**—Blue cloth, stand-up collar, ½-inch mohair lace at top and bottom of collar, figured braiding in centre. Inch mohair braid traced with Russia braid, all round, up the slits, and along the back seams. Five loops of inch mohair braid, at equal distances, down the front on each side with two olivets on each loop, the top loops extend to the shoulder seams, and the bottom to 4 inches. The cuffs pointed with inch mohair braid, traced with Russia braid, and figured braiding at the top and bottom. The mohair braid reaches to 5 inches from bottom of cuff, and the figured braiding at the top to 8 inches. Pockets in front edged all round with inch mohair braid. Figured braiding at the top of slits, and at the top of the shoulder seams. Figured braiding in the centre of the back, at the bottom of the collar, and at the bottom of the jacket figured braiding on the right, left, and between the back seams. Hooks and eyes in front. Pocket inside left breast. Shoulder straps of the same material as the garment, edged with ½-inch black mohair braid, except at the base; black netted button at the top. | 125 | 31.8.98 | 26

In the 5th Lancers, the braiding is of regimental pattern.

61002 / 6685   **382. Frock**—As for Hussars, see paragraph 349. | 126 | 26.3.98 | 19

383. Slings, Sword and Sabretache, Sword Knot—Plain buff leather. | 331 | | 64

61002 / 6890   **384. Belts**—"Sam Browne"
Scabbard—Brown leather } See Appendices VII and VIII.
Sword Knot—Brown leather

The other articles, except the gauntlets, as in Full Dress.

	Pattern.		No. of
	No	Sealed.	Plate.

CLOAK AND CAPE.

6100·2⁄6568 **385. Cloak and Cape**—Blue cloth, of the same pattern as for Officers of Dragoon Guards and Dragoons, lined with scarlet, white lining in the 17th Lancers.   121   11.5.92

6100·2⁄Cav.⁄108   In the 12th Lancers the collar of the cloak is scarlet, and in the 21st Lancers it is lined with French grey.   122   11.5.92

MESS DRESS.

386. Mess Jacket—Blue cloth [scarlet in the 16th Lancers] edged with 1 inch lace (1½ inches for Field Officers) all round, including the collar, and forming dummies at the back seams. Gold chain gimp at the bottom of the collar. Collar, pointed cuffs, and welts in the sleeve and back seams, of the regimental facings. The point of the cuff is 6 inches from the bottom, the lace rounded at the back seam, and turned in at the bottom of the cuff. Two buttons on the sleeve above the lace, no button holes. Hooks and eyes in front. Shoulder cords as for tunic.   128   14.5.97   27

387. Mess Waistcoat—Of regimental pattern.
Other articles as in Full Dress.

REGIMENTAL STAFF OFFICERS.

388. The Adjutant, Riding-master, and Quartermaster wear the same uniform as other Officers of their rank.

HORSE FURNITURE.

6100·2⁄6568 **389.** Cavalry pattern, see Appendix VI. The lambskin (see paragraph 327) is not worn in India.

	Pattern.		No. of Plate.
	No.	Sealed.	

ROYAL ARTILLERY.

GENERAL AND STAFF OFFICERS.

GENERAL OFFICERS.

$\frac{\text{A.O. 26}}{1897}$ **390.** Uniform of their Rank, see paragraphs 74 to 103.

Officers below the Rank of Substantive Colonel, on the Strength of the Royal Artillery, serving on the General, or Personal Staff:—

391. As laid down in paragraphs 166–178.

$\frac{61002}{6104}$ **Officers serving on the Regimental Staff of the Royal Artillery:—Chief Instructors of Gunnery, Officers Commanding Militia and Volunteer Artillery Districts.**

392. Regimental uniform, with the addition of the cocked hat and frock coat, described below.

393. Cocked Hat—As described in paragraph 7, with loop of 1-inch lace, regimental pattern, gold half-ball netted button.

	No.	Sealed.	Plate
393	1	23.8.98	2 & 3
	2	29.11.98	

394. Plume—White swan feathers, drooping outwards, 6 inches long, with red feathers under them long enough to reach the ends of the white ones; feathered stem, 3 inches long. — 54 — 17.12.75 — 2

$\frac{61002}{\text{Arty.}}$ $\frac{}{11}$ $\frac{61002}{6374}$ **395. Frock Coat***—As for Colonel on the Staff, but with regimental buttons. With the frock coat, white gloves and full-dress belts (see paragraph 439) will be worn. — 107 — 27.3.97 — 12

396. Forage Cap—Blue cloth, $3\frac{1}{4}$ inches deep, bell-shaped top, with gold embroidered drooping peak and band of $1\frac{3}{4}$-inch lace; gold purl button and braided figure on the crown. — 33 — 13.11.96 — 8

HORSE FURNITURE.

397. Officers serving on the Regimental Staff of the Royal Artillery, Chief Instructors of Gunnery. } As described in paragraphs 134 and 135.

$\frac{61002}{6104}$ **398.** Officers Commanding Militia and Volunteer Artillery Districts. } Regimental pattern.

ROYAL HORSE ARTILLERY.

FULL DRESS.

399. Busby—Black sable skin, $6\frac{3}{4}$ inches high in front, $7\frac{1}{4}$ inches at the back and $\frac{1}{2}$ inch smaller round the top than the bottom. A scarlet cloth bag, covering the top of the busby, and falling down the right side to the bottom. A screw socket at the top in front. Black leather chin-strap and black enamelled buckle. — 8 — 12.11.87 — 4

$\frac{61002}{6475}$ **400. Line**—Gold cord, $\frac{3}{10}$ inch in diameter, with an acorn at each end, passing round the busby diagonally three times, then round the neck, and looped on the left breast. — 55

$\frac{61002}{6819}$ **401. Plume**—White ostrich feather, 15 inches high from the top of the busby to the top of the plume, encircled by a gilt ring, white vulture feather, bottom in a metal socket with three flames. — 43 — — 4

402. Jacket—Blue cloth, edged all round with gold cord forming a figure 8, $2\frac{1}{2}$ inches deep at the bottom of each back seam. Scarlet cloth collar, square in front, but slightly rounded at the corners; two hooks and eyes, black silk tab with hook and eye. The collar edged all round with gold cord; laced as described below, according to rank; and with a grenade embroidered in frosted silver $2\frac{1}{4}$ inches long at each end. On each side in front, loops of gold cord 15 to 18 in number according to height of wearer, $\frac{3}{10}$ inch in diameter, 1 inch apart from centre to centre, fastening with ball buttons, a crow's foot and curl at the top. Gold cord along the back seams, forming a crow's foot at the top of each seam, and an Austrian knot at each side of the waist. Plaited gold wire shoulder-cord, lined with blue; a small button of regimental pattern at the top. — 129 — 22.2.98 — 28

Field Officers have $\frac{5}{8}$-inch lace all round the collar within the cord; and a chevron of $1\frac{1}{2}$-inch lace on each cuff, with figured braiding above and below the lace, extending to 11 inches from the bottom of the cuff. — 520 — — 63 / 28

Captains and Lieutenants have lace $1\frac{3}{16}$ inch wide round the top only of the collar; and an Austrian knot of gold cord on the sleeve, $7\frac{1}{2}$ inches deep from the bottom of the cuff, traced round with gold braid $8\frac{1}{4}$ inches deep and figured for Captains; $7\frac{1}{2}$ inches deep and plain for Lieutenants. — — — 28

---

* Officers in possession of the old pattern frock coat with roll collar may continue to wear it till 31st December, 1903.

		Pattern.		No. of Plate.
		No.	Sealed.	
	403. **Lace**—Gold, regimental pattern.	136		78
	404. **Buttons**—See Appendix I.			
	405. **Trousers**—Blue cloth, with $1\frac{3}{4}$-inch lace down the side seams.			
	406. **Pantaloons**—Blue cloth, with scarlet stripes $1\frac{3}{4}$ inches wide down the side seams.			
	407. **Boots and Spurs**—See paragraphs 4 and 25.			
	408. **Sword**—Half-basket, steel hilt, with two fluted bars on the outside; black fish-skin grip, bound with silver wire; slightly curved blade, $35\frac{1}{2}$ inches long and $1\frac{1}{4}$ inches wide, grooved and spear-pointed.	336	26.10.63	
	409. **Scabbard**—Steel.	336	26.10.63	64
61002 / Arty. / 16	**410.** **Sword Belt**—Web, as described in Appendix VIII. (2).	337		
	411. **Slings**—Gold lace, lined with blue Morocco leather. Sword slings 1 inch wide; sabretache slings $\frac{3}{4}$ inch.			64
	412. **Sword Knot**—Gold cord, with gold runner and acorn.	317	23.8.98	64
	413. **Shoulder Belt**—Gold lace, 2 inches wide, lined with blue Morocco leather; ornamented buckle and slide, a grenade encircled with a wreath at the end.	339		
	414. **Pouch**—Blue Morocco leather collapsing pouch with two pockets; the flap $6\frac{3}{4}$ inches long at the bottom, $4\frac{1}{8}$ inches deep, covered with blue cloth, and edged with $\frac{3}{4}$-inch lace. For device see Appendix I. Collapsing leaf for loops, swivel loops and collapse stud.	340		
	415. **Sabretache**—Blue Morocco leather, faced with blue cloth; $1\frac{1}{2}$-inch lace round the face, $\frac{1}{4}$ inch from the edge. For device, see Appendix I.	341		
	UNDRESS.			
	416. **Forage Cap**—Blue cloth, with band of $1\frac{5}{8}$-inch gold lace, gold button and braided figure, of special pattern, on the crown. The cap to be $2\frac{5}{8}$ inches high.	56	13.6.98	8
61002 / Art. / 77	**417.** **Field Cap**—As described in paragraph 10, the body of the cap of scarlet cloth. Gold French braid welts on cap and flaps, and at front and back seams. Regimental Badge on the left side. (See Appendix I.)	53	5.4.98	9
	418. **Patrol Jacket**—Blue cloth, rounded in front, and edged with inch black mohair braid all round and up the openings at the sides; five loops of flat plait on each side in front, fastening with netted olivets, and with crow's feet and olivets at the ends. Stand-and-fall collar. The sleeves ornamented with flat plait, forming crow's feet, $6\frac{1}{2}$ inches from the bottom of the cuffs. Double flat plait on each back-seam, with crow's foot at top and bottom, and two eyes at equal distances. Pockets edged with flat plait, forming a crow's foot at each end and an eye top and bottom in the centre. Shoulder-straps, of the same material as the garment, edged with $\frac{1}{2}$-inch black mohair braid, except at the base; black netted button at the top. A false collar of the same pattern as the collar of the mess jacket. No grenade. The jacket to be long enough to reach the saddle, when the Officer is mounted.	130	13.6.98	28
61002 / 6685	**419.** **Frock**—Blue angola, tartan, or serge, full in chest, cut with side bodies, slits at sides, five ball regimental buttons down the front. Two breast patch pockets outside, $6\frac{1}{4}$ inches wide, $8\frac{1}{2}$ inches deep from the top of the flap, the top edge of pocket in line with the second button, with three-pointed flap, small regimental button and hole, loose plait on rear side of pocket, two outside patch pockets below, with three-pointed flap. Two inside breast pockets up and down with hole and button, two inside skirt pockets, with hole and button. Scarlet cloth collar. Shoulder straps, of the same colour and material as the rest of the garment, shaped for shoulder chains, fastened with a small regimental button. Steel shoulder chains, with badges of rank, see Appendix X. Italian cloth or thin serge lining. Sleeves with pointed cuffs, 6 inches high in front and $2\frac{1}{4}$ inches behind, with slit and two small buttons and button holes.	131	13.6.98	19, 63
	420. **Trousers**—Blue cloth, with scarlet stripes, $1\frac{3}{4}$ inches wide, down the side seams.			
	421. **Slings, Sword and Sabretache**—Black patent leather, with mountings as for Full Dress. Sword slings 1 inch wide, sabretache slings $\frac{3}{4}$ inch wide.			64
61002 / 6890	**422.** **Belts**—"Sam Browne"; **Scabbard**—, **Sword Knot**— } Brown leather } See Appendices VII & VIII.			
	423. **Binocular Case**—Black patent leather, solid leather flap, on the flap a gun in gilt or gilding metal.	342	13.6.90	
	424. **Sabretache**—As described in Appendix V. Other articles as in Full Dress.	302	11.5.95	
	CLOAK AND CAPE.			
	425. **Cloak**—Blue cloth, with sleeves. Stand-and-fall collar with three black hooks and eyes in front, and three small flat silk buttons at the bottom to fasten the cape. Round loose cuffs, 6 inches deep. A pocket in each side-seam outside, and one in the left breast inside. Four buttons down the front. A cloth back-strap, to fasten with a large flat silk button at the top of each pocket; a similar button in front on the right to hold the end of the back-strap when it is not buttoned across behind. White shalloon lining. The cloak to reach within	132	13.6.98	

	Pattern.		No. of Plate.
	No.	Sealed.	

8 inches of the ground. Shoulder-straps of the same material as the garment; a small button of regimental pattern at the top. A gusset behind as described in paragraph 14.

426. Cape—Blue cloth, long enough to cover the knuckles, lined with white shalloon. A cloth band round the top, to fasten with a cloth strap and black buckle; and a fly inside the band, with three button holes for attaching cape cloak. Three buttons down the front.   133   13.6.98

Mess Dress.

61002/5374

427. Mess Jacket—Blue cloth, with scarlet collar and pointed scarlet cuffs, laced all round, including top of collar, with ¾-inch gold lace, regimental pattern, forming a bull's eye at the bottom of each back seam; small gold tracing on collar seam; hooks and eyes down the front, a row of small studs on the left side, scarlet lining. Shoulder-cords as for dress-jacket.   134   6.11.96   28

Field Officers have a flat chevron of inch lace, extending to 6 inches from the bottom of the cuff, with braided eyes above and below the lace, the bottom of the braiding to reach just over the top of the scarlet cuff. The top of the braiding extends to 7½ inches from the bottom of the cuff.

Captains have on the sleeve an Austrian knot of ¼-inch gold Russia braid, traced with ⅛-inch braid. A further tracing of eyes above and below the knot. The Austrian knot extends to 7½ inches from the bottom of the sleeve; the figured braiding to 8 inches.

Lieutenants—As for Captains, but without the tracing of eyes.

A silver embroidered grenade is worn on the collar, as laid down for the dress jacket.

428. Mess Waistcoat—Scarlet cloth with collar, ½-inch gold lace, regimental pattern, all round —including collar—row of gold Russia braid to form eyes, down the front, inside the lace, with figures according to pattern, extending to 1 inch and 1½ inches alternately from the edge of the lace. Pockets edged with gold Russia tracing braid forming a crow's foot and eye at each end, and crow's feet in centre. To fasten with hooks and eyes, small studs down the front.   135   12.5.97   28

429. Trousers, Boots, and Spurs—As in Full Dress.

REGIMENTAL STAFF OFFICERS.

430. The same uniform as for the other Officers of their respective honorary rank.

Horse Furniture.

431. Saddle, wallets, shoe cases and lambskin of regimental pattern, other articles as cavalry pattern, see Appendix VI.   606   16.5.98

432. Lambskins are not worn in India.   538   8.12.98

61002/Arty./76

ROYAL FIELD AND ROYAL GARRISON ARTILLERY.

As for Royal Horse Artillery, with the following exceptions :—

433. Helmet, Home Pattern—See paragraph 16. For Helmet Plate, see Appendix I.   3   7.12.98   5
Dimensions of Plate—
From top of crest to bottom of plate, back measurement, 4 inches.
Extreme horizontal width, back measurement, 3¼ inches.

434. Field Cap (Royal Garrison Artillery only)—As described in paragraph 10. Gold French braid welts on cap and at front and back seams. An embroidered badge on the left side, a grenade in gold with a scroll under it, bearing the motto "Ubique" in silver, on a scarlet ground.   57   27.6.96   9

435. Tunic—Blue cloth, with scarlet cloth collar. The collar and sleeves laced and braided according to rank, and a grenade at each end of the collar, as detailed for Royal Horse Artillery. The skirt square in front, open behind, with a blue cloth flap on back of each skirt. Flaps edged with round gold cord, traced inside with gold Russia braid. Skirt lined with black. Scarlet cloth edging down the front, and at the opening behind, nine buttons down the front, two at the waist and three on each flap behind. Shoulder-cords as for Royal Horse Artillery.   136   6.11.96   28

436. Frock—As for Royal Horse Artillery but with universal pattern instead of the special shaped shoulder straps.   520 / 131   13.6.98

437. Girdle, Mounted Officers, Full Dress—Gold lace, 1½ inches wide, lined with blue Morocco leather.   343   7.12.98

61002/Arty./16

438. Sword Belt, Mounted Officers—Web, as for Royal Horse Artillery.

439. Sword Belt, Royal Garrison Artillery, Full Dress { Gold lace, 1½ inches wide, lined with blue Morocco leather.   64

61002/6943

440. Sword Belt, Royal Garrison Artillery, Undress { White Buff leather 1½ inches wide, or web as described in Appendix VIII. (2). See paragraph 28.

441. Slings, All Officers, Full Dress—Gold lace, lined with blue Morocco leather, sword slings 1 inch, sabretache slings ¾ inch wide. Gilt lion-head buckles on the slings.   343   28.7.97   64

	Pattern.		No. of Plate.
	No.	Sealed.	

442. Slings, all Officers, Undress—White buff leather. Sword-slings 1 inch wide, sabretache-slings for Mounted Officers ¾-inch wide. | 345 | 23.8.98 | 64

443. Sword Knot—White buff leather, ½ inch wide, with runner and gold acorn. | 344 | | 64

444. Shoulder Belt—White buff leather, 2 inches wide, gilt stud and hole at each end. | 346 | 28.7.97 |

445. Mess Waistcoat—Scarlet cloth, edged all round, including collar, with ½-inch gold lace, regimental pattern ; pockets edged with gold Russia tracing braid, forming a crow's foot and eye at each end, with crow's feet in centre—to fasten with hooks and eyes, small studs down the front. | 138 | | 28

REGIMENTAL STAFF OFFICERS.

446. The same uniform as the other Officers of their respective honorary rank.

Horse Furniture.

A.O. 167 / 1899 — **447.** For Mounted Officers who provide their own saddlery, Royal Field Artillery,—as for Royal Horse Artillery ; Royal Garrison Artillery,—as for Infantry.

Lambskins are not worn in India, or by the Royal Garrison Artillery at other stations.

MOUNTAIN ARTILLERY.

61002 / 6255 — **448.** *Review Order.*—As for Mounted Officers of Royal Garrison Artillery.

449. *When parading with the men in other than Review Order.*—As for Royal Garrison Artillery with the following exceptions :—

450. Helmet—Indian pattern, with puggaree and Royal Artillery ornaments, see paragraph 1194. | 4 | 15.6.98 | 5

451. Sword Belt—"Sam Browne."

452. Scabbard / **Sword Knot** } Brown leather } As described in Appendices VII. and VIII.

453. Leggings—Brown leather, cut riding pattern, with one long leather lace forming loops which pass through five eyelet holes, secured at the top by a leather strap passing through the top loop and buckling (point of strap to the rear) into a brass buckle ½ inch square.

454. Boots—Ankle, brown leather.

61002 / Arty. — **455. Spurs**—Hunting pattern, steel, straight neck, 1¼-inch, brown top strap and steel foot-chain.

456. Collar—White linen, to show ⅛ inch all round above collar of jacket.

20 / 54 — **457.** *When not parading with the men.*—As for mounted Officers of Royal Garrison Artillery, except that the Undress belt is of "Sam Browne" pattern.

Officers / 103 — **458. Horse Furniture.**—As for Royal Field Artillery.

ROYAL MALTA ARTILLERY.

459. Uniform, &c., as for Officers of Royal Garrison Artillery, except the pouch ornament, waist plate, and helmet plate, which are of special patterns, see Appendix I.

MILITIA.

[Including the Channel Islands Artillery.]

460. Uniform, &c., as for Royal Garrison Artillery, with the following exceptions. The letter **M** is worn below the badges of rank in similar material to those badges. For badges and devices, see Appendix I.

S / Militia. / 5031 — **461.** Candidates for the Line between the ages of 17 and 22 need not provide themselves with Full Dress uniform, patrol jacket, or mess waistcoat, but must not attend in undress uniform at Levées or public ceremonies where full dress is worn.

Adjutant and Quartermaster.

462. An Officer selected from the full pay of the Royal Artillery for the appointment of adjutant or quartermaster to the Militia will wear the uniform of the corps of the Regular Army to which he belongs ; in the case of a quartermaster, he will wear it so long as he is borne on the seconded list of that corps.

32

	Pattern.		No. of Plate.
	No.	Sealed.	

ROYAL ENGINEERS.

GENERAL AND STAFF OFFICERS.*

GENERAL OFFICERS.

463. Uniform as for their rank, see paragraphs 74 to 103.

OFFICERS BELOW THE RANK OF SUBSTANTIVE COLONEL.

A.O. 26 / 1897 **464.** As laid down in paragraphs 166–178.

REGIMENTAL OFFICERS.

465. Cocked Hat—As described in paragraph 7, with loop of 1-inch lace, gold half-ball netted button, and black silk cockade (see also under *Helmet*). — 1 — 23.8.98 — 2 & 3; 2 — 29.11.98

466. Plume—White swan feathers, drooping outwards, 5 inches long. — 58 — — 2

467. Helmet, Home Pattern—See paragraph 16.

†All Officers performing Regimental duty or Garrison duty (other than Staff) will wear the helmet with the tunic; other Officers, if of field rank, will wear the cocked-hat; if below field rank, they will wear the helmet. — 3 — 7.12.98 — 5

468. Helmet Plate—Gilt or gilding metal. Dimensions:—From top of crest to bottom of plate, back measurement, 3⅝ inches. Extreme horizontal width, back measurement, 3¼ inches. For device, see Appendix I.

469. Tunic—Scarlet cloth, with collar and cuffs of Garter blue velvet. The collar edged all round with round-back gold cord; ¾-inch lace all round within the cord for Field Officers, round the top only for Captains and Lieutenants; at each end a grenade, 2¼ inches in length, embroidered in silver. The cuffs pointed and ornamented as described below, according to rank. Nine buttons in front and two at the waist behind. The skirt rounded off in front, closed behind, with a plait at each side, and lined with white. The front, skirt, and plaits edged with Garter blue velvet. Treble twisted round-back gold shoulder cords, lined with scarlet. A small button of regimental pattern at the top. — 139 — 19.3.97 — 29

Field Officers have 1½-inch lace round the top of the cuff; and figured ⅛-inch Russia braiding above and below the lace, extending to 11 inches from the bottom of the cuff. — 539 — 30.9.99 — 63

Captains have an Austrian knot of round-back gold cord on each sleeve, traced all round with braid, outside the braid is another tracing with eyes, the braid extending to 8 inches from the bottom of the cuff.

Lieutenants have a similar knot, but without the figured braiding.

470. Lace / Buttons } Regimental patterns. — 139 — — 78

471. Dress Trousers—Blue cloth, with 1¾-inch lace down the side seams.

472. Pantaloons—Blue cloth with scarlet cloth stripes 2 inches wide.

61002 **473. Boots and Spurs**—As described in paragraphs 4 and 25.

6148 / 61002 **474. Sword / Scabbard** } As described in Appendix VII. — 347 — 13.12.97 — 68; 347 — 13.12.97 — 68

5140 **475. Sword Belt**—Russia leather, 1½ inches wide, with removable flap; two stripes of gold embroidery on belt and slings. Removable slings an inch wide, the front sling lined with Russia leather; and a double swivel on the eye of dee of front sling for hooking up sword; running carriage for back sling. Round billets for sword-slings, and flat billets for sabretache-slings. Three dees on inside of belt, with Russia leather protecting flap inside the belt, to attach sabretache slings. Square wire gilt buckles for sword and sabretache slings. — 348 — 17.3.97 — 64

476. Sword Knot—Gold cord and acorn. — 349 — 17.3.97 — 64

477. Waist Plate—See Appendix I.

61002 / 5809 **478. Shoulder Belt**—Russia leather, 2 inches wide, with three stripes of gold embroidery, the centre one waved, the others straight; engraved buckle, tip and slide. The letters "R.E." within the tip. — 350 — 19.3.97

479. Binocular Case—Black patent leather, to hold a binocular field glass; solid leather flap, with regimental badge. Broad leaf loops, gilt. — 351 — 19.3.97

480. Sabretache—As described in paragraph 21. — 302 — 11.5.95

UNDRESS.

481. Forage Cap—Blue cloth, bell-top, in one piece, 3 inches high, with band of 1¾-inch gold lace. Black patent leather drooping peak and chin straps. The peak ornamented with ½-inch, *full*, gold embroidery. A gold netted button on the crown. Field Officers will have a gold French braid welt round the crown; Officers under the rank of Field Officer, a blue cloth welt. — 59 — 17.3.97 — 8

61002 / Engrs. / 5 ——— * Colonels on the Staff, Commanding Royal Engineers, may continue to wear the uniform in their possession till 31st December, 1901.
† All Officers attending Court or Levées will wear the full dress of their rank (including cocked hat if of field rank) but without sabretache.

	Pattern.		No. of Plate.
	No.	Sealed.	

61002/5636 **482. Field Cap**—As described in paragraph 10, but with gold French braid welts on cap, and at front and back seams. For badge, see Appendix I. — 60 | 14.12.96 | 9

483. Frock Coat for Regimental Field Officers—Blue cloth, single-breasted, with roll collar; ornamentation on sleeve as on the tunic, but in black mohair braid, traced. Eight loops of ¾-inch black braid down the front, with barrel buttons according to regimental pattern. The front edges, collar, back and sleeve seams, and back-skirts trimmed with ⅞-inch black braid traced. Hooks and eyes in front. Two olivets at the back, to support the waistbelt. The skirt lined with black. Shoulder straps of the same material as the garment, edged with ½-inch black mohair braid, except at the base; black netted button at the top. — 140 | 19.3.97 | 29

61002/6282 **484. Frock**—Scarlet. As for Infantry, but with medium buttons. Collar badge, grenade in gold embroidery, 2¼ inches long. Russia gold braid, ⅛ inch wide, round the bottom of collar and round the cuffs forming a crow's foot at the top and extending to 7½ inches from the bottom. — 141 | 29.7.97 | 30

485. Frock—Blue. As for Infantry of the line, but with medium regimental buttons. — 142 | 18.7.96 | 30

486. Trousers—Blue cloth, with scarlet stripe, 2 inches wide, down the side seams.

61002/6943 **487. Sword Belt**—Plain bridle leather, with mountings as for Full Dress, flat billets throughout; or web, as described in Appendix VIII (2). See paragraph 28. — 308 | 9.2.94 | 64 — 309 | 24.11.97 | 64

488. Sword Knot—Brown leather, as described in Appendix VIII.

61002/6890 **489. Belts**—"Sam-Browne."
Scabbard—Brown leather. } See Appendices VII and VIII.
Sword Knot—Brown leather. }
Other articles as in Full Dress.

GREAT COAT AND CAPE.

490. Blue cloth, of the pattern described in paragraph 14, lined with scarlet shalloon. Garter blue velvet collar. The cuffs 5½ inches deep. A button on the pockets at the waist. — 143 | 17.3.97

Shoulder straps of the same material as the garment; a small button of regimental pattern at the top. — 144 | 17.3.97

MESS DRESS.

491. Mess Jacket—Scarlet cloth, with Garter-blue velvet collar and cuffs. Gold Russia braid ⅛ inch wide, all round the jacket and along the bottom of the collar, with small eyes at the ends of the collar and bottom of the front, and a crow's foot at the centre of collar seam and of waist. At each end of the collar a grenade, 2¼ inches in length, embroidered in gold. Hooks and eyes and gilt studs down the front. Pointed cuffs, 5 inches deep, edged—for Field Officers, with 1-inch lace, traced above with Russia braid ⅛ inch, forming a crow's foot at the top; for Captains, with ⅛-inch Russia braid, forming a crow's foot at the top, a row of small eyes above and below the braid, terminating in plain braid round the crow's foot; for Lieutenants, with plain Russia braid, ⅛-inch, forming a crow's foot at the top, the crow's foot extending to 7 inches from the bottom of the cuff; scarlet silk serge lining. Shoulder cords as for tunic. — 145 | 17.3.97 | 30

492. Mess Waistcoat—Scarlet cloth, with hooks and eyes and gilt studs down the front, and edging of gold braid all round and on collar seam. Pockets edged with gold braid, forming crow's feet at ends and centre. The edging is 5½ inches in length and 2¼ inches deep at the fullest dimensions. A fly down the right front 2½ inches wide, and a black silk tab inside collar, fastening with hook and eye. — 146 | 17.3.97 | 30

493. Trousers, Boots, and Spurs—As in Full Dress.

61002/5150 ... 5635 ... 5809 ### WORKING DRESS—SUBMARINE MINING COMPANIES.

494. Field Cap—As for Undress, see paragraph 482.

495. Frock—Blue, as for Undress, see paragraph 485.

496. Trousers—Blue serge, with red stripes 2 inches wide down the side seams. Two cross pockets.

497. Boots, Knee—Canada pattern.

498. Pea Jacket—Blue tweed, lined with black Italian cloth. Double breasted, and made loosely to be worn over Frock. Length, 1 inch longer than Frock. Two rows of large R.E. gilt buttons down the front, four in each row. Buttons to be six inches apart. Two black bone buttons inside. Plain sleeve. One flap pocket on each hip, length 6¾ inches, flap 2½ inches. Pocket inside left breast, stand and fall collar. — 147 | 17.3.97

WORKING DRESS—BALLOON SECTION.

61002/Engrs./4 **499.** For Officers when employed on Ballooning Duties,—Undress Uniform, with blue puttees, lace boots, and, when actually mounted, hunting spurs.

| | Pattern. | | No. of Plate. |
	No.	Sealed.	

HORSE FURNITURE.

$\dfrac{31002}{\text{Engrs.}}$
$\dfrac{}{7}$

Officers who are not provided with saddlery from Store :—

500 **Saddle**—As described in Appendix VI ; or "Hunting." Breastplates as laid down in Appendix VI, but with bosses of Universal pattern. See paragraph 22.

501. **Bridle and Wallets**—Universal pattern, but with regimental bosses, see Appendix VI.

| | 600 | 24.9.97 | |

REGIMENTAL STAFF OFFICERS.

502 Uniform, &c., as for other Officers of their respective honorary rank, with the exception that the cocked hat will be worn with the tunic.

MILITIA.

Uniform, &c., as for Officers of Royal Engineers, with the following exceptions :—

503. **Shoulder Cords and Shoulder Straps**—The letter **M** is worn below the badges of rank, in similar material to those badges.

504. **Shoulder Belt**—On the tip of the belt **M.E.** is substituted for **R.E.**

ADJUTANT AND QUARTERMASTER.

505. An Officer selected from the full pay of the Royal Engineers for the appointment of Adjutant or Quartermaster to the Militia will wear the uniform of the corps of the Regular Army to which he belongs.

	Pattern.		No. of Plate.
	No.	Sealed.	

INFANTRY.

FOOT GUARDS.

FULL DRESS.

506. Cap—Black bearskin, with a plain taper chain with black leather lining.
For Officers not exceeding 5 ft. 6 ins. in height, 8½ inches.

,,	,,	,,	,,	5	,,	9	,,	,,	9	,,	
,,	,,	,,	,,	6	,,	0	,,	,,	9½	,,	
,,	,,	exceeding		6	,,	0	,,	,,	10	,,	

(margin: 61002 / 5950)

507. Plume—Grenadier Guards—White goat's hair, 6 inches long, on the left side. Coldstream Guards—Scarlet cut feather 6 inches long, on the right side. The Scots Guards wear no plume.

508. Tunic—Scarlet cloth; blue cloth collar and cuffs; the collar embroidered in front and round the top; at each end, the badge of the regiment embroidered in silver; the cuffs round, 3¼ inches deep, embroidered round the top. Blue flap on each sleeve, 6 inches long at the seam, 6¾ inches at the points, 2¾ inches wide at the narrowest part, and at the points, 3½, 3¼, and 3¾ inches respectively, beginning at the bottom of the cuff; scarlet flap on each skirt behind, reaching within ½ inch of the bottom of the skirt; 2 buttons at the waist behind, about 3 inches apart. The front, collar, cuffs, and flaps edged with white cloth, ¼ inch wide; the skirts lined with white. Blue cloth shoulder-straps, embroidered with two rows of purl embroidery, except at the base. Small button at the top. [Pattern No. 148, Sealed 7.1.96, Plate 31]

The Grenadier Guards have a grenade at each end of the collar; 9 buttons in front, at equal distances; and 4 bars of embroidery, at equal distances, on each skirt and sleeve flap.

The Coldstream Guards have a Star of the Order of the Garter at each end of the collar; 10 buttons in front, 2 and 2; and 4 bars of embroidery, 2 and 2, on each skirt and sleeve flap. [Pattern No. 149, Sealed 7.1.96, Plate 31]

The Scots Guards have a thistle at each end of the collar; 9 buttons in front, 3 and 3; and 3 bars of embroidery, at equal distances, on each skirt and sleeve flap. [Pattern No. 150, Sealed 7.1.96, Plate 31]

Field Officers and Captains have embroidery round the bottom of the collar and round the skirt and sleeve flaps, and a second bar of embroidery round the cuff. [Plate 31]

509. Embroidery—Gold, of special patterns; that round the collar, cuffs, and flaps to be ½ inch wide.

510. Lace—Gold, of regimental pattern. [Pattern No. 735, Sealed 13.2.1900, Plate 79]

511. Buttons—Regimental pattern, see Appendix I.

512. Trousers—At levées, drawing-rooms, and when full dress is worn in the evening, blue cloth, with gold lace 1½ inches wide down the side seams; on other occasions, blue cloth, with scarlet stripes 2 inches wide.

(margin: 38407 / Dress / 120 / 61002 / 6783)

513. Pantaloons—Blue cloth, with scarlet stripes, 2 inches wide.

514. Boots—As described in paragraph 4, except that Wellington boots are worn in all orders of dress, except marching order.

(margin: 38407 / Dress / 120)

515. Spurs—Brass.

516. Sash—On State occasions, crimson and gold; at other times, crimson silk net.

517. Sword—As described in paragraph 27, steel hilt, with regimental device pierced and chased in the guard; black fish-skin grip, bound with silver wire; the blade embossed with battles and devices according to regimental patterns.

518. Scabbard—Steel, lined with wood, with German silver mouthpiece.

519. Sword Belt—Gold lace, lined with crimson Morocco leather 1½ inches wide, with slings an inch wide. No metal furniture. [Plate 64]

520. Waist Plate—See Appendix I.

521. Sword Knot—Gold cord and acorn. [Pattern No. 352, Sealed 23.8.93, Plate 64]

UNDRESS

522. Forage Cap—Blue cloth, of special pattern, with embroidered peak and plain chin strap, band 1½ inches wide, and regimental badge in front. The Grenadier and Coldstream Guards wear a black band, the Scots Guards a regimental check band, and a gold cord round the edge of the crown. For badge, see Appendix I. [Plate 9]

(margin: 61002 / 6783)

523. Field Cap—As described in paragraph 10, but with welts of regimental pattern. For badge, see Appendix I. [Pattern No. 61, Sealed 9.12.96, Plate 9] [Pattern No. 62, Sealed 9.12.96] [Pattern No. 63, Sealed 9.12.96, Plate 32]

524. Frock Coat—Blue cloth, braided according to regimental pattern. Shoulder-straps of the same material as the garment, edged with ½-inch black mohair braid, except at the base; black netted button at the top.

(margin: 61002 / 5634)

525. Frock, Red—Angola, tartan, or serge, according to climate, full in chest, lined in front with scarlet; blue cloth stand-up collar and shoulder-straps; the shoulder-straps with small regimental button at top. Six large regimental buttons down the front, arranged thus:— [Pattern No. 151, Sealed 9.11.96, Plate 32]

Grenadier Guards—At equal distances apart.
Coldstream Guards—By pairs.
Scots Guards—By threes.

	Pattern.		No. of Plate.
	No.	Sealed.	

A band, 1½ inches wide, round the waist, with special pattern buckle, 2 inches long and 1¼ inches wide, in front. A patch pocket with shaped flap and small button on each breast, and similar pockets, but without a button, below the band. A slit at the cuff, with small buttons and button holes, in the Grenadier Guards two, in the Coldstream Guards two pairs, and in the Scots Guards, three.

526. Frock, Blue—As for Red Frock, but with medium regimental buttons down the front.   152   25.6.96

527. Sword Belt—Buff leather, 1½ inches wide, with slings an inch wide ; or web, as described in Appendix VIII (2). See paragraph 28.   64

528. Sword Knot– Buff leather with gold acorn.   353   23.8.98   64

529. Belts—"Sam Browne"   }
Scabbard—Brown leather   } See Appendices VII and VIII.
Sword Knot—Brown leather }

530. Sabretache—See paragraph 21.

531. Sash—Crimson silk net, as in full dress.

532. Whistle—See paragraph 31.

Other articles as in Full Dress.

61002 *6127* ... *6943*
61002 *5278*
61002 *6890*

GREAT COAT AND CAPE.

533. Grey cloth, of regimental pattern. Shoulder-straps of the same material as the garment; a small button of regimental pattern at the top.

MESS DRESS.

534. Mess Jacket—Scarlet cloth, with Garter blue collar and cuffs. The collar rolled ; regimental badge on collar, 5 inches from seam of shoulder. Cuffs pointed ; Field Officers have on each sleeve, three rows of small gimp cord forming an eye at the top. Captains two rows, and Lieutenants one row.   32

535. Waistcoat—Garter blue cloth, with rolled collar ; 4 mounted regimental buttons for Grenadier Guards and Coldstream Guards, 3 for the Scots Guards.   32

Other articles as in Full Dress.

REGIMENTAL STAFF.

536. THE ADJUTANTS wear the uniform of their rank.

537. THE MEDICAL OFFICERS wear the regimental uniform of their rank, except the bearskin cap, sash, and sword-belt, instead of which the following are worn :—

538. Cocked Hat—As described in paragraph 7, loop of 1-inch gold lace ; plume of black cock's feathers, 6 inches long, drooping from a feathered stem 3 inches long.   1   23.8.98   2 & 3
   2   29.11.98

539. Sword Belt, Shoulder   } As for the Royal Army Medical Corps, but with waist-plates
     Belt, Pouch,   }   and devices on pouches of regimental patterns.

540. QUARTERMASTERS wear regimental uniform of their honorary rank with the following exceptions :—

38407 *Dress* *164*

541. Cocked Hat—As for the Medical Officers, but with upright swan feather, 5 inches long. The feather is white in the Grenadier Guards and Scots Guards ; red in the Coldstream Guards.   1   23.8.98   2 & 3
   2   29.11.98

542. Sash—Crimson silk net.

543. Sword Belt—Black leather.   64

HORSE FURNITURE.

544. Saddle—The saddle described in Appendix VI, or hunting, with plain stirrups and blue girths. See paragraph 22.   600   24.9.97

545. Wallets—Brown leather, with black bearskin covers.   614   23.4.96

546. Saddle Cloth—Blue cloth, edged with gold lace an inch wide ; 3 feet long and 2 feet deep in the Grenadier and Coldstream Guards ; 3 feet long at the bottom and 2 feet 2 inches at the top, and 1 foot 9 inches deep, in the Scots Guards. The Field Officers are distinguished by a second stripe of lace and the badges of rank, embroidered in silver, at each hind corner.

547. Bridle—Brown leather, as described in Appendix VI.

Frontlets and rosettes of blue silk in Review Order. On other occasions they will be of leather.

The bridoon reins are attached to bridoon by buckles of regimental pattern instead of being sewn on.   609   19.11.96

In the Coldstream Guards, the "sham Hanoverian bit" is worn.   611   19.11.96

In the Scots Guards the Star of the Order of the Thistle is worn on the bit, below the frontlet, and on the breastplate.   610   19.11.96

38407 *Dress* *120*

	Pattern.		No. of Plate.
	No.	Sealed.	

INFANTRY OF THE LINE.

(*Exclusive of Highland and Scottish Regiments.*)

FULL DRESS.

548. Helmet, Home Pattern—See paragraph 16.

549. Helmet Plate—In gilt or gilding metal, an eight-pointed star surmounted by the crown; on the star a laurel wreath; within the wreath a garter inscribed, "*Honi soit qui mal y pense*"; within the garter the badge approved for the territorial regiments (see Appendix I). On the bottom of the wreath a silver scroll with the designation of the regiment. The dimensions of the plate are—from top of the crown to bottom of plate, back measurement, 5 inches; extreme horizontal width of star, back measurement, $4\frac{1}{4}$ inches; the bottom central ray of the plate comes halfway over the cloth band of the helmet. Deviations from this pattern are noted in Appendix I. *[No. 3 | 7.12.98 | Plate 5]*

550. Tunic—Scarlet cloth, with cloth collar and cuffs of the colour of the regimental facings. The collar ornamented with $\frac{5}{8}$-inch lace along the top, and gold Russia braid at the bottom, badges as in Appendix I; the cuffs pointed with $\frac{5}{8}$-inch lace round the top, and a tracing in gold Russia braid $\frac{1}{8}$ inch above and below the lace, the lower braid having a crow's foot and eye, and the upper an Austrian knot at the top. Eight buttons in front, and two at the waist behind. The skirt closed behind, with a plait at each side, and lined with white. The front, collar, and skirt-plaits edged with white cloth $\frac{1}{4}$ inch wide. Twisted round gold shoulder cords, universal pattern, lined with scarlet. A small button of regimental pattern at the top. In the Leicestershire Regiment a black line is introduced into the shoulder cord. *[No. 153 | 16.10.95 | Plate 33]* *[No. 515 | 17.8.95 | Plate 63]*

Field Officers have a row of braided eyes below the lace on the collar; two bars of lace along the top of the cuff, showing $\frac{1}{4}$ inch of the facing between the bars; and the braiding on the sleeve is in the form of eyes, above and below the lace for Colonels and Lieutenant-Colonels, and above the lace only for Majors. The lace on the sleeve extends to $8\frac{3}{4}$ inches, and the Austrian knot to $10\frac{3}{4}$ inches, from the bottom of the cuff for Colonels and Lieutenant-Colonels, and 8 and 10 inches respectively for Majors.

Captains have no braided eyes on the collar. The lace and braiding on the sleeves are the same as those of the Majors, except that the tracing is plain, without eyes.

Lieutenants have one bar of lace only on the cuff, the lace extending to $7\frac{1}{2}$ and the Austrian knot to $9\frac{1}{2}$ inches, from the bottom of the cuff. In other particulars the lace and braiding are the same as those for Captains.

551. Facings—Blue cloth for Royal regiments, white cloth for English and Welsh regiments, green cloth for Irish regiments. In the "Buffs" (East Kent Regiment), the facings are of buff cloth. In the Northumberland Fusiliers, Gosling green. In the West Yorkshire Regiment, buff. In the Yorkshire Regiment, grass green. In the Queen's Own (Royal West Kent Regiment) they are of velvet.

552. Lace for Tunics—Gold, $\frac{5}{8}$ inch wide. Rose pattern for English and Welsh regiments; shamrock pattern for Irish regiments. In the following regiments a black line is introduced at the top and bottom of the lace:— *[No. 822 | Plate 79]*

The Norfolk, Somersetshire Light Infantry, East Yorkshire, Leicestershire, East Surrey, Loyal North Lancashire, the York and Lancaster, and the Connaught Rangers.

553. Lace for Full Dress Trousers and Sword Belt—Gold lace, Infantry pattern.

554. Special Badges—See Appendix I.

555. Buttons—Regimental patterns. See Appendix I.

556. Trousers—Blue cloth, with gold lace $1\frac{3}{8}$ inches wide, a crimson silk stripe, $\frac{1}{8}$-inch wide, in the centre, down the side seams.

557. Pantaloons—Blue cloth, with a scarlet welt $\frac{1}{4}$ inch wide down each side seam.

558. Boots and Spurs—As described in paragraphs 4 and 25.

559. Sash—Gold and crimson net, $2\frac{1}{2}$ inches wide, in $\frac{1}{2}$-inch stripes of gold and crimson silk alternately (3 gold and 2 crimson); gold and crimson runner and tassels. Morocco leather lining. *[No. 511 | 2.9.95]*

560. Sword,
Scabbard, } As described in Appendix VII. *[No. 347 | 13.12.97 | Plate 68]*

561. Sword Belt—Gold lace of the same pattern as that for the full-dress trousers, lined with red morocco leather, $1\frac{1}{2}$ inches wide; similar slings; the lace $\frac{7}{8}$ inch wide, sword-piece and hook-gilt billet studs. *[No. 354 | 6.5.99 | Plate 64]*

562. Waist Plate—Round gilt clasp, in silver on a frosted centre the Royal Crest. A wreath of laurel forms the outer circle.

563. Sword Knot—Gold and crimson strap, with gold acorn. *[No. 355 | 23.8.98 | Plate 64]*

564. Sabretache—See paragraph 21.

UNDRESS.

565. Forage Cap—Blue cloth, straight up, $3\frac{1}{4}$ inches high, with black patent leather drooping peak and chin strap. The peak ornamented with $\frac{3}{4}$-inch gold embroidery. Band $1\frac{3}{4}$ inches wide, of black oak-leaf lace, black netted button and braided figure on the crown. In *[No. 64 | 20.6.95 | Plate 9]*

[Left margin notes:]
61002
Infantry
174

A.C.D.
N.F.
698
61002
Infy.
438

| | Pattern. | | No. of Plate. |
	No.	Sealed.	

regiments styled "Royal" and in the King's (Liverpool Regiment) the band is of scarlet cloth, 1½ inches wide. Field Officers have a gold French braid welt instead of blue cloth round the top of the cap. For badges, see Appendix I.

61002 / Infantry / 117

566. Field Cap—Blue cloth, as described in paragraph 10, with welts of regimental pattern. For badges, see Appendix I. In the Royal Dublin Fusiliers a lighter blue cap is worn. — 26 | 2.3.94 | 9

61002 / 5632

567. Scarlet Frock—Angola, tartan, or serge, according to climate, with collar, cuffs, and shoulder straps of the colour of the regimental facings. To be full in chest, cut with broad side body at back, slits at sides, left slit 7½ inches deep, right slit 6 inches deep. Five regimental buttons down the front. Two breast patch pockets outside, lined chamois leather, 6½ inches wide and 8½ inches deep from top of flap, the top edge of the pockets to be in line with second button from the top and 1½ inches from centre of button; pointed flaps, small regimental button, loose plait at the rear of the pockets. Two outside patch pockets below, lined chamois leather, with pointed flaps, 6¼ inches wide at the top and 7 inches wide one inch from the bottom, 7½ inches deep from top of flap, the top of the pockets to be 2¼ inches from centre of bottom button. Two inside breast pockets up and down, with hole and button. Two inside skirt pockets, with hole and button. Shoulder straps with regimental button. Collar badges of similar pattern to those worn on the tunic, but with metal substituted for embroidery. Plain pointed cuff, 6 inches deep in front, and 2½ inches behind. — 154 | 8.9.96 | 33

568. Blue Frock—As for Scarlet Frock, except that the collar, cuffs, and shoulder straps, are of the same material as the rest of the garment. — 142 | 18.7.96 | 33

569. Trousers—Blue cloth, with stripes as on Pantaloons.

570. Sash—Crimson silk net. — 512 | 2.9.95

571. Leggings—As described in paragraph 17.

61002 / 6943

572. Sword Belt—White buff leather, 1½ inches wide, with slings an inch wide, and hook. Flat billets and gilt or gilding metal studs; or web, as described in Appendix VIII (2). See paragraph 28. — 356 | 3.9.91 | 64

573. Waist Plate—Round gilt clasp, badge on centre piece, universal ends. For badges and any deviations from this pattern, see Appendix I.

574. Sword Knot—White buff leather. — 357 | 23.8.98 | 64

61002 / 6899

575. Belts—"Sam-Browne"
Scabbard—Brown leather ⎬ See Appendices VII and VIII.
Sword Knot—Brown leather

576. Whistle—See paragraph 31.
Other articles as in Full Dress.

GREAT COAT AND CAPE.

577. Grey cloth, of the pattern described in paragraph 14. Shoulder straps of the same material as the garment; a small button of regimental pattern at the top. — 100 | 13.2.99

MESS DRESS.

The mess dress worn in all battalions of a regiment must be of the same pattern.

A.O.111 / 1896

578. Mess Jacket—Scarlet cloth, edged all round with white piping. Stand-up or roll collar; pointed cuffs, 6 inches deep at the point and 2¾ inches behind, cloth shoulder straps; the collar, cuffs, and shoulder straps to be of the colour of the regimental facings, and edged like the jacket, except where the facings are white. A loop of gold braid at the bottom of the stand-up collar to fasten across the neck. Small buttons and button-holes down the front. — 157 | 17.7.96 | 33 / 158 | 17.7.96 | 33

61002 / Infy. / 318

Shoulder straps, with badges of rank, in gilt metal or gold embroidery, but of the dimensions laid down in paragraph 2, will be worn with all mess jackets, whether fitted with stand up or roll collar.

61002 / Infantry / 116

In regiments which wear mess jackets with a roll collar, the collar badges may be worn on the collar, 5 inches from the seam of the shoulder.

61002 / 5554

579. Mess Waistcoat—Cloth of the colour of the regimental facings; gold braid edging round the top, down the front and along the bottom of the side seams. The pockets edged with braid, forming crow's feet and eyes at top and bottom and at the ends. A row of studs and hooks and eyes down the front. In regiments with white facings the waistcoat may be of white or scarlet cloth, or a white washing waistcoat, without lappels. Fastened with four half-inch buttons of regimental pattern,—see Appendix I. — 159 | 15.9.91 | 33

61002 / Infantry / 120

In regiments in which the jacket is fitted with a roll collar, the waistcoat may be open in front, with or without a roll collar, and fastened with 4 regimental buttons,—see Appendix I.

580. *The Undermentioned Regiments wear Mess Dress of Authorised Regimental Patterns.*

	Regiment.	Jacket.				Waistcoat.	Pattern.		No. of Plate.
		Collar.	Shoulder Straps.	Cuffs.	Piping.		No.	Sealed.	
61002 Infantry 445	The Royal Scots.	Roll	Regulation ...	Regulation	Regulation ...	Blue cloth, piped white, four buttons; no gold lace.			
61002 Infantry 445	The Royal West Surrey.	Roll	Regulation ..	Regulation	Regulation ...	Open in front			
... 5960	The East Kent Regiment.	Roll, buff, red silk	Buff	Buff, 2½ inches deep, with three-pointed buff flap, 5½ inches deep and 2½ inches wide at the points. On the flap 3 small buttons of regimental pattern, and 3 loops of twisted white cord.	White on front of jacket, cuffs, flaps, and shoulder straps.	Regulation	160	4.5.97	
... 5617	The Royal Lancaster Regiment.	Roll	Regulation ...	Regulation	Regulation ...	Blue cloth, with roll collar, no braid or edging, four small regimental buttons of special pattern in front.	162	3.11.96	
... Infantry 146	The Northumberland Fusiliers.	Roll, green cloth	Scarlet	Scarlet	None	Regulation			
61002 Infantry 445	The Royal Warwickshire Regiment.	Roll	Regulation ...	Regulation	None ...	Roll collar, four buttons, no gold lace.			
61002 Infantry 445	The Royal Fusiliers.	Roll	Regulation ...	Regulation	Regulation ...	Roll collar, four buttons, no gold lace.			
61002 Infantry 445	The Liverpool Regiment.	Roll	Regulation ...	Regulation	Regulation ...	Roll collar, three buttons, no gold lace.			
... Infantry 3	Norfolk Regiment.	Roll, red cloth ...	White ...	White	White round jacket and collar.	Scarlet, with roll collar; piped all round, 4 regimental buttons in front.			
61002 5693	The Lincolnshire Regiment.	Roll, scarlet cloth	Regulation ..	Regulation	Regulation ...	Regulation			
... 6532	The Devonshire Regiment.	Roll, green cloth	Scarlet	Scarlet	White on jacket, collar, and cuffs.	Regulation	161	5.2.98	
... 5967	The Suffolk Regiment.	Roll, yellow ...	Same material as for jacket.	Regulation	$\frac{3}{16}$-inch white ..	Regulation			
... 5079	The Somerset Light Infantry.	Stand-up, blue cloth.	Blue cloth ...	Blue cloth	Gold cord to jacket, cuffs, and shoulder straps.	Blue cloth, closed at the neck, collar cut square, edged all round with ¾-inch gold lace instead of tracing braid, gilt or gilding metal studs.	163	29.11.95	
61002 Infantry 445	The West Yorkshire Regiment.	Roll	Regulation ...	Regulation	Regulation ..	Marcella roll collar, three buttons.			
... 6031	The East Yorkshire Regiment.	Roll, white cloth	Same colour and material as for jacket, piped with white.	Regulation	Shoulder straps piped white.	Regulation, white washing.	164	27.7.81	
... 6670	Bedfordshire Regiment.	Roll, scarlet cloth	Scarlet	White with white slashes, 3 buttons on slashes and loops of twisted white cord.	White round the collar and bottom of jacket.	Scarlet: no collar; white piping all round; four buttons.			See Infantry patterns, Plate 33.

The Undermentioned Regiments wear Mess Dress of Authorised Regimental Patterns—continued.

Regiment.	Jacket.				Waistcoat.	Pattern.		No. of Plate.
	Collar.	Shoulder Straps.	Cuffs.	Piping.		No.	Sealed.	
...⁄5055 The Leicestershire Regiment.	Roll	Regulation ...	Regulation ...	Regulation ..	White cloth of regulation infantry pattern, but traced with 2 rows of gold Russia braid, with a tracing of ⅛-inch black mohair braid between. The "eyes" at the pockets are omitted.	165	6.11.95	
61002⁄Infantry⁄445 The Royal Irish Regiment.	Roll	Regulation ...	Regulation	Regulation ...	Roll collar, 4 buttons, no gold lace.			
...⁄Infantry⁄314 The Yorkshire Regiment.	Roll, green cloth	Green cloth ..	Green cloth ...	None	Green cloth, no collar, open in front, within the edging a second row of gold Russia braid forming eyes down the front and along the bottom to the side seams, with special pattern eyes at bottom corners, otherwise of universal infantry pattern.	166	8.11.95	See Infantry patterns, Plate 33.
...⁄202 Lancashire Fusiliers.	Roll, scarlet silk	Scarlet	White	Round jacket only.	Regulation			
...⁄142 Royal Scots Fusiliers.	Roll, blue ...	Regulation ..	Regulation	Regulation ...	Tartan of regimental pattern, otherwise regulation.			
...⁄122 The Cheshire Regiment.	Roll	Regulation ...	Regulation	On jacket only	Regulation with lappels.			
61002⁄Infantry⁄445 The Royal Welsh Fusiliers.	Roll	Regulation ..	Regulation, with 2 buttons.	Regulation ...	Black cloth, 4 buttons...			
...⁄79 The South Wales Borderers.	Roll, white cloth	Scarlet	White	White round jacket and shoulder straps.	Regulation			
61002⁄Infantry⁄445 The King's Own Scottish Borderers.	Roll	Regulation ..	Gauntlet cuff ...	None	Leslie tartan roll collar, 3 buttons.			
61002⁄5650 The Inniskilling Fusiliers.	Roll, blue... ...	Regulation ...	Regulation ...	None	Regulation, with 4 buttons.			
...⁄Infantry⁄20 The Gloucester Regiment.	Roll, red, with steps, white silk facing.	Scarlet	White	Regulation ...	Scarlet; plain; 3 buttons, opening one inch below stud of shirt.			
...⁄6391 The Worcester Regiment.	Roll, green cloth	Same material as jacket.	Same material as jacket.	Shoulder straps and cuffs piped white.	Regulation			
61002⁄Infantry⁄114 The East Lancashire Regiment.	Roll, white cloth	Regulation ...	White	Regulation ...	Scarlet cloth, piped white.			
...⁄Infantry⁄132 The East Surrey Regiment.	Roll	Regulation ...	Regulation	None	Regulation scarlet cloth, without braid or piping.			
...⁄Infantry⁄220 The Duke of Cornwall's Light Infantry.	Roll, crimson silk	Scarlet cloth ...	White	None	Regulation			
61002⁄Infantry⁄47 The West Riding Regiment.	Roll, crimson ...	Scarlet	White, 2¾ inches deep, with three-pointed scarlet flap, 5½ inches deep and 2¼ inches wide at the points. On the flaps 3 buttons of regimental pattern.	White, round the jacket and flaps.	White, washing, with lappels.			

The Undermentioned Regiments wear Mess Dress of Authorised Regimental Patterns—continued.

Regiment.	Jacket.				Waistcoat.	Pattern.		No. of Plate.
	Collar.	Shoulder Straps.	Cuffs.	Piping.		No.	Sealed.	
61002 / Infantry / 445 — The Border Regiment.	Roll	Regulation ...	Regulation	Regulation	Regulation			
... / Infantry / 263 — The Royal Sussex Regiment.	Roll, blue cloth ...	Blue	Blue, gauntlet shape, with red silk slash, 6 inches deep at the point, 4 buttons on slash.	White on collar, cuffs, and jacket.	Regulation			
61002 / Infantry / 445 — The Hampshire Regiment.	Roll	Regulation ..	Regulation	Regulation	Regulation ...			
... / 118 — South Staffordshire Regiment.	Roll	Regulation ...	Regulation	None	Plain white cloth ...			
... / Infantry / 308 — The Dorsetshire Regiment.	Roll, white cloth	Regulation ...	Regulation	None	Regulation, white, washing, with 4 buttons.			
South Lancashire Regiment.	Roll, white silk ...	Scarlet	White, with slashes and 3 buttons.	White, except round collar.	Regulation			
... / 5031 — The Welsh Regiment.	Roll, crimson silk	Regulation ...	Regulation	Regulation ...	Scarlet cloth, universal infantry pattern, with second row of gold braid forming eyes down the front and along the bottom to the side seams.	167	7.11.95	
61002 / Infantry / 445 — The Oxfordshire Light Infantry.	Roll, scarlet silk	Scarlet	White half gauntlet, 4 buttons in a fly.	None	White washing			
... / 5964 — The Essex Regiment.	Roll, black silk ...	As the jacket ...	As the jacket ..	Regulation on cuffs and shoulder straps.	Regulation			
... / 6572 — The Derbyshire Regiment.	Roll, green cloth	Scarlet	Scarlet	Regulation ..	Regulation			
... / 6577 — The Loyal North Lancashire Regiment.	Roll, white cloth	Scarlet	White	None round bottom of jacket.	Plain scarlet cloth; white silk lining; open in front, fastened with 4 small buttons.			
61002 / Infantry / 126 — The Northamptonshire Regiment.	Roll	Regulation ...	Regulation	None	Regulation			
61002 / Infantry / 445 — The Royal Berkshire Regiment.	Roll	Regulation ...	Regulation	Regulation ...	Blue cloth, 4 buttons, no gold lace.			
... / 6253 — The Royal West Kent Regiment.	Roll, blue velvet	Regulation ...	Blue velvet, gauntlet shape, slashed red silk, 6 buttons in pairs.	Regulation ...	White marcella, with roll collar, 6 buttons.			
61002 / Infantry / 445 — The Yorkshire Light Infantry.	Roll, blue cloth ...	Regulation ...	Regulation	Gold cord round jacket, collar, and cuffs.	Blue cloth, edges and pockets trimmed with gold cord, 3 buttons.			
... / Infantry / 367 — The Shropshire Light Infantry.	Roll, blue cloth ...	Scarlet	Regulation, blue cloth.	None	Plain cloth			
61002 / Infantry / 445 — The Middlesex Regiment.	Roll	Regulation ..	Regulation	Regulation ...	Scarlet cloth.			See Infantry patterns, Plate 33.

G

The Undermentioned Regiments wear Mess Dress of Authorised Regimental Patterns—continued.

Regiment.	Jacket.				Waistcoat.	Pattern.		No. of Plate.
	Collar.	Shoulder Straps.	Cuffs.	Piping.		No.	Sealed.	
... Infantry 417 The Wiltshire Regiment.	Roll, white cloth	Scarlet	White	None	White, washing, with lappels.			
The Manchester Regiment.	Roll	Regulation ...	Regulation ...	Regulation ...	... ...			
61002 Infantry 445 The North Staffordshire Regiment.	Roll	Regulation ...	Regulation ...	Regulation ...	... ...			
... 143 The York and Lancaster Regiment.	Roll, red silk ...	Red	Regulation ...	None	Regulation			
... Infantry 288 The Durham Light Infantry.	Roll, rose-coloured ribbed silk.	Scarlet	White	None and no buttons.	Regulation, with 4 buttons.			See Infantry patterns, Plate 33.
61002 Infantry 445 The Royal Irish Fusiliers.	Roll	Scarlet	Regulation ...	None	Blue cloth, roll collar, 4 buttons.			
... 5060 The Connaught Rangers.	... ...	Regulation ...	Regulation ...	Regulation ...	Green cloth. The pockets, front and bottom to the side seams, edged with ½-inch gold cord, 5 buttons of special pattern down the front.			
... 178 The Leinster Regiment.	Roll, blue cloth ...	Blue	Blue	None	Blue cloth or white, according to climate.			
61002 Infantry 445 The Royal Munster Fusiliers.	Roll	Regulation ...	Regulation ...	None	Blue cloth, roll collar, 3 buttons.			
The Royal Dublin Fusiliers.	Roll	... ...	... ...	... ...	... ...			

581. Trousers—As for Undress.

582. Boots and Spurs—As described in paragraphs 4 and 25.

Regimental Staff Officers.

583. ADJUTANTS wear the uniform of their rank, with pantaloons, boots and spurs, as laid down in paragraphs 557, 558.

584. QUARTERMASTERS wear regimental uniform of their honorary rank with the following exceptions :—

585. Sword Belt—Black morocco leather.

586. Shoulder Belt—Plain black morocco leather, without lace or stripe ; buckle, tip and slide.

587. Pouch—Black patent leather (to hold writing materials), the flap 7 inches long and 3½ inches deep. No device.   358

588. Sash—Not worn.

HORSE FURNITURE.

589. Saddle—The saddle described in Appendix VI ; or Hunting, see paragraph 22.   600   24.9.97

590. Bridle and Breast Plate, Wallets—Brown leather, as described in Appendix VI. On the bosses and within the words "Infantry Mounted Officers," the rose, thistle, and shamrock, with a crown above. Browband and rosettes of the colour of the regimental facings.   603   24.9.97
    607   14.9.96

591. Headrope—According to sealed pattern.

	Pattern.		No. of Plate.
	No.	Sealed.	

LIGHT INFANTRY.

(Exclusive of the Highland Light Infantry.)

592. The uniform and horse furniture are the same as for Infantry of the Line, with the following exceptions :—

593. Helmet—(Home pattern)—See paragraph 16. — No. 3, Sealed 7.12.98, Plate 5

594. Special Badges—See Appendix I.

61002 / 5476 / A.O.148 / 1896

595. Forage Cap—Not worn.

596. Field Cap } Dark green. — No. 26, Sealed 2.3.94
Lanyard }   Plate 64

597. Sword Knot (Undress)—Black leather of regimental pattern.

598. Linen Collars—In Undress the Officers of the Oxfordshire Light Infantry are allowed to wear white linen collars, see paragraph 8.

FUSILIERS.

(Exclusive of the Royal Scots Fusiliers.)

599. The uniform and horse furniture are the same as for Infantry of the Line, with the following exceptions :—

600. Tunic—The Northumberland Fusiliers wear Gosling green facings. The Royal Welsh Fusiliers wear "the flash." — No. 168

601. Cap—Short bear skin, or black racoon skin— — No. 14, Sealed 23.8.98, Plate 6

61002 / 5915 / ... / 5950

For Officers not exceeding 5 ft. 6 in. in height, 8 ⎫
       „   „   5 „ 9 „   „ $8\frac{1}{2}$ ⎬ inches high in front.
       „   „   6 „ 0 „   „   9 ⎪
       „   exceeding   6 „ 0 „   „ $9\frac{1}{2}$ ⎭

A grenade in front, with a badge on the ball; burnished chain, lined with black velvet and leather.

602. Plume—Northumberland Fusiliers, red and white hackle feather, $4\frac{1}{2}$ inches high, the red above; worn on the left side; gilt two-flame socket. Royal Irish Fusiliers, green cut feather, $6\frac{1}{2}$ inches high. — No. 65, Sealed 31.1.74, Plate 6

61002 / Infantry

603. Special Badges—See Appendix I.

HIGHLAND AND SCOTTISH REGIMENTS.

HIGHLAND REGIMENTS, EXCEPT HIGHLAND LIGHT INFANTRY.

FULL DRESS.

61002 / 6812

604. Head Dress—Ostrich feather bonnets, on wire body, about 11 inches in height, white vulture plume on the right side and tails on the left. In the Royal Highlanders, four tails; in the Seaforth, Gordon and Cameron Highlanders, five tails; in the Argyll and Sutherland Highlanders, six tails. Diced border of regimental pattern. — No. 15, Plate 6

605. Doublet—Scarlet cloth, with collar and cuffs of the colour of regimental facings. The collar laced and braided according to rank, as described for Infantry of the Line. Gauntlet cuffs, $3\frac{1}{2}$ inches deep in front and 6 inches at the back, edged with $\frac{5}{8}$-inch lace round the top and down the back seam; 3 loops of gold braid, with buttons on each cuff; 8 buttons in front, and 2 at the waist behind. Inverness skirts, 8, $7\frac{1}{2}$, and 7 inches deep, with skirt-flaps on the first two, $\frac{1}{2}$ inch shorter, the first skirt $1\frac{1}{2}$ inches from centre of bottom button; 3 loops of gold braid, with buttons on each skirt-flap. Pockets in the skirts in front. The front, collar, skirts, and flaps edged with white cloth, $\frac{1}{4}$-inch wide, and the skirts, and flaps lined with white. Twisted round gold shoulder cords, universal pattern, lined with scarlet; a small button of regimental pattern at the top. — No. 169, Plate 34; No. 515, Sealed 17.8.95, Plate 64

Field Officers have a second bar of lace round the top of the cuff, and $\frac{1}{2}$-inch lace round the skirts and skirt-flaps. Colonels have 2 lines of braid, and Lieutenant-Colonels, 1 line within the lace on the cuffs.

Captains have a line of braid within the lace on the cuffs.

Lieutenants have the same lace on the cuffs as Captains, but without the line of braid.

The several bars of lace and lines of braid on the cuffs are to be $\frac{1}{4}$ inch apart.

61002 / Infantry / 188

606. Facings—Blue cloth in the Royal Highlanders and Queen's Own Cameron Highlanders; buff in the Seaforth Highlanders; yellow cloth in the other regiments.

607. Lace—Gold, thistle pattern, $\frac{5}{8}$ inch wide. In the Gordon Highlanders a black line is introduced at top and bottom. — No. 822, Plate 79

608. Special Badges—See Appendix I.

609. Buttons—Regimental patterns. See Appendix I.

610. Pantaloons—Tartan, of authorized pattern.

611. Boots and Spurs—As described in paragraphs 4 and 25.

612. Sash—Crimson silk, Highland pattern. Dimensions, unstretched—15 inches wide in the middle and 7 inches at the commencement of the fringe.

	Pattern.		No. of Plate.
	No.	Sealed.	

613. Belted Plaid, Shoulder Plaid, Kilt, Trews, Hose, Garters, Skean Dhu, Gaiters, Shoes, and Buckles— } Of authorized regimental patterns.

614. Brooch—Of authorized regimental pattern. The diameter not to exceed 3⅞ inches. Undress brooches are not to be worn.

615. Sporrans—Of authorized regimental patterns. The sporran top is not to exceed 6 inches in width. The breadth of the sporran leather is not to exceed 8½ inches. The length of the top and leather together will not exceed 11 inches, or for badger-skin sporrans, 13 inches. Officers may wear undress sporrans resembling those of the men. The bullion tassels on the dress sporrans will not exceed six. They are only to be worn in "Review Order," and must be removable in regiments that do not adopt the undress sporran.

61002
Infantry
230

In the Royal Highlanders—White horse-hair. The sporran top is in frosted gilt metal, edged with thistles. Thistle leaves at each side and in the centre. Above the centre thistle St. Andrew and cross. Five gold bullion tassels suspended by looped gold cord.

In the Seaforth Highlanders—White horse-hair. The sporran top is in burnished gilt metal engraved with a thistle on either side. In the centre, in silver, two sprays of thistle with the scroll inscribed "Cuidich'n Righ" on the lower bend. On the top of the sprays the scrolls inscribed with some of the honours of the Regiment. Between the sprays a stag's head. Above the stag's head two other scrolls inscribed with the remaining honours of the Regiment. Two long black horse-hair tassels with gilt sockets. Sockets engraved with thistles and leaves.

In the Gordon Highlanders—White horse-hair. Gilt metal top, engraved with thistles and ornamental edges. In the centre, badges as for waistplate in silver. Five gold bullion tassels hanging from looped gold cord. The heads of the tassels in dead and bright gold.

In the Cameron Highlanders—Grey horse-hair. Sporran top in frosted gilt metal. In the centre, an elliptical ring, inscribed "The Queen's Own Cameron Highlanders," within an oak-leaf wreath. Within the ring, on a burnished gilt ground, a thistle surmounted by a crown in silver. On either side of the oak-leaf scroll are sprays of thistles. On the lower portion of the wreath and sprays, a scroll inscribed "Peninsula, Egypt, Waterloo." Six gold bullion tassels suspended by blue and gold twisted cords.

In the Argyll and Sutherland Highlanders—Engraved gilt top, special shape (five-sided), square edges with centre in enamel. On the centre, the boar's head and scroll, the coronet with cypher, and the cat and scroll similar in design to the full dress head-dress. Five small gold bullion tassels with netted head suspended by looped gold cords.

616. Claymore—Steel, basket hilt, lined with scarlet cloth; straight cut and thrust blade, 1½ inches wide at the shoulder, and 32 inches long.	359	7.10.63	
617. Scabbard—Steel.	359	7.10.63	
618. Waist Belt—White buff leather, from 2 to 2½ inches wide, with slings 1 inch wide, hanging from two rings. Flat billets and gilt studs attached to the slings by square gilt wire buckles.	395	15.11.98	
619. Shoulder Belt (for Company Officers)—White buff leather, 3 inches wide, with slings 1 inch wide hanging from rings. Round billets and gilt studs attached to the slings by square gilt wire buckles.	361	13.2.96	64

61002
Infantry
99
61002
5154

620. Waist Plate, Breast Plate, Dirk, *Dirk Belt and Plate, } Of authorized regimental patterns. The dirk is not to exceed in length 17¼ inches over all, from extreme end of dirk handle to the point of the sheath. The blade should not be more than 1⅜ inches in breadth at the broadest part.	362	8.3.61	
621. Sabretache—See paragraph 21.	302	11.5.95	

UNDRESS.

622. Glengarry—Blue, of pattern similar to that worn by the men. Plain in the Royal Highlanders and Cameron Highlanders; diced in the Seaforth Highlanders, Gordon Highlanders, and Argyll and Sutherland Highlanders. Bottom of cap bound with black silk. Black silk rosettes, except in the Royal Highlanders. Badges to be worn on the left side. See Appendix I.	88 90 91 92	4.10.98 14.10.98 14.10.98 14.10.98	9
623. Drill and Mess Jacket—Scarlet cloth, with collar and pointed cuffs, of the regimental facings. Edged all round with white cloth, ⅛ inch wide. The cuffs similarly edged round the top. 10 buttons of regimental pattern down the front; two above each cuff at the back of the sleeve. Shoulder cords as on doublet.	170	24.11.91	35

61002
Infantry
189

In the Royal Highlander the jacket will have buff silk lining (except for collar, which is dark blue), and no facing cloth on the inside. Point of cuff at back seam.

In the Seaforth Highlanders the jacket will be lined with buff silk, with buff cloth on inside of jacket in front and inside of collar.

In the Gordon Highlanders the jacket will be lined with red, and the inside of the collar and of the garment on either side with crimson silk instead of facing cloth.

In the Cameron Highlanders the jacket will have buff silk lining, and no facing cloth on the inside.

In the Argyll and Sutherland Highlanders the jacket is lined with pale yellow; the inside of the collar and down the inside of the jacket on either side with facing cloth.

---

* To be worn with slings on Full Dress occasions by Field Officers.

	Pattern.		No. of Plate.
	No.	Sealed.	

624. Scarlet Frock—Red angola, tartan or serge, full in chest, rounded in front, cut with side bodies, slits at side seams, two slits at the back 6 inches deep, five small regimental buttons down the front.   Two breast patch pockets outside, 6¼ inches wide, 8 inches deep from the top of the flap, the top edge of pocket in line with the second button, shaped flap, small regimental button and hole, loose plait on rear side of pocket, two outside pockets below, with shaped flap.   Two inside breast pockets up and down with hole and button, two inside skirt pockets, with hole and button.   Outside pockets lined chamois leather. Shoulder straps of the same material as the garment, fastened with a small regimental button.   Red lining.   Collar of the colour of the regimental facings.   Sleeves with gauntlet cuffs, 6¼ inches high at the back and 4 inches in front.   *(171 23.4.98)*

61002 / 6165

61002 / Infy. / 37

61002 / Infantry / 230

625. Dirk Belt—Plain white or black leather.

626. Sporrans—In the Royal Highlanders—White horse-hair.   Top as for full-dress sporran. Five short black horse-hair tassels in black patent leather sockets.
    In the Seaforth Highlanders—As for full dress.
    In the Gordon Highlanders—White horse-hair.   Top as for full dress.   Two long black horse-hair tassels, suspended from gilt metal sockets and chains.   Sockets engraved with thistles.
    In the Cameron Highlanders—Black horse-hair.   Black leather top.   On the top, in silver, St. Andrew and cross, between sprays of thistle.   Two long white horse-hair tassels in black leather sockets.
    In the Argyll and Sutherland Highlanders—A badger head forms the top.   Six short white horse-hair tassels, with thistle leaf sockets in gilt metal, suspended by looped gold wire cord.

61002 / 6890

627. Belts—"Sam Browne"
Scabbard—Brown leather   } See Appendices VII and VIII.
Sword Knot—Brown leather

... / 6943

628. Sword Belt for wear under the frock—As described in Appendix VIII (2).   See paragraph 28.
    Other articles as in Full Dress.

Great Coat and Cape.

629. As for Infantry of the Line.

Mess Dress.

630. Mess Jacket—See Drill and Mess Jacket, paragraph 624.   *(35)*
631. Mess Waistcoat—Cloth of the colour of the facings, scarlet cloth or regimental tartan ; in other respects, the pattern will be as for the cloth mess waistcoats of Infantry of the Line. In the Gordon Highlanders, the waistcoat will be of scarlet cloth, with roll collar and three small regimental buttons.   *(35)*
632. Trews—See paragraph 613.
633. Boots and Spurs—As described in paragraphs 4 and 25.

REGIMENTAL STAFF OFFICERS.

634. The Adjutants wear the uniform of their rank, with pantaloons, boots and spurs as laid down in paragraphs 610, 611.
635. Quartermasters wear regimental uniform of their honorary rank, with the following exceptions :—
636. Waist Belt—Black morocco leather.
637. Shoulder Belt
Pouch   } As for Infantry of the Line.
638. Sash—Not worn.

Horse Furniture.

639. As described in Appendix VI.

THE HIGHLAND LIGHT INFANTRY.

640. Uniform and horse furniture as for kilted regiments, with the following exceptions :—
641. Chaco—Blue cloth, 4 inches high in front and 6½ inches at the back, the crown 6 inches long and 5½ inches across.   Diced band, black corded boss with device in front, green tuft, plate of special pattern.   Cap lines.   At back, for ventilation, a bronze ornament ; a bronze ornament with hook on each side at the top, to hook up the lines.   Horizontal peak.   Black leather chin strap.
    Colonels and Lieutenant-Colonels have two rows of ⅝-inch lace, thistle pattern, round the top of the chaco ; Majors have one row.   *(16 4.1.62 7)*
642. Chaco Lines—Black round silk cord, with egg moulds and sliders.   *(16 4.1.62 7)*
643. Glengarry—Of dark green cloth, with diced band 1¼ inches wide, and dark green tuft.   *(66 3.8.95 9)*

A.C.D. / H.L.I. / 307

644. Special Badges—See Appendix I.
645. Facings—Buff.

	Pattern.		No. of Plate.
	No.	Sealed.	

_{61002 / 4960} **646. Drill and Mess Jacket**—Scarlet cloth, with collar and cuffs of regimental facings, edged all round with white cloth ⅛ inch wide. Gauntlet cuffs edged round the top. Ten buttons of regimental pattern down the front. Four on the back of each cuff in a fly. Crimson silk lining and inside of collar. Twisted treble gold shoulder cords lined with scarlet. Small regimental button at the top, thistle in silver embroidery below the badges of rank.   172   3.8.95   35

_{61002 / 4960} **647. Mess Waistcoat**—Tartan, of authorized regimental pattern, single-breasted; no collar; open halfway down; three regimental buttons in front. The waistcoat edged all round with ⅛-inch round gold cord. Pockets on each side, edged with similar cord, forming crows' feet in the centre and at the ends.   173   16.9.91   35

648. Trews and Pantaloons—Tartan of authorized regimental pattern.

649. Claymore—Removable basket hilt for Levées, &c. On other occasions a cross-bar hilt.   359   7.10.63

650. The Forage Cap, the Belted Plaid, Kilt, Sporran, Hose, Gaiters, Skean Dhu, Garters, Shoes, and Buckles are not worn.

SCOTTISH REGIMENTS.

THE ROYAL SCOTS, AND THE KING'S OWN SCOTTISH BORDERERS.

651. The uniform and horse furniture are the same as for Infantry of the Line, with the following exceptions :—

_{61002 / 5876} **652. Forage Cap**—Not worn.

653. Glengarry—Blue cloth, of pattern similar to that worn by the men; the bottom of the cap bound with black silk; badge on left side. See Appendix I.   See 88, &c.   9

654. Doublet—As for Highland regiments; blue facings.   169   78

655. Lace for Doublet—Gold, thistle pattern.

656. Special Badges—See Appendix I.

657. Frock—As for Highland regiments.

658. Trews
     Pantaloons } Tartan, of authorized pattern.

659. Sash—Crimson silk, Highland pattern.

660. Claymore and Scabbard—As for Highland regiments, but with a removable basket-hilt for Levées, &c.; on other occasions a cross-bar hilt.   359   7.10.63

661. Sword Belt, Full Dress—Gold lace, thistle pattern, 2 inches wide, with slings 1 inch wide.   360   4.3.85   64

662. Sword Belt, Undress—Buff leather, 2 inches wide, with slings 1 inch wide; flap, and hook. See also paragraph 28.   64

THE ROYAL SCOTS FUSILIERS.

_{61002 / Infantry / 221} **663.** Uniform and horse furniture as laid down for Fusiliers (paragraphs 599 to 603), with the following exceptions :—

_{61002 / 5876} **664. Glengarry**—Blue cloth with diced band of regimental pattern similar to that worn by the men, bottom of cap bound with black silk. Badge on black ribbed silk rosette on left side. See Appendix I.   See 88, &c.   9

665. Doublet—As for Highland regiments; blue facings.

666. Lace for Doublet—Gold, thistle pattern.   34

667. Special Badges—See Appendix I.

668. Frock—Red Angola, tartan, or serge, according to climate; full in chest, pleated at waist to allow of "Sam Browne" belt being worn outside. Very slightly rounded in front, cut with side bodies, slits at side seams, two slits at the back 6 inches deep, six large regimental buttons down the front. Two breast patch-pockets outside, 6¼ inches wide, 8 inches deep from the top of the flap, the top edge of pocket in line with the second button, shaped flap, small regimental button and hole, loose plait in rear side of pocket. Two outside pockets below with shaped flap, on the flap three strands of white braid and three small regimental buttons. Shoulder straps of the same material as the garment and fastened with a small regimental button. Collar of the colour of the regimental facings, with white braid on collar seam, and on the collar a silver grenade with a thistle on the ball. The sleeves with plain cuffs traced to Highland pattern with white braid, 6¼ inches at back and 4 inches in front; on the cuff three strands of white braid and three small regimental buttons.   36

669. Blue Frock—As for Infantry of the line, but without collar badges.

670. Trews
     Pantaloons } Tartan, of authorized pattern.

671. Sash—Crimson silk, Highland pattern.

672. Claymore and Scabbard—As for Highland regiments, but with a removable basket hilt for Levées, &c.; on other occasions a cross-bar hilt.

673. Waistbelt—Full dress, gold lace, thistle pattern, 2 inches wide.

674. Shoulder Belt—White buff leather, 3 inches wide, with slings 1 inch wide, hanging from rings, with a gilt breast-plate 4 inches by 3 inches, and on it the regimental crest in silver.   361   13.2.96   64

	Pattern.		No. of Plate.
	No.	Sealed.	
675. Waistbelt—Worn with shoulder belt, white buff leather, 2 inches wide.			
676. Sword Belt—Undress, white buff leather, 2 inches wide, with slings 1 inch wide, hook for claymore. See also paragraph 28.			64

GREAT COAT AND CAPE.

677. As for infantry of the line, but with a plain gilt grenade and chain under the flap of the collar of the great coat.

THE SCOTTISH RIFLES.

678. Chaco—Rifle green cloth, 4½ inches high in front and 7¾ inches at the back, the crown 6 inches long and 5¾ inches across. Bands of black lace, thistle pattern, 1¾ inches wide round the base, and ⅝ inch round the top. At the sides two small bronze thistle ornaments for ventilation and with hook attachments. Black silk square cord plait in front carried up to the hooks at each side, and a double cord carried round the back over ring at rear, with black egg moulds and slider at left side. Black silk doubled square body line, 76 inches long, with swivel to attach to the ring behind, with black egg moulds and sliders. Horizontal peak, black leather chin strap.	17	11.5.92	7
679. Badges—See Appendix I.			
680. Plume—Black ostrich feathers, a black vulture feather bottom in a bronze corded ball socket with three upright leaves. The height of the plume from the top of the chaco is 7 inches.	17	11.5.92	7
681. Doublet—Rifle green cloth, collar and cuffs of the same material. The collar laced and braided according to rank as described for Infantry of the Line. The lace, black, ⅝ inch wide, thistle pattern. Gauntlet cuffs, 5 inches deep in front and 8 inches at the back, edged with ⅝-inch lace round the top and at either side of the back seam. Three loops of Russia braid on each cuff with a button at the top of each loop. Eight buttons down the front with two hooks and eyes at the waist, and two buttons at the waist behind. Skirts 7¼, 6¾, and 6¼ inches deep with skirt flaps on the first two 6¾ and 6¼ inches deep, the first skirt ¾ inch from centre of bottom button. Three loops of Russia braid, with a regimental button at the bottom of each loop. Pocket inside the left breast and in each front skirt. Two hooks for the support of the sword belt. Black lining. Shoulder straps of the same material as the garment, edged with ⅝-inch lace, except at the base. A small regimental button at the top. Badges of rank in same material as the buttons. For distinctions of rank, as shown on cuffs and skirts, see Highland Regiments.	174	27.10.91	34
682. Lace—Black, thistle pattern.	822		
683. Buttons—Black ; for great coat, bronze. See Appendix I.			
684. Trews ⎫ Tartan of authorised pattern. **Pantaloons** ⎭			
685. Boots and Spurs—As described in paragraphs 4 and 25.			
686. Sword—As described in paragraph 27, steel hilt, with device of bugle and crown.	394	17.6.29	
687. Scabbard.—Steel.			
688. Sword Belt—Black patent leather, 1½ inches wide, with slings 1 inch wide.			64
689. Waist Plate—See Appendix I			
690. Sword Knot—Black leather strap and acorn.	363	23.8.98	64
691. Shoulder Belt—Black patent leather, 3 inches wide, with silver breast ornament, whistle and chain of regimental patterns.			
692. Pouch—Black patent leather, with the thistle in silver on the flap.			
693. Sabretache—See paragraph 21, the thistle in silver on the flap.	302	11.5.95	
694. Gloves—Black leather.			

UNDRESS.

695. Forage Cap—Rifle-green cloth, with band of 1¾-inch black lace, thistle pattern, black purl button and braided figure on the crown ; black leather chin strap ; no peak.	67	23.5.82	9
696. Glengarry—Rifle-green cloth.	See 88, &c.		
697. Patrol Jacket—Rifle-green cloth, 28 inches long from the bottom of the collar behind, for an Officer 5 feet 9 inches in height, with a proportionate variation for any difference in height, rounded in front ; collar and cuffs of Rifle-green cloth. Inch black mohair braid down the front, at the bottom of the skirts, and on the slits. The mohair braid traced inside with Russia braid, forming eyes at each angle of the slits. The back seams trimmed with inch mohair braid, traced on both sides with Russia braid, forming 3 eyes at the top, and 2 eyes at the bottom. On each side in front, five loops of black square cord, fastening with olivets ; each loop forms an eye above and below in the centre, and a drop at the end ; a cap on each drop. Cuffs pointed with inch mohair braid with a tracing of black Russia braid above and below. Collar cut square and edged with inch mohair braid ; tracing below the braid and on the collar seam, forming an eye in the corners ; at the back, below the centre of the collar, the tracing forms a plume 6 inches deep. Black lining, hooks and eyes. A pocket on either side below the fourth loop, and one inside the left breast. Shoulder cords of black chain gimp ; badges of rank as for doublet.	175	24.1.80	9 36
	176	23.3.86	63

61002
Infantry
111

	Pattern.		No. of Plate.
	No.	Sealed.	

698. Frock—Rifle green, the collar seam piped with the same material as the garment. Gauntlet cuffs, piped at the top, 4 inches deep in front, and 5½ inches at the back, with flap and five regimental horn buttons at back seam. A body seam at each side with a slit 4½ inches deep. All seams welted except the side body seams. Back strap, diamond shaped, sewn down the centre, and fastened on each side to a regimental horn button. Five regimental horn buttons down the front. A pocket on each side with pointed flap, and an outside pocket on either breast with pointed flap. An inside pocket in lining of left breast. The jacket lined with alpaca. Shoulder straps of the same material as the garment, a small button at the top.

699. Belts—"Sam Browne"
Scabbard—Brown leather } See Appendices VII and VIII.
Sword Knot—Brown leather

61002 / 6943

700. Sword Belt for wear with the Patrol Jacket and Frock.—Web as described in Appendix VIII (2). See paragraph 28.
Other articles as for Full Dress.

GREAT COAT AND CAPE.

701. Grey cloth, of the pattern described in paragraph 14, with bronze buttons; shoulder straps of the same material as the garment; a small button of regimental pattern at the top.

MESS DRESS.

702. Mess Jacket—Rifle-green cloth; collar and cuffs of Rifle-green cloth. Inch mohair braid all round the body, forming barrels or dummies at bottom of the back seams; a tracing of black Russia braid terminating in an eye at the bottom corners in front. Back seams, trimmed with black chain gimp, forming a crow's foot at the top, and an Austrian knot and curl at the bottom. A tracing of black Russia braid on either side of the gimp on each back seam; on the outside only of the crow's foot an Austrian knot with curl. Pockets trimmed with black chain gimp, forming a double crow's foot and eye; the gimp traced with black Russia braid, with eyes at intervals. Five plaited olivets down the front on the left side; hooks and eyes. Cuffs pointed with black chain gimp forming an Austrian knot in front, and continued to the bottom of the cuff at either side of the back seam. The gimp traced on the outside with black Russia braid. The Austrian knot extends to 7½ inches from the bottom of the cuff. Collar edged all round with ½-inch mohair braid; pockets inside the left breast; black silk lining; a loop at bottom of collar to fasten across the neck; shoulder straps of black chain gimp; badges of rank as for doublet. *(177, 35)*

703. Mess Waistcoat—Rifle-green cloth, single breasted; no collar; open halfway down; edged with ½-inch mohair braid; hooks and eyes; pockets edged with black Russia braid, forming three eyes in the centre at the top, three eyes in the centre at the bottom and, a crow's foot at each end. *(178, 23.5.82, 35)*

704. Trews, Boots, and Spurs—As for Full Dress.

REGIMENTAL STAFF OFFICERS.

705. Uniform as for the other Officers of their rank.

HORSE FURNITURE.

As described in Appendix VI, with the following exceptions:—

706. Bridle, Breast Plate, &c.—Black leather, with silver whole buckles and silver bit bosses; green front and rosettes; black and green horse-hair throat ornament, 18 inches long, with silver ball socket.

54 / Officers. / 41

707. Head Rope—Rifle-green.

708. Pattern of Bit Boss—Within a garter, surmounted by a crown, a bugle, with strings; on the garter, "The Cameronians."

King s Royal Rifle Corps.

49

	Pattern.		No. of Plate.
	No.	Sealed.	

RIFLE REGIMENTS.
(*Exclusive of the Scottish Rifles.*)

THE KING'S ROYAL RIFLE CORPS.
FULL DRESS.

709. Busby—Black Persian lambskin, height in front 5 inches, rising to 6 inches in the centre of each side of the busby and sloping back to the bottom edge. The crown of Rifle-green cloth, with figured ornament. Black silk square cord plait in front, carried up to a small bronze bugle at the centre of the top of each side with two rows of square silk cord at back, ending in a knot, to which is attached a bronze ring. A black corded oval boss on the top in front. Chin strap of black patent leather. Black silk square cord body line with swivel to attach to the ring at the back of the busby, black egg moulds and sliders. — 68 | 9.7.90 | 7

61002 / Infantry / 123

710. Plume—Scarlet ostrich feathers, a black vulture feather bottom in a bronze corded ball socket, threaded pattern, three upright flames. The height of the plume from the top of the busby is 7 inches. — 68 | 7.10.99 | 7

711. Tunic—Rifle-green cloth, edged all round, except the collar, with black square cord. Scarlet cloth collar and cuffs. The collar edged with ½-inch black braid; the cuffs pointed, and ornamented as described below, according to rank. The skirt rounded off in front, closed behind, and lined with black. On each side of the breast, 5 loops of black square cord, with netted caps and drops, fastening with black olivets. On each back seam a line of the same cord, forming a crow's foot at the top, passing under a netted cap at the waist, below which it is doubled, and ending in an Austrian knot reaching to the bottom of the skirt. Shoulder cords of black chain gimp, with small button of regimental pattern at the top. — 179 | 29.3.99 | 36

Field Officers have figured braiding below the braid on the collar; and 1½-inch black braid round the top of the cuff, with figured braiding above and below the braid, extending to 11½ inches from the bottom of the cuff. — 63

Captains have a row of braided eyes below the braid on the collar, and an Austrian knot of black square cord on the sleeve, with a tracing of braided eyes all round it, extending to 9½ inches from the bottom of the cuff.

Lieutenants have a tracing of plain braid only below the braid on the collar, and an Austrian knot on the sleeve, with a tracing of plain braid round it, extending to 8½ inches from the bottom of the cuff.

712. Braid—Black mohair.

713. Buttons—Bronze. See Appendix I.

714. Trousers—Rifle-green cloth, with 2-inch black braid down the side seams; in summer, Rifle-green tartan.

715. Pantaloons—Rifle-green cloth, with stripes as on the cloth trousers.

716. Boots and Spurs—As described in paragraphs 4 and 25, steel spurs in all orders of dress.

717. Sword—As described in paragraph 27; steel hilt, with device of bugle and crown. — 394 | 17.6.29

610 2 / 6943

718. Scabbard—Steel.

719. Sword Belt—Web—as described in Appendix VIII (2).

720. Slings—Sword and Sabretache—Black patent leather, 1 inch wide; silver oval buckles. — 64

721. Sword Knot—Black leather strap and acorn. — 363 | 23.8.98 | 64

722. Shoulder Belt—Black patent leather, 3 inches wide, breast ornament, see Appendix I. Whistle and chain, of regimental patterns.

723. Pouch—Black patent leather, with a silver bugle on the flap. Silver furniture.

724. Sabretache—See paragraph 21; device on flap, a bugle with strings in silver. — 302 | 11.5.95

725. Gloves—Black leather.

UNDRESS.

61002 / Infantry / 156

726. Forage Cap—Rifle-green cloth, with band of 1½-inch black mohair braid, braided figure with netted button on the crown, and black leather chin strap. No peak. — 69 | 5.10.97 | 9

61002 / 6250

727. Field Cap—As for Infantry, but of Rifle-green cloth. For badge, see Appendix I. — 26 | 2.3.94 | 9

728. Patrol Jacket—Rifle-green cloth, 28 inches long from the bottom of the collar behind, for an Officer 5 feet 9 inches in height, with a proportionate variation for any difference in height; rounded in front; collar and pointed cuffs of the regimental facings. Inch black mohair braid down the front, at the bottom of the skirts, and on the slits; the mohair braid traced inside with Russia braid, forming eyes at each angle of the slits. The back seams trimmed with inch mohair braid, traced on both sides with Russia braid, forming three eyes at the top and two at the bottom. On each side in front, five loops of black square cord fastening with olivets. Each loop forms an eye above and below in the centre and a drop at the end. A cap on each drop. Cuffs edged with inch mohair braid, traced with Russia braid, forming a crow's foot and eye at the top and an eye in the angle at the bottom. Collar edged all round with ½-inch mohair braid, traced inside with Russia braid, forming an eye at each end. At the back, below the centre of the collar, the — 175 | 24.1.80 | 36

	Pattern.		No. of Plate.
	No.	Sealed.	

tracing forms a plume, 6 inches deep ; a crow's foot and eye at the bottom. Black lining, hooks and eyes. A pocket on either side below the fourth loop, and one inside the left breast. Shoulder cords as for tunic.

729. Frock—Rifle-green rough serge, cut square in front, lined with black alpaca. Collar fastened by large hook, scarlet piping on the seam. Cuffs pointed, 4½ inches deep in front and 2 inches behind. A patch pocket 6¾ inches wide and 7½ inches deep with square flap and small button on each breast. A similar pocket 7¾ inches wide and 8 inches deep on each side below the waist, the bottom corners rounded off. A pleat on each side in front, four small gathers to give shape to the waist behind, and one from centre of each breast pocket to the top of the pocket below the waist. Waistband 2 inches wide, sewn on centre of back, running through a loop on each side, leather-covered buckle of special pattern. Five horn ball buttons of regimental pattern down the front. Shoulder straps of same material as the garment, with small flat horn button of regimental pattern at the top. *(61002 / 5281)* — No. 180, Sealed 23.4.96

730. Belts—"Sam Browne"
Scabbard—Brown leather } See Appendices VII and VIII.
Sword Knot—Brown leather
Other articles as in Full Dress. *(61002 / 6390)*

GREAT COAT AND CAPE.

731. Grey cloth, of the pattern described in paragraph 14, with bronze buttons. Shoulder straps of the same material as the garment ; a small button of regimental pattern at the top.

MESS DRESS.

732. Mess Jacket—Rifle-green cloth, scarlet collar and cuffs. Black mohair braid all round the body, forming barrels (or dummies) at bottom of back seams. Back seams trimmed with a double row of ¼-inch mohair braid, forming a crow's foot at top, and finishing over the barrels (or dummies) at the bottom. Pockets trimmed with ¼-inch mohair braid, forming a crow's foot at each end and in the centre. Five waved loops of square cord in front, with four rows of knitted olivets, two olivets on each loop. Pointed cuffs of inch mohair braid, with tracing of black Russia braid, forming a row of small eyes on the outside and inside of the cuffs, and extending 7 inches from the bottom of each cuff. Mohair braid, ½ inch wide, all round the collar, trimmed through the centre with plumes, a row of small eyes along top edge ; a loop at bottom of collar to fasten across the neck ; shoulder cords as for tunic. — No. 181, Sealed 17.3.99, Plate 37

733. Mess Waistcoat—Rifle-green cloth, single-breasted, no collar, open halfway down. Hooks and eyes. ½-inch mohair braid on edges, with a ¼-inch braid down the front, one inch from the edge. Scarlet cloth between the two braids, with row of eyes of black Russia braid down front edge on the scarlet cloth. Pockets trimmed with ¼-inch mohair braid, forming a crow's foot at each end, edged all round with scarlet cloth. — No. 182, Sealed 16.9.91, Plate 37

734. Trousers, Boots, and Spurs—As in Full Dress.

REGIMENTAL STAFF OFFICERS.

735. Uniform as for the other Officers of their rank.

HORSE FURNITURE.

As described in Appendix VI, with the following exceptions :—

736. Bridle, Breast Plate, &c.—Black leather, the head-stall lined with scarlet cloth, with scalloped edges ; silver whole buckles and silver bit bosses ; green front and rosettes ; black and scarlet horse-hair horse plume, 18 inches long, with silver ball socket.

737. Head Rope—Rifle-green. *(54 / Officers / 41)*

738. Pattern of Bit Boss—Within a garter, surmounted by a crown, a bugle with strings. On the garter, "King's Royal Rifle Corps."

THE ROYAL IRISH RIFLES.

739. The uniform and horse furniture are the same as for the King's Royal Rifle Corps, with the following exceptions :—

740. Busby—Same as for King's Royal Rifle Corps, with the exception of the badges, and the colour of the boss, which is dark green. — No. 68, Sealed 9.7.90, Plate 7

741. Plume—Same as for King's Royal Rifle Corps, except that the ostrich feathers are black and the vulture feathers are dark green. — No. 68, Sealed 7.10.99, Plate 7 *(61002 / Infy. / 128)*

742. Forage Cap—Band of 1¼-inch black lace, shamrock pattern. — No. 69, 70, Sealed 5.10.97, Plate 9

743. Tunic
Patrol Jacket } Dark-green cloth collar and cuffs. { — 179, 29.3.99, 36 / 175, 24.1.80, 36

744. Buttons—See Appendix I.

	Pattern.		No. of Plate.
	No.	Sealed.	

745. Frock—Rifle-green, slightly rounded in front. Dark-green Russia braid on collar seam. A body seam at each side, with a slit 4½ inches deep. Five bronze regimental buttons down the front. Cuffs, dark-green cloth, pointed, 5 inches deep in front and 1¾ inches at the back. A pocket on each side, and a patch pocket on the left breast. Black alpaca lining. Shoulder straps of the same material as the garment ; a small bronze regimental button at the top.

746. Shoulder Belt— 3 inches wide. Breast ornament, see Appendix I. Whistle and chain of regimental patterns.

747. Pouch—Black patent leather ; in silver, on the flap, a bugle with strings, surmounted by the Sphinx over Egypt.

748. Sabretache—In silver, on the flap, a bugle with strings surmounted by the Sphinx over Egypt. Silver furniture. `302` `11.5.95`

749. Mess Jacket—Rifle-green cloth ; dark-green cloth collar, square in front ; dark-green cloth cuffs ; inch black mohair braid all round the body, forming barrels (or dummies) at bottom of back seams. The mohair braid traced inside with Russia braid, forming an eye at each bottom corner in front. The back seams trimmed with double ¼-inch Russia braid, forming in single braid at the top a crow's foot and eye, and terminating in single braid in an eye at the bottom, above the dummies. On each side, in front, four waved loops of ¼-inch Russia braid, each loop forming a drooping crow's foot at the end ; two double-stitched olivets on each loop. Cuffs pointed with ¼-inch black Russia braid, forming a crow's foot in front, and continued to the bottom of the cuff at either side of the back seam. The crow's foot extends to 6 inches from the bottom of the cuff. The ¼-inch braid traced inside and outside with small Russia braid. A further tracing of small eyes above and below the ¼-inch braid, terminating in a figured braiding below in the front. The collar edged top and bottom with ½-inch mohair braid, with a double row of eyes within the braid, terminating in an eye at each corner of the collar. A loop at bottom of collar to fasten across the neck. Pocket inside the left breast ; black silk lining ; hooks and eyes down the front. Shoulder cords as for tunic. `184` `23.5.82` `37`

750. Mess Waistcoat—Green, instead of scarlet cloth, between the two braids down the front ; the mohair braid on the pockets edged with green. `182` `16.9.91` `37`

HORSE FURNITURE.

751. Bridle, Breast Plate, &c.—The head-stall is not lined. The garter of the bit bosses inscribed " Royal Irish Rifles " ; dark green horse-hair horse plume.

THE RIFLE BRIGADE

752. The uniform and horse furniture are the same as for the King's Royal Rifle Corps, with the following exceptions :—

753. Plume—Black ostrich feathers instead of scarlet. `68` `7.10.99` `7`

754. Forage Cap—No button on the crown.

755. Tunic—Black velvet collar and cuffs. `179` `29.3.99` `36`

756. Patrol Jacket—Rifle-green cloth, of the size and shape described in paragraph 670, with collar and cuffs of black velvet. Inch black mohair braid down the front, at the bottom of the skirts, and on the slits. The mohair braid traced inside with Russia braid, forming eyes at each angle of the slits. The back seams trimmed with inch mohair braid traced on both sides with Russia braid, forming three eyes at the top and two eyes at the bottom. On each side, in front, five loops of black square cord, fastening with olivets. Each loop forms an eye above and below in the centre, and a drop at the end. A cap on each drop, cuffs pointed with inch mohair braid, traced at the bottom with Russia braid, forming an eye in the angle. Collar edged with inch mohair braid ; a tracing below the braid, and on the collar seam, forming an eye in the corners. At the back, below the centre of the collar, the tracing forms a plume 6 inches deep ; black lining, hooks and eyes. A pocket on either side below the fourth loop, and one inside the left breast. Shoulder cords as for tunic. `175` `24.1.80` `36`

757. Frock—Rifle green. Cuffs plain. A body seam on each side, seven regimental horn buttons down the front. Two pockets on each side with pointed flaps. A small button with tab under each flap. A drawing string inside at the waist. Shoulder-straps of the same material as the garment, a small button at the top. `185` `23.3.86`

758. Shoulder Belt—3 inches wide. Breast ornament, see Appendix I. Whistle and chain of regimental patterns.

759. Mess Jacket—Rifle-green cloth ; black velvet collar. Inch mohair braid all round the body, forming barrels (or dummies) at bottom of back seams. The mohair braid traced inside with Russia braid, forming an eye at each bottom corner in front. The back seams trimmed with double ¼-inch black Russia braid, forming in a single braid an Austrian knot at the top. Five plaited olivets on the left side ; hooks and eyes down the front. Cuffs, black velvet, pointed with inch mohair braid, traced at the bottom with Russia braid, forming an eye in the angle. The mohair braid extends to 6 inches from the bottom of the cuff. Collar edged with inch mohair braid ; a tracing of black Russia braid below `186` `16.9.91` `37`

61002 / 6250

	Pattern.		No. of Plate.
	No.	Sealed.	

the mohair braid, and on the collar seam, forming an eye in the corners. Pockets edged with ¼-inch Russia braid forming a crow's foot at each end. Black lining; shoulder cords as for tunic.

760. **Mess Waistcoat**—Rifle-green cloth, single-breasted, without collar, open to the second olivet of the mess-jacket; edged with ½-inch black mohair braid, traced inside with black Russia braid, forming an eye at each bottom corner in front. The pockets edged with black Russia braid, forming plumes at the top and bottom, in the centre, and at each end.   *187   16.9.91   37*

HORSE FURNITURE.

761. **Bridle, Breast Plate, &c.**—The head-stall is not lined; the garter of the bit-bosses inscribed, "Rifle Brigade"; black horse-hair horse plume.

MOUNTED INFANTRY.

61002 / 6585

762. Officers of Mounted Infantry will wear the same dress as that described for Mounted Officers of Infantry, with the following exceptions:—

763. **Breeches**—Bedford cord.

764. **Putties**—Woollen, khaki colour.

765. **Knee Boots**—May be worn in Review Order.   *501   6.11.96*

WEST INDIA REGIMENT.

766. Uniform and horse furniture as for Infantry of the Line, with the following exceptions:—

767. **Lace for Tunic**—Bias and Stand pattern.

768. **Special Badges**—See Appendix I.   *822   79*

769. **Scarlet Frock**—Not worn.

770. **White Trousers**—Are worn on ordinary occasions.

61002 / 5898

771. **Mess Jacket**—Roll collar of scarlet silk, white cuffs.

WEST AFRICAN REGIMENT.

61002 / 6789

772. As for Infantry of the Line, with the following exceptions:—

773. **Helmet**—"Wolseley" pattern, cork covered with khaki, made with six seams, bound buff leather, projecting peak all round, 3 inches wide in front, 4 inches at back, and 2 inches at the sides, ventilated at top with zinc-covered button, side hooks with brown leather chin strap.   *22   13.9.99   11*

61002 / Infy. / 385

774. **Frock**—Scarlet. Not worn.

775. **Boots**—Brown leather.

776. **Putties**—Woollen, khaki colour.

777. **Sword Belt**—"Sam Browne."

778. **Mess Dress**—White mess dress, or cloth mess dress of the pattern worn in the regiment from which the Officer was transferred.

... / 6856

THE CHINESE REGIMENT.
IN COLD WEATHER.

779. **Cap**—As described in paragraph 565 for Infantry of the Line, or sealskin to be worn at night, or when ordered.   *9*

780. **Frock**—Khaki, drab or neutral colour material, thick or thin according to the climate, cut similarly to the frock for officers of Infantry of the Line, but with turn down (Italian) collar, fastened with one hook and eye, and no pockets below the waist. A tab of the same material inside the collar to button across the neck when the collar is turned up.

781. **Buttons**—As described in Appendix I.

782. **Knickerbocker Breeches**—Bedford cord.

783. **Trousers**—Infantry pattern, in Oxford mixture, with ¼ inch red welt down the side seams.

784. **Putties**—Khaki.

785. **Boots**—Ankle, black, lace.

786. **Belt**—"Sam Browne," as described in Appendix VIII.

787. **Sash**—Red.   *397   4.1.1900   70*

788. **Sword**—As described in Appendix VII. (3)   *347   13.12.97*

789. **Scabbard**—As described in Appendix VII. (4)   *398 & 399   4.1.1900*

	Pattern.		No. of Plate.
	No.	Sealed.	

FULL DRESS FOR LEVÉES AND STATE OCCASIONS.

The full dress of the regiment from which Officers have been seconded.

GREAT COAT AND CAPE.

790. As for Infantry of the Line. Fur-lined great coat to be worn at night, and when ordered.	100	13.2.96	

IN HOT WEATHER.

791. Helmet—Wolseley pattern as described in paragraph 773.	22	13.9.99	11
792. Boots—Brown leather.			
793. Off parade, khaki trousers may be worn.			

MESS DRESS.

794. Mess Jacket—Infantry pattern, red cloth, with pale yellow roll collar, cuffs, and shoulder straps.	158	17.7.96	
795. Mess Waistcoat—Red cloth, as for Infantry of the Line.	159	15.9.91	
796. Trousers—Infantry pattern, grey Oxford mixture with ¼ inch red welt down the side seams.			

A.O. 148 / 1896

OFFICERS COMMANDING REGIMENTAL DISTRICTS, AND DEPÔT W. INDIA REGIMENT.

61002 / 6818

61002 / Staff.

39 / 61002 / Infantry / 466

797. The uniform of the regiment of the district, with the following exceptions :—			
798. Cocked Hat—As described in paragraph 7, but with loop of ⅝-inch lace, and netted gold purl head, the plume as for Colonel on the Staff.	1 2	23.8.98 29.11.91	2 and 3
799. Forage Cap—As described in paragraph 11, band of blue cloth—Rifles, black braid. The badge will be that for the forage cap of the regiment of the district.	31	14.7.93	8
800. Frock Coat.—The frock coat as for Colonel on the Staff, *vide* paragraph 123, but with regimental buttons, may be worn.			
801. Shoulder Cords—As described for General Officers, see paragraph 76. Officers commanding districts of rifle regiments will wear shoulder cords of the same pattern, but of mohair braid.	514	21.1.98	62
802. In the case of two regimental districts being under one command, the Officer commanding will wear the uniform of the regiment to which he belonged if its depôt forms part of the regimental district command ; if it does not he will wear the uniform of the senior regiment.			

61002 / 6809

Uniform obtained under the provisions of the Dress Regulations, 1894, may be worn till 31st December, 1901.

MILITIA BATTALIONS.

803. Uniform and horse furniture as for the Line battalions of the Territorial Regiments of which they form part, with the following exceptions :—

804. Shoulder Cords or Shoulder Straps—The letter **M** is worn on the shoulder cords or shoulder straps below the badges of rank, and will follow those badges in material.

61002 / Infantry / 379

805. In the Militia Battalions of the Royal Highlanders, Seaforth Highlanders, and Argyll and Sutherland Highlanders, the Belted Plaid, Kilt, Sporran, Hose, Garters, Skean Dhu, Shoes, and Buckles are not worn. They *may* be worn at balls and levees by officers above the rank of 2nd Lieutenant. Boots will be worn as laid down in paragraph 4.

806. In the Militia Battalions of the Royal Irish Rifles, the device on the flap of the pouch is a bugle with strings, in silver.

ADJUTANT AND QUARTERMASTER.

807. An Officer selected from full pay for the appointment of Adjutant or Quartermaster of Infantry Militia, will wear the uniform of the battalion of Militia to which he is appointed.

CHANNEL ISLANDS LIGHT INFANTRY MILITIA.

808. As for Militia battalions of Light Infantry of the Line, but with gold lace of special pattern, and badges and devices as laid down in Appendix I.

ROYAL MALTA REGIMENT OF MILITIA.

809. As for Militia Battalions of Infantry of the Line, but with badges and devices as laid down in Appendix I.

	Pattern.		No. of Plate.
	No.	Sealed.	

ARMY SERVICE CORPS.

FULL DRESS.

810. Helmet—See paragraph 16. — No. 3, Sealed 7.12.98, Plate 5

811. Tunic—Blue cloth, with collar and cuffs of white cloth. The collar ornamented with ¾-inch lace round the top, and a gold cord similar to that in the shoulder straps round the bottom ; eight buttons in front and two at the waist behind. The skirt rounded off in front, closed behind with a plait at each side, and lined with black silk ; white cloth edging, ⅛ inch wide, all round (except the collar) and up the skirt plaits ; twisted round gold shoulder cords, universal pattern, lined with blue ; a small button, of regimental pattern, at the top. — No. 191, Sealed 15.12.88, Plate 38 ; No. 515, Sealed 17.8.95, Plate 63

  Field Officers have a row of braided eyes below the lace on the collar ; a chevron of 1½-inch lace on each cuff, with figured ⅛-inch Russia braiding above and below the lace, extending to 11 inches from the bottom of the cuff.

  Captains have an Austrian knot of round-back gold cord on each sleeve, traced all round with braided eyes ; no braided eyes on the collar.

  Lieutenants have a similar knot, but without the figured braiding.

812. Lace—Gold, as for Colonel on the Staff, for tunic, mess jacket and waistcoat, and regimental pattern with dark blue stripe in the centre for cap, dress trousers, belts, and slings. For the shoulder belt the stripe is ¼ inch, for the slings ¹⁄₁₆ inch, and for the other articles ⅛ inch in width. — No. 813, Sealed 13.2.1900, Plate 79
(margin: 61002 / 6106)

813. Buttons—Of regimental pattern.

814. Trousers—Blue cloth, with 1½-inch lace down the side seams.

815. Pantaloons—Blue cloth, with two stripes of white cloth, each ¾ inch wide and ⅛ inch apart, down the side seams.

816. Boots and Spurs—As described in paragraphs 4 and 25.

817. Sword—Half-basket, steel hilt, with two fluted bars on the outside ; black fish-skin grip, bound with silver wire ; slightly curved blade, 35½ inches long and 1¼ inches wide, grooved and spear-pointed. — No. 336, Sealed 26 10.63

818. Scabbard—Steel. — No. 336, Sealed 26.10.63

819. Sword Belt—Gold lace, 1½ inches wide, with removable slings 1 inch wide ; a hook on eye of front sling for hooking up sword, running carriage for back sling ; flat billets, square wire buckles ; for mounted officers, three dees on inside of belt, with leather protecting flap to attach sabretache slings. Dark blue morocco leather lining. — No. 364, Sealed 7.5.97, Plate 64
(margin: 61002 / 5831)

820. Sword Knot—Gold and blue cord and acorn. — No. 365, Sealed 23.8.98, Plate 64

821. Shoulder Belt—Gold lace, 2 inches wide, chased buckle, tip, and slide. — No. 366, Sealed 7.5.97
(margin: 61002 / 5831)

822. Binocular Case—Black patent leather, to hold a binocular field glass, solid leather flap reaching to the lower edge of the case. Gilt leaves for loops. — No. 367, Sealed 19.1.98

823. Sabretache (for Mounted Officers)—As described in Appendix V. Slings as for sword slings, but ¾ inch wide. — No. 302, Sealed 11.5.95

UNDRESS.

824. Forage Cap—Officer Commanding A.S.C.—On the Staff of the Army—As described in paragraph 11. Band of white cloth. For badge, see Appendix I. Other Officers— Blue cloth, with gold embroidery ¾ inch wide on peak, and band of 1½-inch lace of regimental pattern. Gold purl button and braided figure on crown. — No. 29, Sealed 14.7.98, Plate 8 ; No. 33, Sealed 13.11.96, Plate 8

825. Field Cap—As described in paragraph 10, but with white cloth top edged with black mohair welts. For badge, see Appendix I. — No. 71, Sealed 17.9.96, Plate 9
(margin: 61002 / 5426 / 61002 / 6057)

826. Frock—Blue as for Infantry of the Line (see paragraph 568) but with shoulder-straps of white cloth with ⅛-blue light down the centre. — No. 142, Sealed 14.9.97

827. Trousers—Blue cloth with stripes, pattern as for pantaloons.

828. Sword Belt—Web, as described in Appendix VIII (2).
(margin: 61002 / 6943)

829. Slings, Sword and Sabretache—White buff leather, sword slings 1 inch, and sabretache slings for Mounted Officers, ¾ inch wide. Flat billets and square wire buckles. — Plate 64

830. Sword Knot—Buff leather, ½ inch wide, with runner and acorn. — No. 368, Sealed 23.8.98, Plate 64

831. Shoulder Belt—White buff leather, 2 inches wide ; no buckle, tip, or slide.

832. Belts—"Sam Browne"
   Scabbard—Brown leather } See Appendices VII and VIII.
   Sword Knot—Brown leather
   Other articles as in Full Dress.

CLOAK AND CAPE.

833. Cloak—Blue cloth, with sleeves. Stand-and-fall collar, with three black hooks and eyes in front, and three small flat silk buttons at the bottom to fasten the cape. Round loose cuffs, 6 inches deep. A pocket in each side seam outside, and one in the left breast inside. Four buttons down the front. A cloth back-strap, to fasten with a large flat silk button at

	Pattern.		No. of Plate.
	No.	Sealed.	

³⁸⁴⁰⁷/_{Dress 110} the top of each pocket; a similar button in front on the right to hold the end of the back-strap when it is not buttoned across behind. White ratinett lining. The cloak to reach within 8 inches of the ground. Shoulder straps of the same material as the garment; a small button of regimental pattern at the top.

³⁸⁴⁰⁷/_{Dress 110} **834. Cape**—Blue cloth, long enough to cover the knuckles, lined with white ratinet; a cloth band round the top to fasten with a cloth strap and black buckle, and a fly inside the band, with three button holes for attaching cape to cloak. Three buttons down the front.

MESS DRESS.

³⁸⁴⁰⁷/_{Dress 110} **835. Mess Jacket**—Blue cloth, edged all round with ¾-inch gold lace, forming a bull's eye or ring at the bottom of each back seam; white collar and cuffs; a line of ⅛-inch gold braid along the collar seam; cuffs pointed and edged with ¾-inch lace, the point extending to 6 inches from the bottom of the cuff; 2 inches deep at the back, a loop of gold braid at bottom of collar to fasten across the neck; a row of studs down the front on the left side, fastened with hooks and eyes, white silk lining, white cloth shoulder straps, edged with ⅛-inch lace. — 192 — 15.12.88 — 38

³⁸⁴⁰⁷/_{Dress 110} **836. Mess Waistcoat**—White cloth with collar, edged with ½-inch gold lace all round, including collar closed at the neck; to fasten with hooks and eyes; studs down the front on the left side. The pockets edged with Russia braid, with crows' feet at ends and centre. — 193 — 15.12.88 — 38

837. Trousers, Boots, and Spurs—As in Full Dress.

HORSE FURNITURE.

838. Field Officers—As for Cavalry, see Appendix VI.

839. Other Mounted Officers, if not provided with saddlery from store—As for Colonel on the Staff, see Appendix VI.

QUARTERMASTERS AND RIDING-MASTERS.

840. Uniform, &c., as for other Officers of their respective honorary rank.

ARMY MEDICAL SERVICE.

ARMY MEDICAL STAFF.

SURGEON - GENERAL.

FULL DRESS.

	Pattern No.	Sealed	No. of Plate
841. Cocked Hat—As for General Officer, see paragraph 74.	1 / 2	23.8.98 / 29.11.98	2 & 3
842. Plume—Black swan feathers, drooping outwards, 10 inches long from the top of a feathered stem 3 inches long.	74	17.12.75	2
843. Tunic—Blue cloth; the skirt rounded off in front and closed behind. Black velvet collar and cuffs; the collar laced round the top and bottom with inch lace; the cuffs pointed, with 2 bars of inch lace round the top showing ¼ inch of black velvet between the bars; a figured braiding of alternate large and small eyes above and below the lace, according to special pattern, the top of the braided figure is 10 inches from the bottom of the cuff. 8 buttons down the front, and 2 at the waist behind. Scarlet cloth edging all round (except the collar) and up the skirt-plaits; and the skirts lined with black silk. Plaited round gold shoulder cords of plaited gold wire basket cord $\frac{3}{16}$ inch in diameter, small gold gimp down centre and small button at the top. Strap of the shoulder cord 2¼ inches wide, terminating in a 4-inch wing.	196	19.12.84	39 / 62
844. Lace—Gold, as for Colonel on the Staff, for tunic and mess jackets, and special pattern (with 2 lines of black silk) for cap and dress trousers.	814		{ 72 / 79 }
845. Buttons—See Appendix I.			
846. Trousers—Blue cloth, with 2½-inch lace down the side seams.			
847. Pantaloons—Blue cloth, with scarlet cloth stripes 2½ inches wide.			
848. Boots and Spurs—As described in paragraphs 4 and 25.			
849. Sword—Mameluke, gilt or gilding metal hilt, with device of sword and baton crossed, encircled with oak leaves; ivory grip; scimitar blade. As described in Appendix VII.	303	27.7.96	66
850. Scabbard—Steel. As described in Appendix VII.	304	4.5.98	66
851. Sword Belt—Black morocco leather, 1½ inches wide, with slings 1 inch wide; 3 stripes of gold embroidery $\frac{3}{8}$ inch wide on belt, and $\frac{3}{16}$ inch wide on slings; a hook to hook up the sword. Billets and gilt studs.	370	19.12.84	64
852. Waist Plate—See Appendix I.			
853. Sword Knot—Gold and black cord and acorn.	374	23.8.98	64
854. Shoulder Belt—Black morocco leather, 2 inches wide, with 4 stripes of gold embroidery, each $\frac{3}{8}$ inch wide; gilt chased buckle, tip, and slide.	371	19.12.84	
855. Pouch (for Note Book and Pencil)—Black morocco leather; the flap 6 inches long and 3½ inches deep, with 3 stripes of gold embroidery $\frac{3}{8}$ inch wide, round the bottom and sides; in the centre, a chased Royal cypher and crown. Gilt leaves for loops, swivel rings.	372	19.12.84	

UNDRESS.

	Pattern No.	Sealed	No. of Plate
856. Forage Cap—As described in paragraph 11. Band of black velvet. For badge, see Appendix I.	29	14.7.98	8
857. Field Cap—As described in paragraph 10, with black top; gold welts on cap and flaps and at front and back seams. Two Army Medical Staff buttons in front. Badge as in Appendix I.	75	7.10.96	9
858. Frock Coat—Blue cloth, single-breasted. Black velvet roll collar and pointed cuffs; the cuffs ornamented with black braid of the same pattern as the cuffs of the tunic. The collar, front, and back skirts edged with ¾-inch black mohair braid; 5 loops of the same braid on each side in front, with 2 olivets on each loop; 2 olivets at the waist behind, encircled with braided crow's foot; the skirts lined with black. Shoulder cords as for tunic.	197		39
859. Waistcoat to be worn with Frock Coat—As for the Mess Waistcoat.	200	19.12.84	
860. Frock—Blue serge, tartan, or angola according to climate, full in chest, with black lining in front; stand up collar and cuffs of the same material as the rest of the jacket. Shoulder straps of black velvet, with small button at the top. Side slits. Five small buttons down the front. A patch pocket with box pleat 6¾ inches wide and 9 inches deep, with shaped flap and small button on each breast. Top edge of pocket flap to be in a line with centre of second button. Two similar pockets below, but without pleat and button. Cuffs, pointed, 5 inches deep in front and 3 inches behind, with an opening at the back extending the depth of the cuff; the cuff fastened with two small buttons. Two inside pockets in lining of skirt in front, fastened with small button.	198	27.5.95	
861. Trousers—Blue cloth, with scarlet stripes 2½ inches wide, and welted at the edges, down the side seams.			
862. Sword—As described in paragraph 27; the hilt of gilt or gilding metal, with device of Royal cypher and crown, and lined with black patent leather.			
863. Sword Belt / Sword Knot—As for Full Dress, except that there is no gold embroidery.	373	8.3.94	64
864. Sword Belt—Web. See paragraph 28.			
865. Belts—"Sam Browne" / Scabbard—Brown leather / Sword Knot—Brown leather — See Appendices VII and VIII. Other articles as in Full Dress.			

NOTE.—When the "Sam Browne" belts are worn the pocket case of instruments is to be carried in the breast pocket of the frock.

(Left margin references: 61002/5518; 38407 Dress 116; 61002/5519; 38407 Dress 116; 61002/6743; 61002/6890; 61002/6874)

	Pattern.		No. of Plate.
	No.	Sealed.	

GREAT COAT AND CAPE.

866. Blue milled cloth, of pattern described for Mounted Officers in **paragraph 14**, lined with scarlet rattinet; black velvet collar; shoulder straps of the same material as the garment; a small Army Medical Staff button at the top.

MESS DRESS.

867. Mess Jacket—Blue cloth, edged all round with inch gold lace, forming a bull's-eye or ring at the bottom of each back seam; black velvet collar and cuffs; $\frac{3}{8}$-inch gimp lace on the collar seam; cuffs pointed and edged with inch lace 6 inches high at the point and $2\frac{1}{4}$ inches behind; a loop of gold braid at bottom of collar to fasten across the neck; a row of studs down the front on the left side, fastened with hooks and eyes. Scarlet silk lining. Shoulder cords as for tunic. [Pattern No. 199 | Sealed 19.12.84 | Plate 40]

868. Mess Waistcoat—Scarlet cloth, closed at the neck, edged with $\frac{3}{16}$-inch gold Russia braid all round and on collar seam. Pockets edged with similar braid, forming a crow's foot at each end. A row of studs and hooks and eyes down the front. [Pattern No. 200 | Sealed 19.12.84 | Plate 40]

869. Trousers, Boots and Spurs—As in Full Dress.

HORSE FURNITURE.

870. Saddle—As described in Appendix VI; or Hunting, see paragraph 22, with saddle cloth described in paragraph 101. [Pattern No. 600 | Sealed 24.9.97]

871. Wallets } Brown leather, see Appendix VI. [Pattern No. 607 | Sealed 14.9.96]
Bridle

872. Browband and Rosettes—Brown leather.

THE ROYAL ARMY MEDICAL CORPS.
COLONEL.

873. Uniform and horse furniture as for Surgeon-General, Army Medical Staff, with the following exceptions:—

874. Cocked Hat—As described in paragraph 7, but with loop of $\frac{3}{4}$-inch Staff lace. [Pattern No. { 1 / 2 | Sealed 23.8.98 / 29.11.98 | Plate } 2]

875. Plume—Black swan feathers, drooping outwards, 8 inches long from the top of a feathered stem 3 inches long. [Pattern No. 74 | Sealed 17.12.75 | Plate 3]

876. Forage Cap—As described in paragraph 11, but with band of dull cherry cloth. For badge, see Appendix I. [Pattern No. 31 | Sealed 14.7.98 | Plate 8]

877. Field Cap—As described in paragraph 10. Dull cherry top, gold welts on cap and flaps and at front and back seams. Two corps buttons in front. For badge, see Appendix I. [Pattern No. 98 | Sealed 31.3.1900 | Plate 9]

878. Tunic—Collar and cuffs of the colour of the facings. The collar ornamented with $\frac{3}{4}$-inch lace round the top, gold Russia braid along the bottom, and a row of eyes below the lace; gauntlet shape cuffs, $3\frac{1}{2}$ inches deep in front and 6 inches at the back, a bar of $\frac{3}{4}$-inch lace at the top and on each side of the back seam. Gold Russia tracing braid inside the lace and figured braiding below. Twisted round gold shoulder cord, universal pattern, lined with blue; small button at the top. [Pattern No. 202 | Sealed 3.2.1900 | Plate 39]

879. Facings—Dull cherry colour.

880. Lace—Two lines of dull cherry instead of black silk. [Pattern No. 814 | Plate 79]

881. Buttons—Corps pattern, see Appendix I. [Pattern No. 814 | Sealed 12.6.99]

882. Frock Coat—The collar and cuffs of blue cloth; shoulder straps of blue cloth edged with $\frac{1}{2}$-inch black mohair braid, except at the base; a black netted button at the top. With the frock coat a false waistcoat of dull cherry cloth is worn; stand up collar edged all round and along the bottom seam with gold Russia tracing braid, similar braid on each side, and a row of gilt studs in front; fastened with hooks and eyes. [Pattern No. 197 / 165 | Sealed (165) 3.2.1900 | Plate 39]

883. Frock—The shoulder straps are of dull cherry cloth. [Pattern No. 198 | Sealed 3.2.1900]

884. Dress Trousers—The lace $1\frac{3}{4}$ inches wide.

885. Pantaloons } The stripes to be of dull cherry cloth, $1\frac{3}{4}$ inches wide, with two [Pattern No. 164 | Sealed 3.2.1900]
Undress Trousers } $\frac{1}{8}$ inch black welts, $\frac{1}{2}$ inch apart.

886. Sword Belt—For wear with the frock, the sword belt may be web, as described in Appendix VIII (2). See paragraph 28. [Pattern No. 305 | Sealed 1.6.98]

887. Sword Knot—Gold and dull cherry lace strap and acorn. [Plate 64]

888. Sword Knot (Undress)—Plain black leather. [Plate 64]

889. Sword—As described in paragraph 27.

890. Scabbard—Steel, as described in Appendix VII.

891. Sabretache—As described in paragraph 21.

GREAT COAT AND CAPE.

892. The collar will be of the same material as the rest of the garment.

	Pattern.		No. of Plate.
	No.	Sealed.	

MESS DRESS.

893. Mess Jacket—Blue cloth, with dull cherry cloth roll collar, shoulder straps and gauntlet shape cuffs, four small buttons in front, no buttons on the cuffs. No piping. Dull cherry silk lining. | 162 | 3.2.1900 | 40 |

894. Mess Waistcoat—Dull cherry cloth, open at the neck, no collar. Four ½ inch corps buttons in front. | 163 | 3.2.1900 | 40 |

HORSE FURNITURE.

895. No saddle cloth.

LIEUTENANT-COLONEL.

896. Uniform and horse furniture as for Colonel, with the following exceptions :—

897. Helmet—Home pattern, as described in paragraph 16. | 3 | 7.12.98 | |

61002 / 6925

898. Helmet Plate—See Appendix I. Dimensions :—
From top of crest to bottom of scroll, back measurement   .... 3¼ inches. | 814 | | |
Extreme horizontal width, back measurement .... 3⅜   ,,

899. Forage Cap—Blue cloth 3¼ inches deep, bell-shaped top, with gold embroidered drooping peak, band of 1¾-inch lace, gold and dull cherry purl button, and gold braided figure on the crown. | 33 | 13.11.96 | 8 |

900. Tunic—The cuffs are trimmed with double eyes instead of figured braiding. | 202 | 3.2.1900 | 39 |

61002 / 5519

901. Patrol Jacket instead of Frock Coat—Blue cloth, with stand-and-fall collar, edged with inch black mohair braid, and a false upright collar of dull cherry cloth, with ¾-inch gold lace round the top, to button on inside collar of jacket. Inch mohair braid traced with Russia braid all round, up the slits, and along the back seams. The tracing forms an eye at each angle of the braid, except at the top of the slits and back seams, where it forms a crow's foot, 1 inch in length, and at the bottom in the centre, where it forms a long crow's foot, 1½ inches in length. Five loops of inch mohair braid at equal distances down the front on each side, with two olivets on each loop ; the top loops extend to the shoulder seams, and the bottom to 4 inches. Cuffs, of the same material as the jacket, pointed with inch mohair braid traced with black Russia braid forming an Austrian knot above and below the mohair braid. The mohair braid reaches to 7 inches from bottom of cuff, and the Austrian knot at the top to 9 inches. Pockets in front edged at the bottom with inch mohair braid ; black silk lining ; pocket inside left breast. Hooks and eyes in front. Shoulder straps of the same material as the garment, edged with ½-inch black mohair braid, except at the base ; black netted button at the top. | 203 | 19.12.84 / 3.2.1900 | 40 |

902. Sword Belt—Full Dress.—Two stripes of embroidery. | 376 | 19.12.84 | 64 |

903. Sword Belt—Undress.—The leather belt is not worn.

904. Shoulder Belt—Three stripes of embroidery. | 377 | 5.1.86 | |

905. Pouch (for Instruments)—Black morocco leather, collapsible, of special pattern, to contain the Regulation instrument case ; the flap 6½ inches long and 4 inches deep, with two stripes of gold embroidery ⅜ inch wide round the bottom and sides. Gilt leaves for loops, swivel rings. | 378 | 19.12.84 | |

MAJOR.

906. Uniform and horse furniture as for Lieutenant-Colonel, except :—

907. Tunic—The eyes on the cuffs are single instead of double. | 202 | 3.2.1900 | 39 |

CAPTAIN.

908. Uniform, &c. (*including Pantaloons, Knee Boots, and Horse Furniture when required to be mounted*), as for Major, with the following exceptions :—

909. Forage Cap—Lace 1½ inches wide.

910. Tunic—The braided eyes on the collar and cuffs are omitted. | 204 | 3.2.1900 | 39 |

911. Leggings—As for Infantry of the Line.

LIEUTENANT.

912. Uniform and horse furniture as for Captain, except :—

913. Tunic—The braid on the cuffs is omitted. | 204 | 3.2.1900 | 39 |

QUARTERMASTER.

914. Uniform, &c., of his honorary rank, with the following exceptions :—

915. Shoulder Belt—Two stripes only of gold embroidery on the outer edges. | 379 | 19.12.84 | |

916. Pouch—Black patent leather pouch, of special pattern, to hold writing materials. Gilt leaves for loops, swivel rings. | 358 | | |

	Pattern.		No. of Plate.
	No.	Sealed.	

MEDICAL OFFICERS OF HOUSEHOLD TROOPS.

917. Medical Officers of Household Cavalry and Foot Guards wear the dress as laid down under Regimental Staff for those services in paragraphs 537–539.

MILITIA MEDICAL STAFF AND MEDICAL STAFF CORPS.

918. Medical Officers of Militia on the Departmental List and Officers of the Militia Medical Staff Corps will wear uniform and horse furniture as for Officers of the Royal Army Medical Corps of corresponding rank, with the exception that the letter **M** will be worn below the badges of rank as authorized for Officers of Militia Battalions.

919. Medical Officers of Militia Battalions who have not elected to serve on the Departmental List will continue to wear the uniform of their regiments, but with cocked hats (with lace of loop and button of regimental patterns), plumes, belts, and pouches as for Officers of corresponding rank in the Royal Army Medical Corps.

920. Medical Officers of Militia who join the Army Medical Reserve of Officers will continue to wear the uniform of their respective corps, but with the badges of rank indicative of their rank in the Army Medical Reserve of Officers, when the latter is higher than their regimental rank.

RETIRED MEDICAL OFFICER APPOINTED TO A CHARGE.

921. Retired Medical Officers appointed to charges under the provisions of Article 487 of the Royal Warrant for Pay, &c., will, while so employed, wear the uniform described for Retired Officers.

	Pattern.		No. of Plate.
	No.	Sealed.	

ARMY CHAPLAINS' DEPARTMENT.

---

922. Forage Cap—Black cloth, with black patent leather drooping peak, ornamented with $\frac{7}{8}$-inch black embroidery. Band $1\frac{3}{4}$ inches wide, of black lace, Staff pattern; black netted button and braided figure on crown.

| | 72 | 19.9.91 | 8 |

$\frac{61002}{5426}$ **923. Field Cap**—Black cloth as described in paragraph 10, with black mohair braid welts on the top of the cap. For badge, see Appendix I.

| | 73 | 7.10.96 | 9 |

924. Frock Coat Black cloth, single-breasted, with stand-up collar, square in front, with an opening $2\frac{1}{2}$ inches in width, for badge, see Appendix I; 6 buttons down the front, and 6 loops of small round braid on each side; the top loops 6 inches long, and those at the waist 3 inches; 2 buttons at the waist behind; the skirt lined with black, and to reach to 2 inches below the knee. Shoulder straps of twisted round black cord, universal pattern, lined with black, with black netted button on the top. Badges of rank in black and gold.

| | 194 | | |

The several classes are distinguished as follows :—

The 1st Class have the collar edged round the top and bottom with $\frac{1}{2}$-inch black braid, and a crown and two stars, embroidered in black and gold on the shoulder straps, and 3 braid loops and buttons on each cuff.

2nd Class, as for 1st Class, but with a crown and one star on the shoulder straps.

3rd Class, as for 1st Class, but with a crown on the shoulder straps.

4th Class, as for 1st Class, but with two stars on shoulder straps, and without braid on collar and cuffs.

925. Buttons—Plain black silk.

926. Patrol Jacket—Black cloth or serge, according to climate; stand-up collar, height not to exceed 2 inches, square in front, with an opening $2\frac{1}{2}$ inches in width, $\frac{1}{2}$-inch mohair braid all round the collar, for badge, see Appendix I. Slits at the back $5\frac{1}{2}$ inches deep, fastened at the bottom with a hook and eye. Inch mohair braid traced with Russia braid down the front, along the bottom, up the slits, and on the back seams. The tracing forms an eye at each angle of the braid. Five bars, each 2 inches wide, of mohair braid, at equal distances down the front on each side; the top bar extends to the shoulder seams, and the bottom to $3\frac{1}{2}$ inches from the tracing. Cuffs pointed, with inch mohair braid, traced with black Russia braid, forming an eye above and below the mohair braid. The mohair braid reaches to $5\frac{1}{2}$ inches from bottom of cuff. Pockets in front, edged top and bottom, with inch mohair braid; black lining. Pocket inside left breast. Hooks and eyes down the front. Shoulder straps of the same material as the garment, edged with $\frac{1}{2}$-inch black mohair braid, except at the base; black netted button at the top. Badges of rank in black and gold.

| | 195 | —.5.89 | |

927. Trousers—Black cloth, with black braid $1\frac{1}{4}$ inches wide down the side seams.

928. Gloves—Black leather.

929. Great Coat and Cape—Black cloth, of the pattern described in paragraph 14, but with badges of rank in black and gold.

	Pattern.		No. of Plate.
	No.	Sealed.	

ARMY ORDNANCE DEPARTMENT.

PRINCIPAL ORDNANCE OFFICER.

COLONEL RANKING AS MAJOR-GENERAL.

FULL DRESS.

930. Cocked Hat—As for General Officer, see paragraph 74. — 1 | 23.8.98 | 2 & 3

931. Plume—White swan feathers, drooping outwards, 8 inches long, with black feathers under them long enough to reach to 2 inches below the ends of the white ones; feathered stem 3 inches long. — 76 | | 2

932. Tunic—Blue cloth; the skirt rounded off in front and closed behind. Scarlet cloth collar and cuffs; the collar laced round the top and bottom with ¾-inch lace, a figured braiding of small eyes between the rows; the cuffs pointed, with two bars of ¾-inch lace round the top, showing ¼ inch of scarlet cloth between the bars; a figured braiding of alternate large and small eyes above and below the lace. The top of the braided figure is 10 inches from the bottom of the cuff in front and 4 inches behind. Eight buttons down the front, and two at the waist behind. The front and skirt plaits edged with scarlet cloth, ¼ inch wide; and the skirts lined with black silk. Gold shoulder cords of plaited gold wire basket cord, $\frac{3}{16}$ inch in diameter, small gold gimp down the centre, strap of the shoulder cord 2¼ inches wide, terminating in a 4-inch wing. [sidebar: 38407 / Dress / 165] — 205 | 8.7.97 | 41 ; 62

933. Lace—On tunic and mess jacket, gold, as for Colonel on the Staff; on other articles gold, departmental pattern, with a scarlet stripe in the centre, ¼ inch wide for the shoulder belt, $\frac{1}{16}$ inch for slings, and ⅛ inch for other articles. — 815 | 13.2.1900 | 72, 79

934. Buttons—See Appendix I.

935. Trousers—Blue cloth, with 1½-inch lace down the side seams. [sidebar: 38407 / Dress / 165]

936. Pantaloons—Blue cloth, with scarlet cloth stripes as for Undress trousers.

937. Boots and Spurs—As described in paragraphs 4 and 25.

938. Sword—Mameluke gilt hilt, with device of sword and baton crossed, encircled with oak leaves; ivory grip; scimitar blade, see Appendix VII. — 303 | 27.7.96 | 66

939. Scabbard—Steel, see Appendix VII. — 304 | 4.5.98 | 66

940. Sword Belt and Slings—Gold lace, 1½ inches wide, with slings 1 inch wide, lined with red morocco leather, a gilt hook to hook up the sword. Square gilt wire buckles. — 380 | 26.5.82 | 64

941. Sword Knot—Gold and red cord and acorn. — 381 | 26.5.82 | 64

942. Waist Plate—See Appendix I. [sidebar: 61002 / 6000]

943. Shoulder Belt—Gold lace, 2 inches wide, lined with red morocco leather; gilt buckle, tip, and slide. — 382 | 26.5.82

944. Binocular Case—Black patent leather, to hold a binocular field glass, solid leather flap, reaching to the lower edge of the case. Gilt leaves for loops. — 367 | 19.1.89

UNDRESS.

945. Forage Cap—As described in paragraph 11. Band of blue cloth, piped with scarlet at the top and bottom. For badge, see Appendix I. — 28 | 14.7.98 | 8

946. Field Cap—As described in paragraph 10, but with scarlet welts on the cap, and on the front and back seams. Gold welts round the top of the flap. Two departmental buttons in front. For badge, see Appendix I [sidebar: 61002 / 5410] — 77 | 23.9.96 | 9

947. Frock Coat—Blue cloth, single-breasted. Blue velvet roll collar and pointed cuffs; the cuffs ornamented with black braid of the same pattern as the cuffs of the tunic. The collar, front, and back skirts edged with ¾-inch black mohair braid; five loops of the same braid on each side in front, with two olivets on each loop; two olivets at the waist behind, encircled with a braided crow's foot; the skirts lined with black. Shoulder cords as for tunic. [sidebar: 61002 / 5517] — 197

948. Waistcoat to be worn with Frock Coat—Blue cloth, without collar, edged with gold Russia braid, and fastening with hooks and eyes. A pocket on each side. [sidebar: 61002 / 4684]

949. Frock—Blue, as for Infantry of the Line (see paragraph 568), but with scarlet shoulder straps with a blue light ¼ inch wide. [sidebar: 61002 / 5749] — 142 | 27.4.97

950. Trousers—Blue cloth, 2 stripes of scarlet cloth with welted edges, $\frac{11}{16}$ inch wide and ⅛ inch apart, down each side seam.

951. Shoulder Belt / Sword Belt and Slings / Sword Knot } As for Full Dress, except that plain buff leather will be substituted for gold lace. See also paragraph 28. [sidebar: ... / 5665 / ...] — 383 | | 64

952. Belts—"Sam-Browne" / **Scabbard**—Brown leather / **Sword Knot**—Brown leather } See Appendices VII and VIII. [sidebar: 6943 / 61002 / 6890]

953. Sword—As described in paragraph 27.
Other articles as in Full Dress.

	Pattern.		No. of Plate.
	No.	Sealed.	

GREAT COAT AND CAPE.

A.O.148/1896   **954.** Blue milled cloth, lined with red, of pattern described in paragraph 14. Shoulder straps of the same material as the garment; a small button of departmental pattern at the top.

MESS DRESS.

955. Mess Jacket—Blue cloth, edged all round with ¾-inch gold lace, forming a bull's-eye or ring at the bottom of each back seam; scarlet cloth cuffs and collar, ⅜-inch gimp lace on the collar seam, cuffs pointed and edged with ¾-inch lace, figured braiding of large and small eyes above and below the lace; a loop of gold braid at bottom of collar, to fasten across the neck; a row of studs down the front, on the left side, fastened with hooks and eyes; red silk lining. Shoulder cords as for tunic. | 206 | 16.9.91 | 41

956. Mess Waistcoat—Blue cloth, closed at the neck, edged all round, and at the bottom of the collar with gold Russia braid. The pockets edged with Russia braid, with crow's foot at ends and centre. A row of gilt studs and hooks and eyes down the front. | 207 | 16.9.91 | 41

957. Trousers, Boots and Spurs—As in Full Dress.

HORSE FURNITURE.

958. Saddle—As described in Appendix VI; or Hunting, see paragraph 22, with saddle cloth described in paragraph 101. | 600 | 24.9.97

959. Wallets Bridle } Brown leather, see Appendix VI. | 607 | 14.9.96

960. Browband and Rosettes—Blue.

COLONEL.

961. Uniform and horse furniture as for Principal Ordnance Officer, with the following exceptions :—

962. Cocked Hat—As described in paragraph 7, but with loop of ¾-inch lace.

963. Plume—White swan feathers, 6 inches long, with black feathers under them long enough to reach 2 inches below the ends of the white ones. | 1 & 2 / 76 | 29.11.98 / 23.8.98 | 2 & 3 / 2

964. Forage Cap—Officers serving on the Staff of the Army, as for Principal Ordnance Officer. Other officers—blue cloth, 3¼ inches deep, bell-shaped top, gold embroidered drooping peak, band of 1½ inch gold lace, gold purl netted button and braided figure on the crown.

965. Tunic—The collar ornamented with ¾-inch lace round the top, gold Russia braid along the bottom, and a figured braiding of alternate large and small eyes below the lace; and the braiding below the lace on the cuffs to be of small eyes only. Twisted round gold shoulder cords, universal pattern, lined with blue; small button of departmental pattern at the top. | 208 | 8.7.97 | 41 / 63

966. Frock Coat.—The collar and cuffs are of cloth, and braided in the same pattern as the collar and cuffs of the tunic. Shoulder straps of blue cloth edged with ½ inch black mohair braid except at the base; a black netted button at the top.

967. Sword
968. Scabbard } As described in Appendix VII. | 347 | 13.12.97 | 68

969. Sword Knot—Red and gold lace strap and acorn. | 385 | 27.5.92 | 64

970. Pouch—Black patent leather, of special pattern to hold writing materials. | 358

··/5665   **971. Mess Jacket**—The lace ¾ inch wide; a line of gold Russia braid along the bottom of the collar, with an eye in the centre. No figured braiding on the cuffs. Shoulder cords as for tunic. | 206 | 16.9.91 | 41

972. Sabretache—As described in paragraph 21. | 302 | 11.5.95

973. Horse Furniture—No saddlecloth.

LIEUTENANT-COLONEL.

974. Uniform and horse furniture as for Colonel, with the following exception :—

975. Tunic
Frock Coat } The figured braiding on the collar, and above and below the lace on the sleeve, to be small eyes. | 209 | 8.7.97 | 41

976. Helmet—As for Infantry of the Line, with helmet plate as in Appendix I. } Officers not serving on the Staff of the Army. | 3 | 7.12.98 | 5

977. Frock Coat.—Not worn.

61002/6943   **978. Sword Belt**—The leather undress belt is not worn.

MAJOR.

979. Uniform and horse furniture as for Lieutenant-Colonel, with the following exceptions :—

980. Tunic, Frock Coat } The eyes below the lace on the sleeve are omitted. | 210 | 8.7.97 | 41

CAPTAIN.

981. Uniform, &c., as for Major not serving on the Staff of the Army, with the following exception :—

982. Tunic—The braided eyes on the collar are omitted; the braid above and below the lace on the sleeve is plain, without eyes. | 211 | 8.7.97 | 41

	Pattern.		No. of Plate.
	No.	Sealed.	
LIEUTENANT.	212	8.7.97	41

983. Uniform, &c., as for Captain, with the following exception :—

984. Tunic—There is only one bar of lace on the sleeve.

MEMORANDUM.

61002
Depart-
ments
30

985. Officers appointed to the directing staff of the Army Ordnance Department, under the terms of the Royal Warrant of 16th June, 1896, will provide themselves with the undress uniform of the Department, but will wear in review and mess order the uniform of the unit to which they belong.

986. Officers appointed for permanent service in the Department will wear the uniform of the Department in all orders of dress.

987. Commissaries and Deputy Commissaries will wear the uniform laid down for Captains, and Assistant Commissaries that for Lieutenants.

38407
Dress
112

988. Inspectors of Ordnance Machinery, 1st, 2nd, and 3rd class, will wear the uniform laid down for Major, Captain, and Lieutenant respectively.

ARMY PAY DEPARTMENT.

COLONEL.

FULL DRESS.

	Pattern.		No. of Plate.
	No.	Sealed.	

61002
Depts.
19

989. Cocked Hat—As described in paragraph 7, but with loop of ¾-inch lace, and blue instead of crimson bullions. — No. 1, 2; Sealed 23.8.98, 29.11.98; Plate 2 & 3

990. Plume—White swan feathers 6 inches long, with yellow feathers under them long enough to reach 2 inches below the white. — No. 78; Plate 2

991. Tunic—Blue cloth, the skirt rounded off in front and closed behind. Yellow cloth collar and cuffs; the collar laced round the top with ¾-inch lace, with a tracing of small braided eyes below the lace; gold Russia braid at the bottom; the cuffs pointed with two bars of ¾-inch lace, showing ¼ inch blue cloth between the bars; a tracing of small eyes in gold Russia braid above and below the lace, forming an Austrian knot at the top, and a crow's foot and eye at the bottom. The lace extends to 4½ inches behind and 8 inches in front, and the Austrian knot to 10 inches from the bottom of the cuff. Eight buttons down the front, and two at the waist behind. The front, collar, and skirt plaits edged with yellow cloth, ¼ inch wide, the skirts lined with black silk. Twisted round gold shoulder cord, universal pattern, lined with blue. A small button of departmental pattern at the top. — No. 213, 515; Sealed 14.3.78, 17.8.95; Plate 42, 63

992. Lace, Gold—On tunic and mess jacket, as for Colonel on the Staff; on other articles, departmental pattern, with a yellow stripe in the centre, ¼ inch wide for shoulder belt, $\frac{1}{16}$ inch slings, and ⅛ inch for other articles. — No. 816; Sealed 13.2.1900; Plate 72, 79

993. Buttons—See Appendix I.

994. Dress Trousers—Blue cloth, with 1¾-inch lace down the side seams.

995. Boots and Spurs—As described in paragraphs 4 and 25.

996. Sword } Scabbard }—As described in Appendix VII. — No. 347; Sealed 13.12.97; Plate 68

997. Sword Belt and Slings—Gold lace, 1½ inches wide, with slings 1 inch wide, lined with yellow morocco leather. Gilt oval wire buckles. — No. 386; Sealed 11.10.89; Plate 64

998. Waist Plate—See Appendix I.

999. Sword Knot—Yellow and gold cord and acorn. — No. 387; Sealed 5.3.78; Plate 64

1000. Shoulder Belt—Gold lace, 2 inches wide, lined with yellow morocco leather; gilt buckle, tip, and slide. — No. 388; Sealed 11.10.89

1001. Pouch—Black patent leather, of special pattern, to hold writing materials. — No. 358

1002. Sabretache (for Mounted Officers)—As described in paragraph 21. — No. 302; Sealed 11.5.95

UNDRESS.

61002
Staff
39

1003. Forage Cap—As described in paragraph 11. Band of yellow cloth. For badge, see Appendix I.

61002
5426

1004. Field Cap—As described in paragraph 10, but with yellow top. Black mohair braid welts on cap and flaps, and at front and back seams. Two departmental buttons in front. For badge, see Appendix I. — No. 31, 79; Sealed 14.7.98, 21.9.96; Plate 8, 9

1005. Frock Coat—Blue cloth, single-breasted; blue cloth roll collar and cuffs; the cuffs ornamented with black braid of the same pattern as the cuffs on the tunic, pointed with two bars of ¾-inch mohair braid round the top, ¼ inch apart, a black Russia braiding of small eyes above and below the lace, terminating at the top in an Austrian knot, and at the bottom in a double crow's foot and eye. The collar, front, and back skirts edged with ¾-inch black mohair braid, five loops of same braid on each side in front, with two olivets on each loop. Two olivets at the waist behind, encircled with a crow's foot. Skirts lined with black. Blue cloth shoulder straps, edged with ½-inch black mohair braid, except at the base; black netted button at the top. — No. 201; Plate 42

61002
5523

1006. Frock—Blue Angola, tartan or serge, as for Infantry of the Line, but with shoulder straps with yellow piping ⅜ inch wide. — No. 142; Sealed 18.11.96

61002
4683

1007. Trousers (and Pantaloons when required)—Blue cloth, with two yellow cloth stripes, ⅝ inch wide and ⅛ inch apart.

1008. Knee Boots and Spurs, when required—As described in paragraphs 4 and 25.

61002
6943

1009. Shoulder Belt, Sword Belt and Slings Sword Knot, } Same as for Full Dress, except that plain buff leather will be substituted for gold lace. See also paragraph 28. — Plate 64

61002
6890

1010. Belts—"Sam Browne" **Scabbard**—Brown leather **Sword Knot**—Brown leather } See Appendices VII and VIII. Other articles as in Full Dress.

GREAT COAT AND CAPE.

1011. Blue milled cloth, as described in paragraph 14. White lining; shoulder straps of the same material as the garment; a small button of departmental pattern at the top.

	Pattern.		No. of
	No.	Sealed.	Plate.

MESS DRESS.

1012. Mess Jacket—Blue cloth, with yellow cloth collar and cuffs; the collar edged with ¾-inch lace, round the top, and gold Russia braid at the bottom; the cuffs pointed and edged with ¾-inch lace, extending to 6 inches from the bottom of the cuff in front, and 2 inches behind. The jacket edged all round with gold lace, ¾ inch wide, forming a ring or bull's-eye at bottom of each back seam. Gilt or gilding metal studs down the front, on the left side; hooks and eyes in front. Blue silk lining. Shoulder straps of blue cloth edged with ½-inch lace, a small button at the top. — 214 — 11.10.89 — 42

1013. Mess Waistcoat—Blue cloth, slightly open at the neck, edged all round, and at the bottom of the collar with gold Russia braid. The pockets edged with Russia braid, with crow's foot at ends and centre. A row of studs and hooks and eyes down the front. — 207 — — 42

1014. Trousers, Boots, and Spurs—As in Full Dress.

(margin: 38407 Dress. 115 ; 61002 Depts. 19)

HORSE FURNITURE.

1015. Saddle—As described in Appendix VI; or Hunting, see paragraph 22. — 600 — 24.9.97

1016. Wallets / Bridle } Brown leather, see Appendix VI. — 607 — 14.9.96

1017. Browband and Rosettes—Blue.

LIEUTENANT COLONEL.

1018. Uniform and horse furniture (when forage allowance is specially authorized) as laid down for Colonel, with the following exceptions :—

1019. Forage Cap
1020. Frock Coat
Sword Belt—Undress buff leather
} As for Colonel. Worn only by Officers in financial charge of districts, and Staff Paymaster at Headquarters.

1021. Forage Cap—For other Officers. Blue cloth, 3¼ inches deep, bell-shaped top, gold embroidered drooping peak, a band of 1⅛-inch lace, with ⅛-inch yellow stripe in the centre, gold purl button and braided figure on the crown. — 33 — 13.11.96

MAJOR.

Uniform as for Lieutenant-Colonel, with the following exceptions :—
1022. Tunic—The braid below the lace on the cuffs is plain, without eyes. — 215 — 14.3.78 — 42

CAPTAIN.

1023. As for a Staff Paymaster, with the following exceptions :—
1024. Tunic—The braided eyes on the collar are omitted; the braid above and below the lace on the sleeve is plain, without eyes. — 216 — 14.3.78 — 42

PROBATIONERS.

1025. Officers whilst on probation for the Army Pay Department will, if on full pay, continue to wear the uniform of the corps to which they belong. On the completion of the period of probation, they will wear the undress uniform of the department, and will not be required to provide themselves with the full dress till permanently appointed. Officers appointed on probation, from half-pay, who may not be in possession of the uniform of their late corps, will provide themselves with the undress uniform laid down for a Captain of the Army Pay Department.

OFFICERS APPOINTED ON TEMPORARY AUGMENTATION.

1026. These Officers are not required to provide departmental uniform.

ARMY VETERINARY DEPARTMENT.

	Pattern.		No. of Plate.
	No.	Sealed.	

DIRECTOR GENERAL.

FULL DRESS.

61902
Departments.
13

1027. Cocked Hat—As for General Officer, see paragraph 7, but with loop of four-fold gold chain gimp, gold bullion tassels.

1028. Plume—Red swan feathers, drooping outwards, 8 inches long.

1029. Tunic—Blue cloth, the skirt rounded off in front and open behind. Maroon velvet collar and cuffs, ¾-inch lace all round the collar. The cuffs pointed and edged with round-back gold cord, forming a triple Austrian knot, traced with gold Russia braid inside and out, and extending to 11 inches from the bottom of the cuffs; 8 buttons down the front and two at the waist behind; a blue flap on each skirt behind, edged with round-back gold cord, 3 buttons on each flap. The front, collar, and skirts edged with maroon velvet, the skirts lined with black silk. Twisted-round gold shoulder cord, universal pattern, lined with blue; a small button of departmental pattern at the top.

1030. Lace for Tunic and Mess Jacket—Gold, as for Colonel on the Staff. For other articles, departmental pattern, a maroon stripe in the centre, ¼ inch wide for shoulder belt, $\frac{1}{16}$ inch for slings, and ⅛ for other articles.

1031. Buttons—See Appendix I.

... 18

1032. Trousers—Blue cloth, 1¾-inch gold lace, with ⅛-inch maroon silk stripe in centre, down the side seams.

1033. Pantaloons—Blue cloth, with scarlet cloth stripes 1½ inches wide.

1034. Boots and Spurs—As described in paragraphs 4 and 25.

1035. Sword
Scabbard }—Cavalry pattern. See Appendix VII.

... 18
61002
6847

1036. Sword Belt and Slings—Gold lace, 1½-inches wide, with slings 1 inch wide; maroon morocco leather lining. Oval gilt wire buckles.

1037. Waist Plate—See Appendix I.

1038. Sword Knot—Gold and crimson cord and acorn.

1039. Shoulder Belt—Gold lace, 2 inches wide, gilt chased buckle, tip, and slide. The Royal cypher with crown above the tip. Lining similar to that on sword belt.

1040. Pouch to be worn at Levées, Balls, and State Occasions—Maroon velvet collapsing pouch; the flap 5¾ inches long and 3 inches deep. The flap ornamented with ¾-inch gold lace with $\frac{1}{16}$-inch maroon silk stripe in centre; in the middle of flap, embroidered in gold, an oak-leaf wreath enclosing the Royal cypher and crown. Gilt leaves for loops.

... 18

1041. Sabretache—See paragraph 21.

No.	Sealed.	No. of Plate.
1	23.8.98	2 & 3
2	29.11.98	
80	25 8.80	2
217	25.8.80	43
515	17.8.95	63
817	6 3.99	79
314	11.9.96	67
		64
324	23.8.98	64
389		
390		
302	11.5.95	

UNDRESS.

61002
Staff.
39
61002
5558

1042. Forage Cap—As described in paragraph 11, band of maroon cloth. For badge, *see* Appendix I.

1043. Field Cap—As described in paragraph 10, with maroon cloth top. Gold French braid welts on cap, and at front and back seams. Two departmental buttons in front. For badge, see Appendix I.

1044. Frock Coat—Blue cloth, single-breasted. Blue cloth roll collar, the cuffs pointed, with two bars of ¾-inch black mohair braid, ¼ inch apart; a tracing of small eyes in Russia braid above and below the mohair braid, terminating at the top in an Austrian knot, and at the bottom in a double crow's foot and eye, the top of the tracing to be 10 inches from the bottom of the cuff. The collar, front, and back skirts edged with ¾-inch black mohair braid; 5 loops of the same braid on each side in front, with 2 olivets on each loop; 2 olivets at the waist behind, encircled with braided crow's foot; the skirts lined with black. Shoulder straps of blue cloth, edged with ½-inch black mohair braid, except at the base; a black netted button at the top.

1045. Waistcoat (to be worn with Frock Coat)—Blue cloth, without collar, edged with gold Russia braid, and fastening with hooks and eyes. A pocket on each side.

61002
6036

1046. Frock—Blue, Angola, tartan or serge, full in chest; collar and cuffs of same material as the jacket. Five large indented departmental buttons down the front. On and below each breast a patch pocket with box pleat, shaped flap, and small button. A band, 2 inches wide, round the waist, to buckle in front; buckle of special design. A 3-inch box pleat down the back, and a pleat at each side in front, from collar to skirt. Pointed cuffs, 5½ inches deep in front and 2¼ inches behind; two small departmental buttons, and button holes. Shoulder-straps of maroon cloth with ⅜-inch blue stripe down the centre. Small indented button at the top. Black silk lining.

1047. Trousers—Blue cloth, with scarlet cloth stripes, 1¾ inches wide, down each side seam.

1048. Boots and Spurs—As described in paragraphs 4 and 25.

1049. Sword Belt and Slings—Same as for Full Dress, except that plain bridle leather will be substituted for gold lace. See also paragraph 28.

No.	Sealed.	No. of Plate.
31	14.7.98	8
81	1.12.96	9
201		
		43
218	9.6.97	
		64

	Pattern.		No. of Plate.
	No.	Sealed.	

1050. **Sword Knot**—Brown leather strap and acorn. See Appendix VIII. | | | 73

$\frac{61002}{6890}$ | 1051. **Belts**—"Sam Browne" } See Appendices VII and VIII.
Scabbard—Brown leather }

1052. **Instrument Case**—Black morocco leather, of special pattern. Swivel loops, flat leaf. Other articles as in Full Dress. | 391 | 16.12.79 |

CLOAK AND CAPE.

$\frac{61002}{5868}$ | 1053. Blue cloth, lined with scarlet shalloon. Pattern as for Cavalry. See paragraph 320. Buttons indented.

MESS DRESS.

1054. **Mess Jacket**—Blue cloth, edged all round, including the collar, with $\frac{3}{4}$-inch gold lace, forming two bull's-eyes at bottom of back seams. Gold Russia braid at bottom of collar. The collar and cuffs of maroon velvet; the cuffs pointed, with $\frac{3}{4}$-inch lace round the top, extending to 5 inches from the bottom of the cuff in front and $1\frac{3}{4}$ inches behind. Studs down the front on the left side. Hooks and eyes in front, scarlet lining. Shoulder cords as for tunic. | 219 | 25.5.97 | 43

1055. **Mess Waistcoat**—Blue cloth, closed at the neck, edged with $\frac{3}{4}$-inch gold lace, to fasten with hooks and eyes. Studs down the front, on the left side. The pockets edged with gold Russia braid, forming a crow's foot at each end. | 220 | 25.8.80 | 43

1056. **Trousers, Boots, and Spurs**—As in Full Dress.

HORSE FURNITURE.

1057. As for Colonel on the Staff. See Appendix VI.

VETERINARY-LIEUTENANT-COLONEL.

1058. Uniform and horse furniture as for the Director-General with the following exceptions:— { 1 | 23.8.98 | 2 & 3
1059. **Cocked Hat**—As described in paragraph 7, but with loop of gold chain gimp in four rows. { 2 | 29.11.98 |
1060. **Plume**—6 inches long.

VETERINARY-MAJOR.

1061. Uniform, &c., as for a Veterinary Lieutenant-Colonel, with the following exceptions:—
1062. **Helmet**—As described in paragraph 16. | 3 | 7.12.98 | 5
1063. **Helmet Plate**—As for Infantry (for centre see Appendix I).
1064. **Forage Cap**—Blue cloth, with band of $1\frac{1}{2}$-inch gold lace, gold purl button, and braided figure on the crown; no peak. | 82 | 19.9.91 | 5
1065. **Patrol Jacket instead of Frock Coat**—Blue cloth, stand-up collar, rounded in front, $\frac{1}{2}$-inch | 221 | | 44
mohair braid at top and bottom of collar. Inch mohair braid traced with Russia braid all round up the slits and along the back seam, the Russia braid forming small eyes at each angle. Five loops of inch mohair braid at equal distances down the front on each side, with 2 olivets on each loop. The cuffs pointed, with inch mohair braid, extending to 7 inches from the bottom of the cuff, traced with Russia braid forming an Austrian knot at the top, extending to 9 inches from the bottom of the cuff in front, and $2\frac{1}{4}$ inches behind. Pockets in front edged top and bottom with inch mohair braid. Hooks and eyes in front. Black lining, pocket inside left breast. Shoulder straps of same material as the garment, edged with $\frac{1}{2}$-inch black mohair braid, except at the base; black netted button at the top. | | | 64
1066. **Sword Belt, Undress.**—White buff leather, $1\frac{1}{2}$ inches wide, gilt mountings. See also paragraph 28. | | | 64
$\frac{61002}{6847}$ | 1067. **Sword Slings, Undress**—White buff leather, 1 inch wide. Oval gilt wire buckles.
1068. **Sword Knot, Undress**—White buff leather strap and gold acorn.
1069. **Shoulder Belt, Undress**—White buff leather, 2 inches wide, with chased buckle, tip, and slide; the Royal cypher above the tip.

VETERINARY-CAPTAIN.

1070. Uniform, &c., as for a Veterinary-Major, with the following exception:— | 217 | 25.8.80 | 43
1071. **Tunic**—$\frac{1}{2}$-inch lace at the top and gold Russia braid at the bottom of the collar; a double Austrian knot on the sleeves, 9 inches deep, traced as for a Veterinary-Major.

VETERINARY-LIEUTENANT.

1072. Uniform, &c., as for a Veterinary-Captain, with the following exception:—
1073. **Tunic**—A single Austrian knot on sleeves, 7 inches deep. | 217 | 25.8.80 | 43

MEMORANDUM.

1074. The gold-lace pouch and sword belts, as for Director-General, will be worn by Executive Officers at Levées, Balls, and on State occasions only.

PROBATIONERS.

1075. Probationers will wear the undress of the Army Veterinary Department.
1076. Veterinary Officers gazetted to the Household Cavalry wear uniform as laid down for Regimental Staff Officers under that Service.

	Pattern.		No. of Plate.
	No.	Sealed.	

6l0C2 / 6693

OFFICERS PROMOTED FROM THE RANKS, OR OFFICERS WHO HAVE NOT PREVIOUSLY SERVED IN ANY CORPS OR DEPARTMENT, AND APPOINTED TO A POSITION THE UNIFORM FOR WHICH IS DESCRIBED AS "REGIMENTAL UNIFORM" OR THAT "OF THE CORPS OR DEPARTMENT IN WHICH THEY LAST SERVED."

1077. Uniform as for Officers of the Garrison Staff not on the Cadres of Units, with the following exceptions:—

1078. Helmet—(instead of cocked hat)—As for Infantry of the Line. See paragraph 16.

1079. Helmet Plate—The Royal Arms.   Dimensions :—
From top of crest to end of scroll, back measurement, 3 inches.
Extreme horizontal width, back measurement, 3¼ inches.

(Pattern No. 3, Sealed 7.12.98, Plate 5)

61902 / 6048

OFFICER COMMANDING DISCHARGE DEPOT, AND RECRUITING STAFF OFFICER.

1080. Uniform and horse furniture of the regiments from which the Officers are appointed, or of the regiments in which they last served.

61002 / 6325

OFFICERS APPOINTED TO THE REGIMENTAL STAFF OF A PROVISIONAL BATTALION.

1081. The uniform of the regiment from which they are appointed.

PROVOST MARSHAL AND MILITARY MOUNTED POLICE.

1082. Cocked Hat—As described in paragraph 7. *(Pattern No. 1, Sealed 23.8.98)*

1083. Plume—Black swan feathers, drooping outwards, 6 inches long, with white swan feathers under them. *(Pattern No. 2, Sealed 29.11.98, Plate 2 & 3)*

61002 / 6337

1084. Forage Cap—Scarlet cloth, with gold-embroidered drooping peak and band of 1¾-inch lace, gold purl button and braided figure on the crown, a blue cloth welt round the top of the cap and a blue light ⅛-inch deep above and below the lace. *(Pattern No. 83, Sealed 14.7.98, Plate 9)*

61002 / 6337

1085. Tunic—Blue cloth, with scarlet edging down the front and at the opening of the back, scarlet collar and cuffs, plain flaps on the skirts edged scarlet, three buttons on each flap and two at the waist behind. The collar edged with ¾-inch gold lace round the top and a gold cord ¼ inch in diameter at the bottom. Twisted round gold shoulder cords, universal pattern. *(Pattern No. 261, Sealed 7.10.98, Plate 44)*

Officers of the rank of Major have an Austrian knot of round-back gold cord on each sleeve, traced all round with braided eyes, a row of braided eyes below the lace on the collar. *(Plate 63)*

Officers of the rank of Captain have a similar knot, but the braiding is plain ; no braid on the collar.

Officers of the rank of Lieutenant have a similar knot, but without the braid tracing.

1086. Lace—Gold, as for Colonel on the Staff.

1087. Buttons—See Appendix I. *(Plate 72)*

1088. Patrol Jacket—Blue cloth, 28 inches long from the bottom of the collar behind, for an Officer 5 feet 9 inches in height, with a proportionate variation for any difference in height, rounded in front, and edged with inch black mohair braid all round and up the openings at the sides. On each side in front, four double drop loops of ¼-inch flat plait, with eyes in the centre of each loop ; the top loops extend to the shoulder seams, and the bottom to 4 inches ; four netted olivets on the right side, to fasten through the loops on the left. On each sleeve, an Austrian knot of flat plait 7 inches high from the bottom of the cuff. Double flat plait on each back seam, with crow's foot at top and bottom, and two double eyes at equal distances. Pockets fitted with flaps in and out. Hooks and eyes in front.   Shoulder straps of the same material as the garment, edged with ½-inch black mohair braid, except at the base ; black netted button at the top. *(Pattern No. 222, Sealed 15.9 91)*

1089. Frock—As for Hussars, see paragraph 349, with a scarlet chevron an inch wide on the top edge of each cuff. *(Pattern No. 126, Sealed 26.3.98, Plate 19)*

61002 / 6943

1090. Sword Belt—Russia leather, 1½ inches wide, with slings 1 inch wide, two stripes of gold embroidery on belt and slings, a hook to hook up the sword. Gilt lion head buckles. See also paragraph 28. *(Pattern No. 310, Sealed 26.11.97, Plate 64)*

	Pattern.		No. of Plate.
	No.	Sealed.	

1091. Field Cap,
    Sword Belt, "Sam-Browne," Sword Knots, and Scabbards,
    Spurs, Trousers, } As for Colonel on the Staff.
    Pantaloons and Knee Boots,
    Great Coat and Cape,

HORSE FURNITURE.

1092. As for Colonel on the Staff.

PROVOST MARSHAL AND ASSISTANT PROVOST MARSHAL ON ACTIVE SERVICE.

1093. Regimental uniform with distinctions as for Officers of the General Staff.
61002/6337 **1094. Chevrons**—On the frock a scarlet chevron an inch wide is laid on the upper edge of each cuff.
.../6911 **1095.** When on duty, a scarlet brassard 3½ inches wide, fastened with three scarlet silk-covered buttons, is worn on the arm above the elbow. On the brassard the Royal Cypher and Crown in gold embroidery. | 262 | 17.10.98 |

GOVERNORS OF MILITARY PRISONS.

61002/6337 **1096.** The uniform of the unit in which they last served, or uniform as for Infantry of the Line, with the following exceptions :— | | 7.12.98 | |
1097. Helmet—Blue cloth, as laid down in paragraph 16. Gilt or gilding metal plate—the Royal Arms. At stations abroad the white helmet will be worn, see paragraph 1187. | 3 | 23.8.98. | 5
1098. Tunic—Blue cloth, with scarlet cloth collar and cuffs. Badges of rank according to the rank last held in the Army.
1099. Lace—Gold, as for Colonel on the Staff.
1100. Buttons—See Appendix I.
1101. Forage Cap,
    Patrol Jacket, } As for Provost Marshal. | 26 | 2.3.94
    Trousers, undress,
1102. Waist Plate—See Appendix I.
1103. Great Coat and Cape—Blue cloth.
1104. Mess Jacket—Blue cloth, with scarlet collar and cuffs as for Infantry.
1105. Mess Waistcoat—Scarlet, in other respects as for the cloth mess waistcoats of Infantry of the Line, see paragraph 579.

INSPECTORS OF ARMY SCHOOLS.

FULL DRESS.

61002/6140 **1106. Helmet,**
    Sword,
    Sword Knot, } As for Infantry of the Line. | 3 / 347 / 355 / 347 | 7.12.98 / 13.12.97 / 23.8.98 / 13.12.97 | 5 / 68 / 64 / 68
    Scabbard,
    Boots,
1107. Tunic—Same pattern as for Lieutenants of Infantry of the Line, but of blue cloth, with scarlet cloth collar, cuffs and edging. Twisted round gold shoulder cords, universal pattern, lined with blue, a small button at the top. | 153 | 16.10.95 | 33 / 63
1108. Lace—Gold, rose pattern. For cap lace, see paragraph 1115. | 818 | 8.11.99 | 79
1109. Buttons—See Appendix I.
1110. Trousers—Blue cloth, with two stripes of scarlet cloth, each ¾ inch wide, with light blue cloth between, ¼ inch wide.
61002/5420 **1111. Sword Belt**—Black morocco leather, 1½ inches wide, with slings an inch wide, 2 stripes of gold embroidery, ⅜ inch wide on belt and 3/16 inch wide on slings ; a hook to hook up the sword. Billets and gilt studs. | | | 64
1112. Waist Plate—See Appendix I.
61002/5420 **1113. Shoulder Belt**—Black morocco leather, 2 inches wide, with two stripes of gold embroidery each ⅜ inch wide on the outer edges. Chased buckle, tip and slide. | 392 | 13.5.91 |
1114. Pouch—Black patent leather, special pattern ; flap, 5 inches long, 3½ inches deep. Gilt leaves for loops. | 393 | 13.5.91 |

UNDRESS.

1115. Forage Cap—Blue cloth with gold embroidered Staff peak and band of 1½-inch gold lace (departmental pattern) with light blue stripe in centre ⅛ inch wide, gold netted button and braided figure on the crown. | 33 | 13.11.96 | 8
61002/5420 **1116. Field Cap**—As described in paragraph 10, but with light blue top and gold French braid welts round the top and flaps and down the front and back seams. For badge, see Appendix I. | 84 | 25.9.97 | 9
1117. Frock, Blue—As for Infantry of the Line (see paragraph 568), but ¼-inch blue light on shoulder-straps. | 142 | 21.7.97 |
1118. Sword Belt, Web—See paragraph 28.
    Other articles as for Full Dress.

	Pattern.		No. of Plate.
	No.	Sealed.	

GREAT COAT AND CAPE.

1119. As for Infantry of the Line, but of blue milled cloth with black lining.

MESS DRESS

1120. Mess Jacket—Pattern as for Infantry of the Line. Blue cloth with roll collar faced with silk of same colour, scarlet cuffs. Shoulder-straps of the same colour and material as the jacket. | 158 | 17.7 96 | 33
1121. Mess Waistcoat—As for Infantry of the Line. | 159 | 15.9 91 | 33
1122. Trousers and Boots—As for Field Dress.

OFFICERS OF THE ROYAL MILITARY COLLEGE, SANDHURST.

GOVERNOR.

1123. The uniform and horse furniture of his rank as a General Officer.

ASSISTANT COMMANDANT AND SECRETARY.

1124. Cocked Hat—As described in paragraph 7, but with loop of ½-inch lace. | 1 / 2 | 23.8.98 / 29.11.98 | 2 & 3
1125. Plume—Red and white swan feathers, drooping outwards, 6 inches long. | 30 | 17.12.75 | 2
1126. Tunic—Scarlet cloth of the same pattern as for an Officer of Infantry of the Line of corresponding rank, with blue cloth collar and cuffs. | 153 | 16.10.95 | 33
1127. Lace—Gold, two-vellum pattern. | 822 | | 79
1128. Buttons—See Appendix I.
The other articles as for Infantry of the Line.
1129. HORSE FURNITURE—As for Infantry, see Appendix VI

QUARTERMASTER.

1130. Uniform, &c., as for the Commandant and Secretary, with the following exceptions :—
1131. Helmet—As for Infantry of the Line.
1132. Helmet Plate—Universal pattern. For badge, see Appendix I. | 3 | 7.12.98 | 5

(left margin: 61002 / 6637)

RIDING-MASTER.

1133. Uniform and horse furniture of the regiment from which appointed, or of the regiment in which he last served.

STAFF COLLEGE.

COMMANDANT.

1   . If a General Officer, the uniform and horse furniture of his rank. If under the rank of General Officer, the uniform and horse furniture as for a Colonel on the Staff.

MILITARY PROFESSORS AND INSTRUCTORS AT THE ROYAL MILITARY COLLEGE, AND MILITARY PROFESSORS AT THE STAFF COLLEGE.

1135. The uniform they are authorized to wear, irrespective of their appointments as Professors or Instructors.

Schools, Colleges, &c.—Tower of London.

| | Pattern. | | No. of Plate. |
	No.	Sealed.	

ROYAL MILITARY ACADEMY, WOOLWICH.

GOVERNOR AND COMMANDANT.
1136. The uniform and horse furniture of his rank as a General Officer.

ASSISTANT COMMANDANT AND SECRETARY.
61002/6083 **1137.** Uniform and horse furniture of his rank in the Royal Artillery or Royal Engineers according to the corps from which the Officer is appointed, with Cocked Hat as described in paragraph 7. Officers appointed from the Royal Artillery will wear the frock coat and forage cap described in paragraphs 395, 396.

ADJUTANT AND QUARTERMASTER.
1138. The regimental uniform of his rank.

OFFICERS OF THE SCHOOL OF MUSKETRY.

COMMANDANT.
1139. The uniform and horse furniture of his rank.

CHIEF INSTRUCTOR, AND DEPUTY ASSISTANT ADJUTANT-GENERAL.
1140. The uniform of their rank.

CAPTAIN-INSTRUCTOR, LIEUTENANT-INSTRUCTOR.
1141. Regimental uniform.

QUARTERMASTER AND ACTING ADJUTANT.
1142. As laid down for Garrison Quartermasters in paragraphs 144–160.

ROYAL MILITARY SCHOOL OF MUSIC.

COMMANDANT.
1143. The uniform and horse furniture of his rank.

QUARTERMASTER AND ADJUTANT, DIRECTOR OF MUSIC.
1144. As laid down for Garrison Quartermaster in paragraphs 144-160.

OFFICERS OF THE DUKE OF YORK'S ROYAL MILITARY SCHOOL, CHELSEA, AND OF THE ROYAL HIBERNIAN MILITARY SCHOOL, DUBLIN.

1145. The uniform of the regiment in which they last served.
1146. If not in possession of such uniform, the uniform laid down in paragraphs 136–143 for Officers under the rank of Colonel on the Staff not on the Cadres of Units.
61002/6531 **1147.** The Adjutant and Quartermaster will wear the uniform laid down in paragraphs 144–160 for Garrison Quartermaster.

61002/6955 ## OFFICERS OF THE TOWER OF LONDON.

CONSTABLE, LIEUTENANT, AND MAJOR.
1148. The uniform of their rank in the army.

OTHER OFFICERS.
1149. The uniform for the branch of the service to which they belong.

	Pattern.		No. of
	No.	Sealed.	Plate.

OFFICERS OF THE ROYAL HOSPITALS AT CHELSEA AND KILMAINHAM.

OFFICERS SERVING ON THE STAFF OF THE HOSPITAL.

61002 / 6486

1150. The uniform of their rank, or of the regiment in which they last served; or

1151. The uniform laid down, in paragraphs 136–143, for Officers under the rank of Colonel on the Staff, not on the Cadres of Units.

1152. The Quartermaster will wear the uniform of the regiment in which he last served, or that laid down in paragraphs 144–160, for Garrison Quartermaster.

CAPTAIN AND LIEUTENANTS OF INVALIDS.

1153. Cocked Hat—As described at paragraph 7, but with loop of ½-inch lace.   *1 — 23.8.98 — 2 & 3*

1154. Plume—White swan feathers, drooping outwards, 6 inches long.   *2*

61002 / 6656

1155. Tunic—Blue cloth; the skirt 12 inches deep for an Officer 5 feet 9 inches in height, with a proportionate variation for any difference in height. Plain scarlet cloth collar and cuffs, without badges of rank on the collar. A blue flap on each sleeve, 6 inches long and 2½ inches wide, with three small buttons, and a similar flap, 9 inches long, with two buttons, on each skirt behind; eight buttons down the front, and two at the waist behind; a gold cord loop, with a small button, on each shoulder. The front flaps and back skirts edged with scarlet cloth, ⅛ inch wide, and the skirts lined with black.   *2 — 29.11.98*

1156. Lace—Gold, two-vellum pattern.

1157. Buttons—Windsor pattern.

1158. Trousers—Blue cloth, with scarlet stripes, 1¾ inches wide, down the side seams.

1159. Dress Trousers,
    Sword,
    Scabbard,   As for Infantry.   *68*
    Sword Belts,   *68*
    Sword Knots,   *64*
    Sashes,   *64*

1160. Waist Plate—Round clasp, see Appendix I.

61002 / 4877

1161. Forage Cap—Blue cloth, 3¼ inches deep, bell-shaped top, with gold embroidered drooping peak and band of 1¾-inch lace, gold purl button and braided figure on the crown.   *33 — 13.11.96 — 8*

.. / 6531

1162. Great Coat and Cape—Blue cloth, as described at paragraph 14; lined with scarlet rattinet, black velvet collar.

OFFICERS ON THE ACTIVE LIST ON HALF-PAY.

61002 / 6325
61002 / Staff
65

1163. Officers on the Active List on half-pay, until retired or brought back to full-pay, or if brought back to full pay for temporary duty, may wear the uniform in which they last served.

RESERVE OF OFFICERS.

A.O. 81 / 1900

1164. Officers of the reserve of officers, when employed on army service, will provide themselves with undress and mess dress. Those serving with units will wear the uniform of the unit to which they are attached; those on staff employ, that of their rank. The letter " R " will be worn on the shoulder-straps below the badges of rank, in similar material to those badges.

1165. Officers of the Reserve of Officers are not required to provide themselves with any uniform until their services are actually required, but are authorised to wear uniform in accordance with following regulations:—

OFFICERS RETIRED FROM THE REGULAR FORCES WITH LIABILITY TO SERVE IN CASE OF NATIONAL EMERGENCY.

The uniform of the Regiments in which they last served, but with the letter **R** on the shoulder cords or shoulder straps below the badges of rank.

OFFICERS RETIRED FROM THE REGULAR FORCES WITHOUT LIABILITY TO FURTHER SERVICE, OR FROM THE INDIAN MILITARY FORCES, BUT WHO HAVE BEEN SUBSEQUENTLY GRANTED COMMISSIONS AS OFFICERS OF THE " RESERVE OF OFFICERS."

The uniform in which they last served, with the following exceptions:—

61002 / 6325

Shoulder Cords or Shoulder Straps—The word " **RESERVE** " is worn below the badges of rank in similar material to those badges.   *521 — 20.10.80*

Waist Plate—On the outer circle " Reserve of Officers."

OFFICERS OF THE MILITIA, YEOMANRY, AND VOLUNTEERS WHO MAY BE PERMITTED TO HOLD COMMISSIONS AS OFFICERS OF THE " RESERVE OF OFFICERS " IN ADDITION TO THEIR COMMISSIONS IN THE MILITIA, YEOMANRY AND VOLUNTEERS.

The uniform of their corps.

OFFICERS RETIRED FROM THE MILITIA, YEOMANRY, AND VOLUNTEERS WHO MAY BE GRANTED COMMISSIONS AS OFFICERS OF THE " RESERVE OF OFFICERS."

The uniform of the corps in which they last served, with the word " **RESERVE** " below the badges of rank in similar material to those badges.

	Pattern.		No. of Plate.
	No.	Sealed.	

RETIRED OFFICERS.*

1166. Officers on the Retired List,† *i.e.*, the Officers included in the classes specified below, whose names are retained in the Army List, may wear the uniform in which they last served, but with the letter **R** on the shoulder cords or shoulder straps below the badges of rank.

61002
6325

    a. Officers retired on retired pay, or on full pay or with gratuity, and who are liable for service, in case of national emergency, with the "Reserve of Officers."

    b. Officers retired after 15 years' service, who are permitted to retain their rank.

    c. Officers compulsorily retired on account of age or continuous non-employment.

    d. Field Officers who have commuted pensions.

    e. Officers who are Companions of the Bath.

77070
13

    f. Officers who join the Reserve of Officers on retirement, and who serve in the Reserve until compulsorily retired at the age of 50.

MILITIA.

1167. Officers on retirement after 15 years' commissioned service, including Army service, who are permitted to retain their rank, may wear the uniform of the Militia unit in which they last served, with the addition of the letters **MR** on the shoulder cords or shoulder straps below the badges of rank.

DEPARTMENTS.

1168. *a.* Officers who have retired, or who may retire, with the honorary or corresponding rank of Field Officer.

    b. Officers retired after 15 years' service, who are permitted to retain their rank.

    c. Officers compulsorily retired on account of age.

    d. Officers retired on full pay.

    e. Officers with the honorary or corresponding rank of Field Officer, who have commuted pensions.

    f. Officers who are Companions of the Bath.

    May wear the uniforms of their respective departments, but with the letter **R** or the letters **MR** below the badges of rank.

1169. The above regulations do not apply to Officers who retired prior to the 1st July, 1881. These Officers can only be allowed to wear uniform if the regulations existing at the time of their retirement permitted it.

1170. Whenever retired Officers require to renew their uniforms, the latest approved patterns will be followed.

1171. The letters **R** and **MR** will be in silver embroidery on shoulder cords; in gilt or gilding metal on cloth shoulder straps. In the case of Officers retired from Rifles, the letters will be in bronze.

MILITARY KNIGHTS OF WINDSOR.
FULL DRESS.

1172. Cocked Hat—Black silk, gold lace loop and gilt button, two bullion tassels.	1	23.8.98	2 & 3
1173. Plume—Upright swan feather, 8½ inches long; the bottom scarlet, the top white.			2

1174. Dress Coat—Scarlet cloth, double-breasted; blue cloth Prussian collar; blue cloth cuffs, turnbacks and skirt linings, ten button-holes down the front at regular distances; two rows of large buttons, square end to collar, with two cord holes and two small buttons on each side; scarlet flap on each skirt, with four cord holes and four large buttons on each flap, two buttons at the waist behind; scarlet flap on each cuff, with four small buttons and button-holes, each skirt ornamented at its termination with an embroidered St. George's cross.

1175. Buttons—See Appendix I.

1176. Epaulettes—Gold bullion, gilt crescents, St. George's shield with badges of rank above.

61003
109

1177. Trousers—Blue cloth with scarlet cloth stripe 1¾ inches in width.

1178. Sash—Crimson silk net, bullion tassels. Worn round the waist.

1179. Sword—Crossed hilt; gilt mountings.

1180. Scabbard—Black leather.

1181. Sword Belt—Black enamelled leather, with frog.

UNDRESS.

1182. Forage Cap—Blue cloth, scarlet cloth band, scarlet piping round top of crown; plain black patent leather drooping peak; embroidered St. George's cross on band. For badge, see Appendix I.

1183. Frock Coat—Blue cloth, single-breasted; eight buttons down the front at regular intervals; short side edges, two buttons on each skirt, two small buttons on cuffs; Prussian collar.

1184. Scales—Gilt crescents, with embroidered St. George's cross; V.R. and badges of rank above.

1185. Trousers—As for Full Dress.

1186. Cloak—Blue cloth, lined with scarlet; deep cape, lined with black, black velvet collar, gilt rose clasp, and five gilt buttons down the front.

---

* Instructions for the wearing of uniform by Retired Officers of the Indian Army are contained in the Army Regulations, India, Vol. VII.

† Officers retired from the Household Cavalry with permission to wear uniform, will not wear breeches and jack boots, but will wear overalls.

	Pattern.		No. of Plate.
	No.	Sealed.	

UNIFORM FOR SERVICE ABROAD.

HELMET.*

1187. A helmet of the following description is worn by all Officers :—
Cork, covered with white cloth in six seams, bound with buff leather at the bottom ; above the peak, and going round the helmet, a buff leather band, 1 inch wide, stitched top and bottom. The head-piece let in with zigzag ventilator ; back peak to centre of crown 12 inches, front peak to centre of crown 10¾ inches, side to centre of crown 9 inches, side hooks, curb-chain, the links ⅜ inch wide, the chain lined with white leather. At top of helmet a collet, riveted on to a collar ⅜ inch wide, to receive spike and base. A hook at the side, to which the chin-chain is attached when not required to be worn under the chin. Rifle regiments will have a chin-chain on Morocco leather of the colour as the regimental facings, lined with black velvet. A leather chin-strap, ⅜ inch broad, is worn in all orders of Dress except Review Order.

(Pattern No. 4, Sealed 15.6.98, Plate 10)

A.O. 83 / 1896

1188. With khaki uniform the helmet is worn with a khaki cover, and khaki-covered zinc button, or a khaki helmet may be worn. Spikes and chains will not be worn unless specially ordered, but they may be worn by Officers not parading with their men on such occasions as may be directed by Officers commanding, subject to the instructions of the General Officer commanding the station.

(Pattern No. 5, Sealed 15.6.98, Plate 10)

PUGGAREES.

1189. Puggarees are worn with helmets at all stations abroad.

(Pattern No. 5, Sealed 15.6.98, Plate 10)

BADGES.

1190. In the branches of the Service in which helmet badges are issued to men, badges, as a general rule of similar design to the field cap badge, will be worn on the puggaree by Officers, see Appendix I.

(Pattern No. 21, Sealed 12.9.99)

FURNITURE.

1191. Metal furniture will be in gilt or gilding metal, except in Rifle regiments, when it will be bronze.

ORNAMENTS.

GENERAL, STAFF, AND DEPARTMENTAL OFFICERS, except Officers of the Army Ordnance Department not serving on the Staff of the Army, and Army Veterinary Department, when plumes are not worn.

1192. A spike of bright metal, on a dead base,—acanthus leaf pattern.

(Pattern No. 4, Sealed 20.3.99, Plate 10)

Dimensions :—
Height of spike from base, 3⅜ inches.
Total height of spike and base, 4⅛ inches.
Diameter of spike at point of contact with leaf base, 1 inch.
Diameter of base, 3¼ inches full.
The base has eight principal points, with an interval of about 1¼ inches between each point.

CAVALRY.

1193. Spike and base as in paragraph 1192.

ROYAL ARTILLERY, ARMY SERVICE CORPS, ROYAL ARMY MEDICAL CORPS, AND ARMY VETERINARY DEPARTMENT.

1194. In the Royal Horse Artillery, Royal Field Artillery, Army Service Corps, Royal Army Medical Corps, Army Veterinary Department, a ball in a leaf on the cup, pattern of base as in paragraph 1192. The height of the ball and cup is 1¾ inches. In the Royal Garrison Artillery the ball in leaf cup is mounted on the dome base as in paragraph 1195.

(Pattern No. 3, Sealed 4.8.81, Plate 10)

---

* Officers should be careful that their Tradesmen do not supply them with "smart" looking helmets instead of those capable of affording protection from the sun. In fitting themselves with helmets, they should take care that the back part comes well down so as to shield the back of the neck, and that the temples are well covered. The sealed pattern should be strictly adhered to.

	Pattern.		No. of Plate.
	No.	Sealed.	

ROYAL ENGINEERS, INFANTRY, AND ARMY ORDNANCE DEPARTMENT AND CORPS, except Officers of the Army Ordnance Department serving on the Staff of the Army.

1195. Spike of bright metal, mounted on a bright dome base.

Dimensions :--
Height of spike from place of insertion in dome, 2¾ inches.
Total height of spike and dome, 3¼ inches.
Diameter of spike at point of contact with dome, 1 inch.
Diameter of dome, 1⅞ inches full.
Circumference of dome at point of contact with helmet, 5⅞ inches.

| 4 | 20.3.99 | 10 |

A O. 83 / 1896

PLUMES.

1196. General and Staff Officers—White swan feathers, drooping outwards, with red feathers under, reaching to the end of the white ones. Military Secretaries and Aides-de-Camp wear the red feathers outside the white. Officers of Royal Engineers (other than Staff) not performing regimental or garrison duty, a plume of white cock's feathers. The leaf pattern of base is to be worn with the plume.

Departmental Officers who wear the cocked hat at home—Plumes of the description and colour laid down in these Regulations for their respective services.

The leaf pattern of base will be worn with the plumes.

Plumes are attached to the helmet by means of a screw passing through a socket, 1½ inches high, leaf pattern, and fastened by a nut.

The feathers of plumes will be for general officers, 10 inches; colonels, 8 inches; and officers under the rank of colonel, 6 inches in length.

| 85 | | 2 |

61002 / 6975

HELMET CURTAIN.

1197. A detachable khaki helmet curtain may be worn when the severity of the climate necessitates it.

PITH HAT.

1198. Pith, covered with khaki, brim about 3½ inches in width, khaki-covered zinc ventilator at the top, green lining.

| | | 11 |

61002 / 6759

KHAKI UNIFORM.
ALL STATIONS EXCEPT CANADA.

A.O. 83 / 1896

1199. Khaki uniform will be worn at all stations abroad except in Canada. It will be fitted loosely to admit warm clothing being worn underneath if necessary, in cold weather or on active service.

1200. Frock—Khaki drill or serge, full in chest, cut with patrol-shaped back and side bodies; patch pocket, with pointed flaps and small button on each side of breast outside, and with a one-inch box pleat down the centre. The pockets to be 6½ inches deep and 6¼ inches broad at the top. Top edge of pocket flap to be one inch below the centre of the second button. Two inside pockets in lining of skirt in front fastened with small khaki covered button. Two pleats about 3 inches long on each side of neck in front running slightly diagonally from collar seam in the direction of arm-hole, also two pleats underneath the breast pockets, to give shape to the waist and fulness to the breast. Five small buttons down the front. The back to have a yoke, sufficiently wide to cover shoulder seams, ending under the shoulder straps, and not too deep. Sleeves with three pleats, with pointed cuffs 5 inches high at the point and 2 inches behind. Shoulder straps of same material as the frock, and fastened at the top with a small button. In the Royal Horse Artillery and Cavalry, shoulder chains are worn. A slit up each side of sufficient depth to suit the height of the wearer. Inside waistbelt fastened with a buckle.

| 223 | 6.7.97 | 45 |

61002 / 5973

... / 6805

Stand-and-fall collars for all ranks of the same material as the frock, fastened with two hooks. In the services hereafter specified a gorget patch 2½ inches long and 1¼ inches wide, is worn, pointed at the outer end, sewn on to each side of the collar in front, and meeting at the fastening.

| | | 63 |

61002 / 6835
A.O. 83 / 1896

General Officer.—Scarlet cloth, a loop of gold three Russia braid along the centre, with a gold net button near the point.

Staff Officers.—As above, but with loop of scarlet silk, Russia, instead of gold, and gorget (20-*line*) button near the point.

Army Service Corps.—Blue cloth with loops of white braid, a gorget corps button near the point.

Army Medical Service—Blue cloth with loops of black Russia tracing, a gorget corps button near the point.

Army Ordnance Department.—Blue cloth edged with ⅛-inch scarlet piping except the sides by the hooks and eyes, a gorget departmental button near the point.

224	23.5.96	
225	23.5.96	
226	13.6.96	45
227	23.4.96	
228	27.7.97	

61002 / 5938

	Pattern.		No. of Plate.
	No.	Sealed.	

Army Pay Department.—Blue cloth with a ½-inch yellow light, a gorget departmental button near the point. — **229** — 27.7.97

Army Veterinary Department.—Maroon cloth, a gorget departmental button near the point. — **230** — 29.10.97 — 45

Inspectors of Army Schools.—Blue cloth with light blue loop, a gorget departmental button near the point. — **231** — 27.7.97

All other Officers, plain collars, without any patch.

On the shoulder straps, in addition to the badges of rank, distinctive letters or numerals, indicating the Corps, Regiment or Department, are worn, as laid down for the men in the Clothing Regulations.

The buttons will be of regimental or other pattern as worn on the cloth uniform.

1201. Frock for Foot Guards—Pattern as for *serge* frock for the Foot Guards, see paragraph 526. — **232** — 6.7.97 — 45

1202. Frock for Highland and Scottish Regiments.—As described in paragraph 1210 with the following exceptions :—

The pocket flaps are pointed out at the ends and hollowed in the centre, and are fastened with ½-inch buttons of zinc or bone mould, covered with the same material as the frock.

The yoke to the back is omitted.

The cuffs are gauntlet shape, 5 inches deep at the hind arm seam, and 3¼ inches at the fore arm seam.

The skirts are rounded off in front.

1203. Spine Protector—A spine protector may be worn when the severity of the climate necessitates it.

1204. Trousers—Khaki drill. Footstraps, if worn, will be of black leather.

1205. Pantaloons—Brown cord.

(N.B.—With mounted Officers other than those of mounted branches, it is optional when on parade whether they wear khaki or brown cord pantaloons, but Officers of a unit must be dressed alike.

On parade, dismounted Officers of infantry wear trousers with puttees.)

1206. Puttees—Woollen, khaki coloured.

1207. Boots—Black or brown leather ; mounted Officers may wear knee boots or butcher boots with spur rests, or puttees and shooting boots, provided that all Officers of a unit be dressed alike.

1208. Belts—The "Sam Browne." See Appendix VIII.

Scabbard—Brown leather. See Appendix VII.

Sword Knot—Brown leather. See Appendix VIII.

1209. Haversack, Khaki Drill—As described in paragraph 15.

1210. Collars—White linen are optional, but all Officers of a unit must be dressed alike. See paragraph 8. — — — 70

1211. Medals and Medal Ribbons—See paragraphs 35 and 36.

MESS DRESS.

1212. Mess Dress—Units may decide to wear either white waistcoat, kamarband instead of waistcoat, white mess dress with kamarband, or white jacket with kamarband and cloth overalls or trousers.

1213. Mess Jacket—White drill, without braid or buttons ; roll collar or stand-up collar fastened in front with a loop of white braid ; shoulder-straps of similar material, with a small button at top ; one inside breast pocket. Sleeves cut plain with pointed cuffs, 5 inches high at point, and 2⅗ inches behind. — **233** — 23.4.96

1214. Trousers—White drill, with black leather footstraps for mounted Officers.

1215. Kamarbands—Silk, of the following colour :—

		Pattern No.	Sealed
Staff	Red.		
Cavalry, except Hussars	Colour of plume or tunic.	237	7.10.96
Hussars	Colour of busby bag or tunic.		
Royal Artillery	Blue.		
Foot Guards	Blue.	238	13.6.98
East Kent Regiment	Buff.	239	13.6.96
Northumberland Fusiliers	Olive green.		
Scottish Rifles	} Green.	240	9.7.98
Royal Irish Rifles		241	9.7.98
Light Infantry Regiments		242	22.5.96
King's Royal Rifle Corps	Green and red.	243	27.2.82
Rifle Brigade	Green and black.	244	27.2.82
Army Chaplains' Department	Black.		
Army Service Corps	Blue and white.	245	1.1.92

Marginal references:
61002/5847
61002/6140
61002/6127
A.O. 83/1896
61002/5973
38407 Dress/169
61002/5751
61002/6876
A.O. 83/1896
61002/6127
61002/5528

	Pattern.		No. of Plate.
	No.	Sealed.	

Royal Army Medical Corps .... Dull cherry.	237	7.10.96	
Army Ordnance Department.... Red.			
Army Pay Department .... Blue.	246	7.10.96	
Army Veterinary Department Maroon.	247	7.10.96	
All other regiments and corps Red.	237	7.10.96	

When the kamarband is worn, black neckties with white linen collars will be worn.

1216. Linen Collars—See paragraph 8.

1217. Medals and Medal Ribbons—See paragraphs 35 and 36.

WHITE UNIFORM.

<table>
<tr><td>A.O. 83
1896
61002
6936</td><td>

1218. White uniform may be worn under the authority of General Officers Commanding

1219. Frock—Plain white drill, full in chest. Shoulder straps of the same colour and material as the garment, fastened at the top with a small regulation button, and bearing distinctive metal letters or numerals indicating the corps, regiment, or department. Stand-up collar of the same material as the jacket, rounded off in front, with one hook. Five small buttons of regulation pattern down the front. One inside breast pocket. Cuffs pointed, 5 inches high at the point, and 2½ inches behind. The frock to be of sufficient length to just clear the saddle when mounted.

</td><td>234</td><td>23.4.96</td><td></td></tr>
</table>

1220. Frock for Highland and Scottish Regiments—As above, with the following exceptions :—
Cuffs to be gauntlet-shape, 5 inches deep at the hind-arm seam, and 3¼ inches at the fore-arm seam.
Skirt rounded in front to clear the top of the sporran. — **235** — **13.3.97**

61002 / 6601
1221. Aiguillettes—Officers serving on the General or Personal Staff will wear the Staff Aiguillette, as described in paragraph 162, with White Uniform, when this uniform is worn in Review Order.

1222. Trousers—Plain drill, with black leather footstraps for mounted Officers.

DOMINION OF CANADA, EXCEPT BRITISH COLUMBIA.

Uniform as worn in United Kingdom, with winter clothing as follows:—

61002 / 6763
1223. Fur Cap—Astrachan folding cap, colour of fur to match that of fur trimmings of great coat. The body of the cap is similar in outline and folding arrangement to the field cap, 7 inches high. A detachable fur flap on each side to protect the ears ; the flaps 4½ inches long at the top and rounded at the bottom ; the deepest point of the bottom curve 3½ inches from the top edge, fur on each side, and to hold them in position (whether down or up) they are connected by a strip of narrow black elastic tape attached to the lowest point of each curve. To attach the flaps to the cap, a piece of black silk, fitted with two hooks, is stitched to the top of each flap, two eyes corresponding in the lining of the cap. The hooks and eyes should be so placed that when the flap is hooked on, the fur edge of the top meets the fur edge of the lower rim of the cap, so that none of the silk strip may be seen, and the eyes should be placed sufficiently high to avoid pressure of the hooks and eyes on the sides of the head, when the flaps are worn. The straight top edge of the fur flaps should be cut at a slant, so that the flaps, when attached, hang with a slight inclination to the front, in order to allow them to lie flat to the ears when the elastic tape is under the chin. Officers of the Royal Artillery and Royal Engineers wear a gold embroidered upright grenade in the front of the cap, midway between top and bottom, when folded as usually worn. — **11**

Other officers wear, midway in the front of the fur cap, a badge of the same design as they wear on the field cap.

61002 / 6763
1224. Great Coats*—Heavy milled cloth of the colour authorised for the ordinary great coats for each Service, double breasted. Stand and fall collar, high enough (when fully extended) to reach to the top of the ears. Shape generally like that of frock coat, but made somewhat looser (so as to fit over a mess or patrol jacket) and to reach within a foot of the ground. The sleeves lined with "glassade" or "lustreine," the body and skirts lined with worsted "venetian." The collar covered with black astrachan fur in the case of blue coats, and with grey astrachan fur in the case of grey coats. The lappels lined — **236** — **18.3.99** — **45**

---

* Officers now in possession of existing pattern of winter uniform may be allowed to wear it out.

	Pattern.		No. of Plate.
	No.	Sealed.	

<table>
<tr><td>

...
6822

with similar fur on the inside (*i.e.*, on the surface next to the breast when the lappels are closed across it). The fur on the collar and lappels doubled over the cloth to form an edging 1 inch wide on the inside of the collar, and on the outside of the lappels, the edging to be continued to the waist. The cuffs trimmed with similar fur 5½ inches deep all round. Four loops of ¼-inch black square cord down the front on each side. Each loop forms an eye in the centre above and below, and a crow's foot at the end. A black netted olivet on each loop near the crow's foot. Two olivets at the waist behind. Pocket inside the left breast. Pockets in the plaits of the skirts behind. Three hooks and eyes on the collar. Shoulder straps of the same cloth as the garment, with a black netted button at the top.

...
6786

    For Officers of Rifle Regiments, the fur will be black.

...
6786

1225. Knee Boots—Brown leather (black for Rifle regiments) similar to those worn by the rank and file, the official description of which is "boots, knee, Canada pattern." The boots are worn outside the ordinary pantaloons or trousers. Officers can procure them on repayment from the Army Clothing Department, or from the Army Ordnance Department at Halifax, Nova Scotia.

1226. Fur Gauntlets—Astrachan backs, leather palms. Colour of fur and leather to correspond with colour of fur trimming on great coat. Gauntlets to reach up to the top edge of the fur cuff on the great coat.
</td><td></td><td></td><td></td></tr>
</table>

BRITISH COLUMBIA.

61002
6763

1227. Uniform as worn in the United Kingdom.

INDIA.

61C02
6179

1228. The uniform for Officers of the Indian Army is described in Army Regulations, India, Vol. VII.

MISCELLANEOUS ARTICLES FOR ACTIVE SERVICE.

1229. Sealed patterns of the following articles to serve as a guide to Officers proceeding on Active Service may be seen at the War Office :—

	No.	Sealed.	
Bed valise.	546		
Bullock trunk.	545		
Cooking pot.	540		
Goggles.	543	13.12.84	
Khaki spine protector.	542	27.3.85	
Mess tin.	541	26.11.97	
Veil.	544	9.6.96	
Water bottle.	532	15.12.97	

61002
6908

UNIFORM OF OFFICERS, ARMY POST OFFICE CORPS, ON MOBILISATION.

	No.	Sealed.	No. of Plate.
1230. Helmet—Colonial pattern. See paragraph 1188.	4	15.6.98	10
1231. Field Cap—Blue cloth, as for Infantry of the Line, with white cloth welts.	26	2.3.94	9
1232. Frock—Blue serge, full in chest. Collar and cuffs of same material. Five buttons of special pattern down the front. On and below each breast a patch pocket with box pleat, shaped flap and small button. A band, inside the frock, 2 inches wide round the waist, with a buckle in front. A 3-inch box pleat down the back and a pleat at each side in front from collar to skirt. Pointed cuffs, 5½ inches deep in front and 2¼ inches behind. Shoulder straps of scarlet cloth with ¼ inch white stripe down the centre. Small button at top.			
1233. Trousers—Blue cloth with scarlet welts ¼ inch wide down each side seam.			
1234. Khaki Frock and Trousers—Universal pattern. See paragraphs 1200 and 1204.	223	6.7.97	45
1235. Badges and Buttons—As described in Appendix I.			
1236. Boots—Ankle.			
1237. Sword Belt—"Sam Browne" belt, universal pattern. See Appendix VIII.	397	4.1.1900	70

APPENDICES.

1. The Specifications and Instructions in these Appendices are intended to assist the Trade to supply garment or other articles of equipment to Officers strictly according to Regulation Pattern.

2. The Sealed Patterns of Officers' Uniform and Equipment are open to inspection at the War Office, where every information on the subject will be afforded to manufacturers and others concerned.

3. Should any manufacturer desire to provide himself with patterns for his own guidance, such patterns will, upon application, be duly examined at the War Office, and, if found correct, passed and certified as being in conformity with Sealed Pattern.

4. All communications should be addressed to the Under Secretary of State, War Office, London, S.W.

APPENDIX I.

BADGES AND DEVICES.

I. Deviations from the universal patterns of Helmet-plate and Waist-plate are noted in the annexed Table.

II. The Badges authorized to be worn on the collars of Tunics or Frocks, may be worn on the collars of Mess Jackets; exceptions are noted in the following Table.

III. Except where otherwise stated, the Field Cap or Glengarry Badge is worn on the Puggaree. For position of Field Cap Badge see paragraph 10 and plate 9.

IV. All Badges are in *metal*, unless otherwise stated.

V. Field Cap Badges are 1⅜ inches in height, Collar Badges 1¼ inches, unless otherwise laid down.

Badges—Staff.

	Regiment.	On Buttons.	On Collar.	On Full Dress Head-dress.	On Waist Plate.	On Forage Cap.	On Field Cap.	No. of Plate.
61002 / 6470	Field Marshal.	Crossed batons and crown within a laurel wreath.	... ...	... ...	... ...	The Royal Crest with crossed batons. In gold embroidery.	As for forage cap.	46
	General Officers.	Crossed sword and baton within a laurel wreath.	... ...	... ...	... ...	In gold embroidery, the Royal Crest with crossed sword and baton, blade of the sword in silver.	As for forage cap.	46
	Colonel on the Staff.	Burnished. The Garter surmounted by a Crown. The Royal Cypher within the Garter.	... ...	... ...	... ...	O. C. Royal Artillery:—The Royal Artillery puggaree badge. O. C. Royal Engineers:—The Royal Engineer puggaree badge. O. C. Regimental District:—Regimental pattern. O. C. Army Service Corps, if Col. on the Staff:—The A.S.C. field cap badge. Other Colonels on the Staff:—The Royal Crest in gold embroidery.	As for forage cap.	46
	Officers under the rank of Colonel on the Staff, not on the cadre of a unit.	Burnished. The Garter surmounted by a Crown; within the Garter, the Royal Cypher.	... ...	... ...	On a gilt or gilding metal frosted rectangular plate, in silver, the Royal Cypher and Crown encircled with oak leaves; on the bottom of the wreath a scroll inscribed *Dieu et mon droit*.	The Royal Crest in gold embroidery.	The Royal Crest in gold embroidery.	46
61002 / Staff. / 4	Garrison Staff.	... ...	... ...	... ...	Gilt or gilding metal rectangular burnished plate; on the plate, in silver, the Royal Cypher, surmounted by a Crown; an oak branch on each side, and below, a scroll inscribed *Dieu et mon droit.*	... ...	In gilt or gilding metal, the Royal Cypher and Crown.	46
61002 / Staff. / 39	Staff Officers wearing Regimental Uniform.	Regimental Badges and Devices.... ...	... ...	... ...	... ...	On the Staff Forage Cap; the Royal Crest in gold embroidery.		
61002 / 6470	A.D.C's. to the Queen.	As for Colonel on the Staff.	... ...	... ...	As above.	... ...	The Royal Crest in gold embroidery.	46

Badges—Cavalry.

Regiment.	On Buttons.	On Collar of Tunic and Frock.	On Full Dress Head-dress.	On Waist Plate.	On the Pouch.	On Field Cap.	No. of Plate.
61002 / 5736 **1st Life Guards.**	The letters "L.G." reversed and intertwined, surmounted by a Crown. Between the letters and the Crown the number of the regiment.	... ...	Within a wreath of oak leaves and laurel, on a frosted gilt centre surmounted by a Crown, the Star of the Order of the Garter. Around the centre, the Collar of the Order, with the George upon the lower ends of the stems of the wreath. The colours of the Garter, cross, and field are carried out in enamel. The star in silver, the remainder gilt.	On frosted gilt rectangular plate, the star and collar of the Order of the Garter (no motto or centre), surmounted by a Crown. On either side of the collar the letters, "L.G." reversed and intertwined. Below the letters a scroll upon a twig of laurel. The left scroll inscribed "Waterloo," the right, "Peninsula." On the undress belt a burnished plate is worn with a similar device, but with the motto and centre of the star omitted.	As for Waist plate.	The Star of the Order of the Garter, a Crown above in gilt metal.	47
61002 / 5632 **2nd Life Guards.**	Edge scalloped. The Imperial Crest between the letters "L.G." Below the Crown the figure 2.	... ...	As for 1st Life Guards, except that the field of the cross is in silver.	As for 1st Life Guards full dress waist-plate.	As for 1st Life Guards.	In gold and silver embroidery, the Royal Crest; below the crest, in gold embroidery, the letters "L.G." reversed and intertwined; within the letters the figure "2."	47
61002 / 6156 **Royal Horse Guards.**	The letters "R.H.G." surmounted by a Crown.	... ...	The Star of the Order of the Garter.	On a dead gilt frosted rectangular plate, the Royal Crest.	The Royal Arms on a scarlet cloth ground.	The Star of the Order of the Garter.	47
61002 / Cavalry 125 **1st (King's) Dragoon Guards.**	The Star of the Order of the Garter surmounted by a Crown. Within the Garter the letters "K.D.G."	The Austrian Eagle. On the tunic, in gold embroidery. On the frock, in gilt or gilding metal.	On the Garter star, in silver, the Garter with motto in gilt or gilding metal, pierced on a ground of blue enamel. Within the Garter on a ground of red enamel, the Royal Cypher in silver. On the puggaree, the Austrian Eagle in gilt or gilding metal.	On a frosted gilt or gilding metal rectangular plate with burnished edges, in silver, the Royal Cypher and Crown. Within an oak-leaf wreath, a scroll on the bottom of the wreath inscribed *Dieu et mon droit*.	In gilt or gilding metal, the Royal Cypher and Crown.	The Austrian Eagle in gold embroidery.	47
61002 / Cavalry 86 **2nd Dragoon Guards (Queen's Bays).**	Star of Order of the Garter surmounted by a Crown; within the Garter the word "Bays."	In gilt or gilding metal, within a laurel wreath, the word "Bays." Between the ends of the wreath, a Crown.	On the Garter star, the Garter, with motto pierced on a blue enamel ground; within the Garter the Royal Cypher in silver on a ground of red enamel.	As for 1st Dragoon Guards.	As for 1st Dragoon Guards.	As for collar.	47
61002 / Cavalry 79 61002 / 6918 **3rd (Prince of Wales's) Dragoon Guards.**	Within the Garter and motto the Prince of Wales's plume. For the Field Cap the Garter is omitted, and the Plume is silver,—mounted.	The Prince of Wales's plume. The Coronet in gilt or gilding metal, the plume and motto in silver.	On the Garter star, in silver, the Garter, with motto in gilt or gilding metal, pierced on a ground of blue enamel; within the Garter, in silver, the Prince of Wales's plume, on a scarlet enamel ground.	As for 1st Dragoon Guards.	As for 1st Dragoon Guards.	As for collar, with scroll below in gilt or gilding metal, inscribed 3rd Dragoon Guards.	47
61002 / Cavalry 85 **4th (Royal Irish) Dragoon Guards.**	The Star of the Order of St. Patrick, with "R.I.D.G." above the motto.	In silver, the Star of the Order of St. Patrick.	On the Garter star, in gilt or gilding metal, a circle inscribed *Quis separabit*, MDCCLXXXIII, on a blue enamelled ground. Within the circle, on a white ground, the Cross of St. Patrick. On the cross a shamrock-leaf in green enamel, with a red enamelled Crown on each petal.	As for 1st Dragoon Guards, but with shamrock instead of oak-leaf wreath.	As for 1st Dragoon Guards.	As for collar, with gilt or gilding metal scroll on the bottom of the star, inscribed "4th Royal Irish D. Guards."	48
61002 / Cavalry 54 **5th (Princess Charlotte of Wales's) Dragoon Guards.**	Star of Order of the Garter surmounted by a Crown. The Garter inscribed *Vestigia nulla retrorsum*. Within the Garter "5" D.G.	In gilt or gilding metal, a circle surmounted by a Crown. The circle inscribed *Vestigia nulla retrorsum*, on a frosted ground. On a burnished centre, in silver, the white horse with "V." above and "D.G." below.	On the Garter star, in gilt or gilding metal, an elliptical ring, inscribed "P.C.W. Dragoon Guards." Within the ring "5" in silver.	As for 1st Dragoon Guards.	As for 1st Dragoon Guards.	As for collar.	48

Badges—Cavalry.

	Regiment.	On Buttons.	On Collar of Tunic and Frock.	On Full Dress Head-dress.	On Waist Plate.	On the Pouch.	On Field Cap.	No. of Plate.
61002 Cavalry 93 / 61002 Cavalry 133	6th Dragoon Guards (Carabineers).	The Garter inscribed "Carabineers," surmounted by a Crown. Within the Garter "VI" D.G.	In gilt or gilding metal, upon crossed carbines the Garter and motto surmounted by a Crown. In silver, within the Garter, on a frosted ground, "VI" D.G.; below the garter a scroll inscribed "Carabiniers."	In silver, the Garter, with motto in gilt or gilding metal, pierced on a ground of blue enamel. Within the Garter, on a ground of red enamel, the figure "6" in silver. The star has plain rays.	As for 1st Dragoon Guards. For the undress belt, the whole plate is burnished.	As for 1st Dragoon Guards.	As for collar.	48
61002 Cavalry 133	7th (Princess Royal's) Dragoon Guards.	"P.R.D.G." surmounted by Princess Royal's Coronet.	In silver, the Earl of Ligonier's Crest—a lion issuing from a coronet, with a scroll below inscribed, *Quo fata vocant.*	On the Garter star, in silver, an elliptical ring, with "The Princess Royal's Dragoon Guards" in burnished gilt or gilding metal on a silver blue enamel ground. Within, on a ground of red enamel, the figure "7" in silver.	In gilt or gilding metal the letters, P.R.D.G.	As on waist plate...	As for collar, but the scroll inscribed "7 Dragoon Guards."	48
61002 Cavalry 81 ... 95	1st (Royal) Dragoons.	The Royal Crest. The Crown upon and the Lion within a Garter inscribed "Royal Dragoons."	On the tunic and mess jacket, in gold embroidery an eagle on a bar, below the bar "105" in silver. Upon the eagle a wreath in silver. On the frock a similar badge in metal, except that the bar is in silver.	In gilt or gilding metal, the Garter star. On the star the Crest of England on a burnished silver ground within an elliptical ring in silver inscribed "The Royal Dragoons."	As for 1st Dragoon Guards.	The Royal Cypher and Crown in gilt or gilding metal.	In gilt or gilding metal, the Royal Crest. A silver scroll below, inscribed "The Royal Dragoons."	48
61002 Cavalry 88 ... 112	2nd Dragoons (Royal Scots Greys).	Edge burnished and scalloped. An eagle above "Waterloo." Below "Waterloo," the letters "R S.G."	On the tunic, a grenade in silver embroidery. On the frock, in silver, an eagle above "Waterloo."	A grenade in gilt or gilding metal. On the grenade the Royal Arms. In the centre below, St. Andrew and Cross, between sprays of rose, thistle, and shamrock; on a scroll beneath the word "Waterloo."	On a seeded gilt rectangular plate with burnished edges, the Star and Collar of the Order of the Thistle; above the Star, a Crown. The Star and circle with motto in silver, the remainder of the device in gilt metal.	In gilt or gilding metal, an eagle over "Waterloo."	In silver, an eagle above "Waterloo," with a gilt or gilding metal scroll below, inscribed "Royal Scots Greys."	48
61002 Cavalry 130	3rd (King's Own) Hussars	Full dome, gilt, burnished.	The white horse, in silver.	... ...	... ...	In gilt or gilding metal, the Royal Cypher and Crown.	As for collar, with a scroll below. In gilt or gilding metal, inscribed "3rd King's Own Hussars."	48
61002 Cavalry 89	4th (Queen's Own) Hussars.	Full dome, gilt, burnished.	In gilt or gilding metal, a circle inscribed "Queen's Own Hussars," with two sprays of laurel below. Above the circle, a Crown. Within the circle, "IV," ornamented in silver.	... ...	... ...	In gilt or gilding metal, the Royal Cypher and Crown.	As for collar.	48
61002 Cavalry 115	5th (Royal Irish) Lancers.	On crossed Lances a circle surmounted by a Crown, with a shamrock wreath below. On the circle, "Fifth Royal Lancers." Within the circle the Harp.	The Harp and Crown in gilt or gilding metal.	On a gilt or gilding metal plate, universal pattern, in silver, the Royal Arms; below, the harp between sprays of shamrock. Across the bottom of the plate "Fifth Royal Irish Lancers." Above "Fifth," two scrolls inscribed "Blenheim," "Oudenarde." Above "Lancers," two scrolls inscribed "Ramillies," "Malplaquet." On the puggaree, on crossed lances, a circle inscribed *Quis separabit.* Within the circle, the figure "5."	... ...	In gilt or gilding metal, the Royal Cypher and Crown.	Crossed lances and "5" in gold embroidery, the upper pennons in scarlet, and the lower in white silk.	48
38407 Dress 157 / 61002 Cavalry. 166	6th (Inniskilling) Dragoons.	Scalloped edge. The Castle of Inniskilling, with "VI" below. For the tunic and frock the design is in silver. On other buttons in gold.	In silver, the Castle of Inniskilling. In embroidery for the tunic and mess jacket. In metal for the frock.	On a gilt or gilding metal beaded Garter star, an elliptical ring inscribed "Inniskilling Dragoons" in burnished letters on a frosted ground. Within the ring, in silver, the Castle over "VI" on a frosted gilt or gilding metal ground.	On a matted gilt or gilding metal plate with burnished edges, in silver, an oak-leaf wreath with a scroll inscribed "Inniskilling Dragoons" on the lower bend. Within the wreath, the Castle over "VI."	In dead gilt or gilding metal, the Royal Cypher and Crown.	As for collar badge, with a scroll below in gilt or gilding metal, inscribed "Inniskilling."	49

Badges—Cavalry.

Regiment.	On Buttons.	On Collar of Tunic and Frock.	On Full Dress Head-dress.	On Waist Plate.	On the Pouch.	On Field Cap.	No. of Plate.
61002 Cavalry. 162 **7th (Queen's Own) Hussars.**	Full dome, gilt, burnished.	In gilt or gilding metal, a circle inscribed "7th Queen's Own Hussars," surmounted by a Crown, within the circle, in silver, the letters "Q.O." reversed and intertwined.	On the puggaree. As for collar, but larger.	... ...	... ...	The letters "Q.O." in gold embroidery, reversed and intertwined.	49
61002 Cavalry. 74 **8th King's (Royal Irish) Hussars.**	Full dome, gilt, burnished.	The Harp and Crown, the Harp in silver, the Crown in gilt or gilding metal.	... ...	... ...	In gold embroidery the Crest of England, and Harp and Crown, the Royal Cypher in silver embroidery. Round the Royal Cypher a wreath of shamrocks with eight scrolls in gold embroidery. The scrolls embroidered in silver, with the battles as on the colours. A similar scroll below the Harp and Crown inscribed *Pristinæ virtutis memores.* A similar device is worn on the sabretache, but with the regimental motto above the device and surmounted by a Crown.	As for collar, with scroll in gilt or gilding metal below, inscribed "8th King's Royal Irish Hussars."	49
61002 Cavalry 126 **9th (Queen's Royal) Lancers.**	On crossed lances, surmounted by a crown, the letters "A.R.," reversed and intertwined. Below the letters the figure 9.	In silver, the figure "9" on crossed lances, above the "9" a crown, below the "9" a scroll inscribed "Lancers."	In gilt or gilding metal the universal plate with the Royal Arms, on either side on sprays of laurel scrolls inscribed with the honours of the regiment. On a scroll below, "Royal Lancers." In silver, on the centre of the plate, "A.R.," reversed and intertwined.	... ...	In gilt or gilding metal "A.R.," reversed and intertwined, with a crown above.	As for collar, but larger.	49
61002 Cavalry 80 **10th (Prince of Wales's Own Royal) Hussars.**	Full dome, gilt, burnished.	The Prince of Wales's Plume. The Plume and motto in silver. The coronet in gilt or gilding metal.	... ...	... ...	Within a laurel wreath, the Prince of Wales's Plume in silver, with the Royal Cypher and Crown underneath in gilt or gilding metal.	As for collar, with a gilt or gilding metal scroll below, inscribed "10th Royal Hussars."	49
61002 Cavalry 68 **11th (Prince Albert's Own) Hussars.**	Full dome, gilt, burnished.	On a ground of crimson cloth, in gold and silk embroidery, the Crest and Motto of the late Prince Consort. The motto on a blue velvet scroll.	On the puggaree, as for collar, but in gilt or gilding metal.	... ...	... ...	As for collar.	49
61002 Cavalry 78 **12th (Prince of Wales's Royal) Lancers.**	Scalloped edge; "12" resting on crossed lances surmounted by a Crown.	The Prince of Wales's Plume. The Plume and motto in silver. The coronet in gilt or gilding metal.	In silver, the Royal Arms, with the Prince of Wales's Plume above and the sphinx over Egypt below; the scroll inscribed *Dieu et mon droit* resting on two sprays of rose, thistle, and shamrock intertwined. Below, on three gilt or gilding metal scrolls, the battles as on the colours; the outer ends of the scrolls finish in sprays of laurel.	... ...	The Royal Cypher, surmounted by a Crown.	As for collar, with gilt or gilding metal scroll below, inscribed "XII Royal Lancers."	49
61002 Cavalry 57 ... 117 **13th Hussars.**	Full dome, gilt, burnished.	In gilt or gilding metal a circle, inscribed *Viret in æternum,* surmounted by a crown; around the circle a laurel wreath, with "Hussars" on a tablet on the lower bend; within the circle "XIII." in silver.	... ...	... ...	In gilt or gilding metal the Royal Cypher surmounted by a Crown.	As for collar.	49

Badges—Cavalry.

	Regiment.	On Buttons.	On Collar of Tunic and Frock.	On Full Dress Head-dress.	On Waist-Plate.	On the Pouch.	On Field Cap.	No. of Plate.
61002 / 6783 / 61002 / Cav. / 131	14th (King's) Hussars.	Full dome, gilt, burnished.	The Eagle in gilt or gilding metal.	On puggaree:—The Eagle in silver on a gilt or gilding metal shield inscribed "14th Hussars."	... ...	In gilt or gilding metal, the Royal Cypher and Crown.	The Eagle in gold embroidery, 2 inches in height.	50
61002 / Cavalry / 56	15th (King's) Hussars.	Full dome, gilt, burnished.	In gilt or gilding metal the Royal Crest, with a scroll below, in silver, inscribed "Merebimur."	... ...	... ...	... ...	In gilt or gilding metal the Garter and Motto; below the Garter "XV K.H."; below the letters a scroll, inscribed "Merebimur," in silver, filled in blue enamel. Within the Garter, in silver, the Royal Crest.	50
... / 114	16th (Queen's) Lancers.	A Crown with "Q. L." below. 16	In silver, the figures "16" and a scroll below inscribed "Queen's Lancers" on a pair of crossed lances, between the pennons, a Crown; the lower part of the pennons in silver, the remainder of the lances and the Crown in gilt or gilding metal.	The universal plate in gilt or gilding metal. On the plate, in silver, the Royal Arms. On the lower part of the plate, scrolls inscribed with the honours of the regiment. In the centre of the plate at the bottom a scroll inscribed "16th Lancers."	... ...	In gilt metal the Royal Cypher and Crown.	As for collar.	50
61002 / Cavalry / 92	17th (Duke of Cambridge's Own) Lancers.	Full dome, gilt, burnished, with the death's head.	In silver, the death's head and scroll, inscribed "Or Glory."	In silver, the Royal Arms with the death's head and scroll, inscribed "Or Glory," and the letters "D.C.O." below. On the right a branch of laurel, and on the left a branch of oak; on the sprays are six scrolls inscribed with battles as on the colours. A scroll at the bottom of the plate inscribed "17th Lancers."	... ...	The Royal Cypher and Crown in gilt or gilding metal.	As for collar.	50
61002 / Cavalry / 76	18th Hussars.	Full dome, gilt, burnished.	In gilt or gilding metal, within a laurel wreath, a circle inscribed *Pro patria conamur*, surmounted by a Crown. On the right side of the wreath a scroll inscribed "Waterloo," on the left side a scroll inscribed "Peninsula." Within the circle, in silver, "18" H.	... ...	... ...	The Royal Cypher and Crown in gilt or gilding metal.	As for collar.	50
61002 / Cavalry / 87 / ... / 135	19th (Princess of Wales's Own) Hussars.	Full dome, gilt, burnished.	The Dagmar Cross, in silver.	... ...	... ...	The Royal Cypher and Crown in gilt or gilding metal.	In silver, the elephant with a scroll below inscribed "19th P.W.O. Hussars."	50
61002 / Cavalry / 134	20th Hussars.	Full dome, gilt, burnished.	In gilt or gilding metal the letters "xHx" surmounted by a Crown.	... ...	... ...	The Royal Cypher and Crown in gilt or gilding metal.	As for collar.	50
61002 / Cavalry / 108 / ... / 120 / ... / 175	21st Lancers.	Scalloped edge. Between the numerals "XXI," a pair of upright lances. Between the pennons, a Crown.	In gilt or gilding metal a pair of crossed lances; between the pennons a Crown; upon the staves "XXI." The lower part of the pennon in silver.	In silver, on crossed lances, the Royal Arms with a scroll below, inscribed "Khartoum." Below the scroll the Imperial Cypher. On the right a spray of laurel with a scroll below, inscribed "21st (Empress of," and on the left, palm leaves with a scroll below, inscribed "India's) Lancers."	... ...	The Imperial Cypher and Crown in gilt or gilding metal.	In gilt or gilding metal, a pair of crossed lances; between lances the Imperial Cypher and Crown; upon the staves, "XXI." The lower part of the pennons in silver.	50

Badges—Royal Artillery, Royal Engineers, Foot Guards.

Regiment.	On Buttons.	On Collar of Tunic and Frock.	On Full-Dress Head-Dress.	On Waist-Plate.	On the Pouch.	On Field Cap.	No. of Plate.
Royal Horse Artillery. Field Artillery. Garrison Artillery. 61002 / 6266	A Gun and Crown in gilt burnished metal.	A grenade embroidered in frosted silver for the tunic, and in gold embroidery for the frock.	(*Not worn by R.H.A.*) In gilt or gilding metal. The Royal Arms with gun below. *Ubique* above, and *Quo fas et gloria ducunt* below the gun. On the puggaree, a grenade in gilt or gilding metal.	Royal Field and Garrison Artillery, full dress:— Gilt or gilding metal snake hook fastening, inscribed *Ubique*, and two oval gilt or gilding metal plates bearing the Royal Crest. Undress:— Gilt rectangular seeded plate, with burnished edges; on the plate, the centre of the Royal Arms, surmounted by a Crown; on either side a spray of rose, shamrock, and thistle. *Ubique* on a scroll below.	An embroidered device of the Royal Arms above oak and laurel wreath with *Ubique* between. Below the wreath the gun in gilt or gilding metal above the motto *Quo fas et gloria ducunt,* in gold embroidery. The Crown the centre of the Royal Arms, and the mottoes on a scarlet velvet ground. A similar device is worn on the sabretache.	A grenade in gold embroidery, with a scroll under it, bearing the motto *Ubique* in silver embroidery, on a scarlet ground.	51
··· 5834 / 61002 / 6266 **Royal Artillery (Militia).**	As above.	As above.	The letter M, in silver, is added below the gun and above the bottom scroll.	As above.	As above.	The grenade only in gold embroidery.	
61002 / Artillery / 33 **Royal Malta Artillery.**	As for Royal Artillery.	As for Royal Artillery.	Within a wreath, surmounted by a Crown, the Garter inscribed "Royal Malta Artillery." Within the Garter the Maltese Cross. The gun below the wreath.	As for Royal Artillery, but smaller. "Malta" substituted for *Ubique,* and the Maltese Cross for the Royal Crest.	As for helmet-plate. The gun in gilt or gilding metal. The Cross in silver and the rest of the device in gold embroidery.	In gilt or gilding metal a circle inscribed "Royal Malta Artillery," surmounted by a Crown. Within the circle the Maltese Cross in silver; upon the Cross, in gilt or gilding metal, the gun.	51
61002 / 6267 **Royal Engineers.** 61002 / 5891	The Garter, inscribed "Royal Engineers" surmounted by a Crown. Within the Garter, the Royal Cypher.	A grenade in embroidery 2¼ inches in length. In gold, on the frock and mess jacket, In silver, on the tunic.	As for R.A., but with the gun omitted. On the puggaree. In gilt or gilding metal, within a laurel wreath the Garter, inscribed "Royal Engineers," surmounted by a Crown. Within the Garter the Royal Cypher pierced.	On a burnished rectangular plate, in silver, within a laurel wreath, the device as on the buttons; the Garter and Cypher are pierced.	As for full dress head-dress, but smaller.	A grenade in gold embroidery, with a scroll under, bearing the motto *Ubique* in silver embroidery on a light blue ground.	51
Royal Engineers (Militia).	As for Royal Engineers, but with "Militia Engineers" on the Garter.	As for Royal Engineers.	As for Royal Engineers, but with "Militia" added on a smaller scroll.	As for full dress head-dress.	As for full dress head-dress.	As for Royal Engineers, but with the abbreviated designation of the corps substituted for *Ubique* on the scroll.	
61002 / 6238 **Grenadier Guards.** 61002 / 617	The Royal Cypher reversed and interlaced, surmounted by the Crown; a grenade beneath the Cypher in the centre.	A grenade in silver embroidery, on a gold lace ground. On the frock for service abroad a grenade in gold embroidery.	On the bearskin—no badge. On the white helmet, in gilt metal, the Royal Cypher reversed and entwined on a ground of red enamel within the Garter, surmounted by the Crown. The motto pierced on a ground of blue enamel.	A grenade in silver. On a frosted gilt centre, the Royal Cypher reversed and intertwined. On the circle "Grenadier Guards."	Medical Officers: In gilt metal, the Royal Cypher reversed and intertwined, surmounted by the Crown; a grenade beneath the Cypher in the centre.	A grenade in gold thread embroidery, on blue cloth ground, on field and forage cap.	52
61002 / Infantry / 229 **Coldstream Guards.** 61002 / 6832	The Star of the Order of the Garter.	In silver embroidery on a gold lace ground, the Star of the Order of the Garter. A similar badge on the collar of the frock; the Garter and motto in gold; the cross in scarlet silk.	On the bearskin—no badge. On the white helmet, in silver, the Star of the Order of the Garter.	In silver, on a frosted gilt ground, the Star of the Order of the Garter; "Coldstream Guards" on the outer circle.	Medical Officers: In silver, the Star of the Order of the Garter.	In silver, the Star of the Order of the Garter. The Garter and motto in gilt metal, the cross in red enamel. A similar badge on the forage cap.	52
Scots Guards.	The Star of the Order of the Thistle, with Crown in place of the upper point of the Star.	The Thistle in silver embroidery on a gold lace ground.	On the bearskin—no badge. On the white helmet—the Star of the Order of the Thistle.	In cut silver on a gold ground, the Star of the Order of the Thistle. In gilt metal, the Thistle and Motto within the Star. On the circle "Scots Guards."	Medical Officers: The Star of the Order of the Thistle, as on the waist plate.	In silver, the Star of the Order of the Thistle; the circle with motto, and the centre in gilt metal. Height 1 inch. A similar badge on the forage cap, but larger.	52

Badges—Infantry.

Regiment.	On Buttons.	On Collar. See paragraph 567.	On Helmet-Plates; Ornaments for Bear or Racoon-Skin Caps, and Highland Head-dress.	On the Waist Plate.	On the Forage Cap.	On the Field Cap (or Glengarry).	No. of Plate.
61002 / 63C2 The Royal Scots (Lothian Regiment).	The badge of the Order of the Thistle; below the badge, "The Royal Scots."	The Thistle, in gold embroidery, on a blue cloth ground.	The Garter and universal wreath are omitted. The Star of the Order of the Thistle, in gilt or gilding metal. On the star, a silver circle, pierced *Nemo me impune lacessit;* the ground of green enamel. Within the circle, on a convex ground of green enamel, the Thistle, in silver. On the universal scroll "The Royal Scots."	Special pattern. On a gilt or gilding metal rectangular plate, 2⅝ by 2⅜ in., the badge in silver as approved for the glengarry.	Not worn.	In silver, the Star of the Order of the Thistle; in gilt or gilding metal on the Star a raised circle inscribed *Nemo me impune lacessit.* Within the circle, on a ground of green enamel, the Thistle in gilt or gilding metal.	53
61002 / 6918 The Queen's (Royal West Surrey Regiment).	Within a circle surmounted by the Crown, the Paschal Lamb. On the circle "The Royal West Surrey Regiment." Below the circle, a scroll inscribed "The Queen's." For the field cap and mess dress, plain gold —the Lamb in silver, —mounted.	The Paschal Lamb, in frosted gilt or gilding metal. In silver a scroll below inscribed "The Queen's."	On a scarlet velvet ground, the Paschal Lamb in silver. On the universal scroll "The Royal West Surrey Regiment."	On a frosted gilt or gilding metal centre, the Paschal Lamb in silver. On the circle, *Pristinæ virtutis memor.*	In gold embroidery, on a blue cloth ground, the Paschal Lamb: the flag in silver with crimson cross.	As for left collar badge, but 1¼ inches in height.	53
61002 / 5510 ... Infantry 197 61002 / 6918 The Buffs (East Kent Regiment).	A circle surmounted by the Crown. On the circle "The East Kent Regt. The Buffs"; within, the Dragon; below, on a scroll, *Veteri frondescit honore.* For the field cap and mess waistcoat, plain gilt. The Dragon over a scroll, inscribed "The Buffs," in silver, —mounted.	The Dragon, in silver.	On a black velvet ground, the Dragon, in silver. On the universal scroll, "The East Kent Regiment." Above the Garter a scroll inscribed "The Buffs."	On a frosted gilt or gilding metal centre, the Dragon, in silver. On the circle "The East Kent Regt. The Buffs."	The Dragon, in gold embroidery.	The Dragon, in silver. On a scroll beneath, "The Buffs."	53
61002 / 6024 The King's Own (Royal Lancaster Regiment).	The Lion of England with Crown above and Rose below. On circle "The King's Own Royal Lancaster Regt."	The Lion, in silver.	In silver, on a crimson velvet ground, the Lion of England. On the universal scroll "Royal Lancaster Regt."	In silver, on a frosted gilt or gilding metal centre, the Lion. Below the Lion, in gilt or gilding metal and red enamel, the Rose of Lancaster. On the circle, "The King's Own Royal Lancaster Regt."	In gold embroidery, the Lion, with the Rose of Lancaster below.	The Lion in silver. Below the Lion, "The King's Own."	53
61002 / 6331 61002 / 6918 The Northumberland Fusiliers.	St. George and the Dragon within a Garter inscribed *Quo fata vocant.* For the field cap and mess dress, the centre is in silver, —mounted.	A grenade in gold embroidery, with St. George and the Dragon in silver on the ball.	A grenade in gilt or gilding metal. On the ball, a Garter inscribed *Quo fata vocant.* Within the Garter —St. George and the Dragon.	In silver, on a frosted gilt or gilding metal centre, St. George and the Dragon, with scroll above inscribed *Quo fata vocant.* On the circle "Northumberland Fusiliers."	A grenade, in gold embroidery, with St. George and the Dragon in silver, on the ball.	A grenade in gilt or gilding metal; on the ball in silver, St. George and the Dragon within a circle inscribed "Northumberland Fusiliers."	53
61002 / 5954 ... 6918 The Royal Warwickshire Regiment.	An antelope with collar and chain within a circle, inscribed "The Royal Warwickshire Regiment." The circle surmounted by the Crown. For the field cap and mess dress, the button is mounted, the Antelope in silver.	In frosted silver, the Antelope, with gilt or gilding metal collar and chain.	On a black velvet ground, the Antelope, in silver, with gilt or gilding metal collar and chain. On the universal scroll "The Royal Warwickshire Regiment."	The Antelope, in silver, with gilt or gilding metal collar and chain, on a frosted gilt or gilding metal centre. On the circle, "The Royal Warwickshire."	In gilt or gilding metal, the Garter, with motto *Honi soit qui mal y pense,* within a wreath of laurel, in gold embroidery. The Garter surmounted by the Crown in gold embroidery, with a crimson cap. Within the Garter, on a silver blue enamelled ground, the Antelope in silver, with gilt collar and chain.	In silver, the Antelope, with collar and chain. On a scroll below, "Royal Warwickshire."	53
61002 / 6484 The Royal Fusiliers (City of London Regiment).	The Garter inscribed *Honi soit qui mal y pense;* on the Garter at the top, the Crown; within, the Rose.	A grenade, in embroidery, with the White Rose, in silver, on the ball.	In gilt or gilding metal, a grenade; on the ball, the Garter surmounted by the Crown. The Garter pierced with the motto; the ground of blue enamel. Within the Garter, the Rose; below the Garter, in silver, the White Horse. On the puggaree a similar badge, but smaller, and without the White Horse.	In silver, on a frosted gilt or gilding metal centre, the White Rose, with Crown above. On the circle "The Royal Fusiliers."	A grenade, in gold embroidery, with a Crown on the flame; recessed in the ball, the garter pierced with the motto; the ground of blue enamel. The White Rose, in silver, in the centre of the Garter.	As for collar.	53

Badges—Infantry.

Regiment.	On Buttons.	On Collar. See paragraph 567.	On Helmet-Plates; Ornaments for Bear or Racoon skin Caps, and Highland Head-dress.	On the Waist Plate.	On the Forage Cap	On the Field Cap (or Glengarry).	No. of Plate.
61003 5063 ... 6330 ... 6918 **The King's (Liverpool Regiment).**	A circle surmounted by the Crown within a laurel wreath: the circle inscribed "The Liverpool Regiment:" within the circle, the White Horse, with a scroll above inscribed *Nec aspera terrent.* Scroll on wreath at the bottom inscribed "The King's." For the field cap and mess dress, the button is mounted, design as for collar badge, a scroll above inscribed, "Nec aspera terrent."	In silver, the White Horse. A gilt or gilding metal scroll below, inscribed "The Kings."	In silver, on a crimson velvet ground, the White Horse, with scroll above inscribed in old English capitals, *Nec aspera terrent.* On the universal scroll "The Liverpool Regiment."	In silver, on a frosted gilt or gilding metal centre, the White Horse, with a scroll above, inscribed in old English capitals, *Nec aspera terrent.* On the circle, "The King's —The Liverpool Regt."	In gilt or gilding metal, the Garter pierced with the motto *Honi soit qui mal y pense;* the ground of blue velvet. Within the Garter, on a crimson velvet raised ground, the White Horse, in silver, and a gilt or gilding metal scroll below, inscribed "King's" in old English capitals.	In silver, the White Horse. A gilt or gilding metal scroll below, inscribed "The King's."	53
61002 Infantry 284 61002 6783 **The Norfolk Regiment.**	On the circle "The Norfolk Regiment"; within the circle the figure of Britannia holding an olive branch in the right hand; the trident rests against the left shoulder.	The figure of Britannia, in gilt or gilding metal on the tunic and frocks. On the mess jacket, in gold embroidery.	The figure of Britannia, in silver, on a black velvet ground. On the universal scroll "The Norfolk Regiment."	The figure of Britannia, with Castle of Norwich below, in silver, on a frosted gilt or gilding metal centre. On the circle, "The Norfolk Regiment."	The figure of Britannia, in gold embroidery; the shield embroidered in gold and silk.	In gilt or gilding metal, the figure of Britannia; a tablet below, inscribed "The Norfolk Regt."	53
61002 6026 61002 7 6918 **The Lincolnshire Regiment.**	Within a laurel wreath, a circle surmounted by the Crown. On the circle "The Lincolnshire Regt."; within, the Sphinx over Egypt. For the field cap and mess dress, plain gilt; the Sphinx over Egypt in silver,—mounted.	On a silver eight-pointed star, a circle in gilt or gilding metal, inscribed "Lincolnshire Regiment." Within the circle, on a ground of blue velvet, the Sphinx over Egypt, in silver.	In silver, on a black velvet ground, the Sphinx over Egypt. On the universal scroll "The Lincolnshire Regt."	In silver, on a frosted gilt or gilding metal centre, the Sphinx over Egypt. On the circle "The Lincolnshire Regiment."	In gilt or gilding metal, on a silver eight-pointed star, a circle inscribed "Lincolnshire Regiment." Within the circle, on a raised ground of blue velvet, the Sphinx over Egypt, in silver.	As for centre of helmet-plate. A gilt or gilding metal scroll below, inscribed "Lincolnshire." Egypt.	54
61002 Infantry 10 61002 6918 **The Devonshire Regiment.**	On an eight-pointed star a circle surmounted by the Crown. On the circle "The Devonshire Regt.," within, the Castle of Exeter. For the mess dress, the design is in silver,—mounted.	In gilt or gilding metal, on a bright cut silver eight-pointed star, a circle surmounted by the Crown. On the circle "The Devonshire Regiment"; within, in silver, the Castle of Exeter with scroll inscribed *Semper fidelis,* on a ground of blue velvet.	The Castle of Exeter, with scroll inscribed *Semper fidelis,* in silver, on a black velvet ground. On the universal scroll "The Devonshire Regt."	As for helmet-plate on a frosted gilt or gilding metal centre. On the circle "The Devonshire Regiment."	As for collar badge, except that the circle is pierced with the designation of the Regiment, the ground is of blue velvet, the Crown on a crimson velvet cushion.	As for collar badge.	54
61002 Infantry 64 61002 6918 **The Suffolk Regiment.**	Within a laurel wreath, the Castle and Key with scroll above inscribed "Gibraltar," and above the scroll, the Crown. Below the Castle and Key, two scrolls, the upper inscribed *Montis Insignia Calpe,* the lower "The Suffolk Regt." For the mess waistcoat the wreath is omitted, and the design is in silver,—mounted.	The Castle and Key, in gold embroidery.	In silver, on a black velvet ground, the Castle and Key, with scroll above inscribed "Gibraltar," and scroll below inscribed *Montis Insignia Calpe.* On the universal scroll "The Suffolk Regiment."	In silver, on a frosted gilt or gilding metal centre, the Castle and Key with scroll above inscribed "Gibraltar," and scroll below inscribed *Montis insignia Calpe.* On the circle "The Suffolk Regiment."	In gold embroidery, on a raised blue cloth ground, the Castle and Key within a wreath of laurel; above the Castle the Crown; below, a scroll in blue velvet inscribed "Gibraltar." The Crown on a crimson cushion.	In silver, within a circle inscribed:— *Montis insignia calpe,* the Castle and Key, surmounted by a scroll inscribed "Gibraltar"; above the circle, the Crown; surrounding the circle, an oak-leaf wreath. Below the circle, upon the wreath, a scroll inscribed :—"The Suffolk Regiment."	54
61002 Infantry 8 61002 6918 **The Prince Albert's (Somersetshire Light Infantry).**	Within a laurel wreath, a circle surmounted by a mural crown. On the circle, "The Prince Albert's"; within, a bugle with strings. For the field cap—plain gilt, with the bugle in silver,—mounted. For the mess dress—the bugle surmounted by a mural crown, with a scroll above, inscribed "Jellalabad" — the whole in silver,—mounted.	In gold and silver embroidery, on a ground of green cloth, a bugle with strings, surmounted by a mural crown embroidered in silver; above the crown, in gold embroidery, a scroll inscribed "Jellalabad."	In silver, on a black velvet ground, a bugle with strings, surmounted by a mural crown with scroll above inscribed "Jellalabad"; the Sphinx over Egypt within the strings of the bugle. On the scroll, "Somersetshire Light Infantry."	On a frosted gilt or gilding metal centre, badge as for helmet-plate. On the circle, "The Prince Albert's," with two transverse twigs of laurel in the lower bend.	Not worn.	In silver, a bugle: within the strings, the Cypher of H.R.H. the late Prince Consort. Above the bugle a mural crown surmounted by a scroll inscribed "Jellalabad."	54
61002 6360 61002 6918 **The Prince of Wales's Own (West Yorkshire Regiment).**	The Tiger, within a circle, inscribed at the top, "India," and at the bottom, "Waterloo." Outside the circle, "Prince of Wales's Own, West Yorkshire." For the field cap, plain gilt, the tiger in silver,—mounted.	The Prince of Wales's Plume, in gold and silver embroidery.	In silver, on a black velvet ground, the White Horse, with motto *Nec aspera terrent* on a scroll above. On the universal scroll "The West Yorkshire Regiment."	The Royal Tiger, in silver, on a frosted gilt or gilding metal centre. On the circle "West Yorkshire Regiment."	On a blue cloth ground, the White Horse in silver; above, the Prince of Wales's Plume, in gold and silver embroidery; below, a gold embroidered scroll, inscribed "West Yorkshire."	In silver, the White Horse above a gilt or gilding metal scroll, inscribed "West Yorkshire."	54

Badges—Infantry.

Regiment.	On Buttons.	On Collar. See paragraph 567.	On Helmet-Plates; Ornaments for Bear or Racoon skin Caps and Highland Head-dress.	On the Waist Plate.	On the Forage Cap.	On the Field Cap (or Glengarry).	No. of Plate.
61002 / Infantry / 9 — The East Yorkshire Regiment.	A laurel wreath on an eight-pointed star. The White Rose, in silver, within the wreath.	In gilt or gilding metal, an eight-pointed star; on the star a laurel wreath; within the wreath, on a ground of black enamel, the White Rose, in silver.	In gilt or gilding metal, on a ground of black enamel, a laurel wreath on an eight-pointed star. Within the wreath the White Rose, in silver. On the universal scroll, "The East Yorkshire Regt."	On a frosted gilt or gilding metal centre, badge as for helmet-plate. On the circle, "The East Yorkshire Regiment."	In gilt or gilding metal, star, etc., as for helmet-plate, but larger.	In gilt or gilding metal, badge as for centre of helmet-plate, but with a gilt or gilding metal ground; a scroll below, inscribed "East Yorkshire."	54
61002 / 6151 / ... / Infantry / 404 — The Bedfordshire Regiment.	On an eight-pointed star, a Maltese cross. On the cross, a circle inscribed "Bedfordshire." Within the circle, a Hart crossing a ford.	In dead gilt or gilding metal, a Hart crossing a ford; the water in silver. On a scroll below "Bedfordshire."	In silver, on a black velvet ground an eight-pointed star; on the star, in gilt or gilding metal, a Maltese cross. Within a gilt or gilding metal circle on the cross, in silver, a Hart crossing a ford, the Hart on blue enamel. On the universal scroll, "The Bedfordshire Regt."	On a frosted gilt or gilding metal centre, badge as for helmet-plate, except that the Garter, inscribed *Honi soit qui mal y pense*, is substituted for the circle on the centre of the cross. On the circle "Bedfordshire Regiment."	In gilt or gilding metal, a Maltese cross on an eight-pointed star. On the cross, the Garter, with motto; within the Garter, on a raised ground of blue enamel, the Hart crossing a ford, in silver. The ground of the ford in gilt or gilding metal. A silver scroll inscribed "Bedfordshire" below the Garter.	As for Forage Cap, but the cross, etc., in silver, and the scroll in gilt or gilding metal.	54
61002 / 6496 — The Leicestershire Regiment. 61002 / 6918	Within a laurel wreath, the Royal Tiger, with scroll above, inscribed "Hindoostan," and scroll below, inscribed "Leicestershire." [For the field cap, plain gilt, the Tiger in silver, —mounted.	The Royal Tiger in silver, within a wreath in gilt or gilding metal.	On a black velvet ground, the Royal Tiger in silver, with silver scroll above, inscribed "Hindoostan." On the universal scroll, "Leicestershire Regiment."	In silver, on a frosted gilt or gilding metal centre, the Royal Tiger, with the Irish Harp below, and scroll above inscribed "Hindoostan." On the circle "Leicestershire Regiment."	An eight-pointed star in gilt or gilding metal; on the star, in silver, the Royal Tiger, with the Harp below. Above the Tiger, a scroll inscribed "Hindoostan"; below and at either side of the Harp, a scroll inscribed "Leicestershire Regiment."	In gilt or gilding metal, the Tiger. In silver, above the Tiger, a scroll inscribed "Hindoostan"; below the Tiger, another scroll inscribed "Leicestershire."	54
61002 / 5468 — The Royal Irish Regiment. 61002 / 6918	Within a shamrock wreath, a circle inscribed *Virtutis Namurcensis Præmium.* Within the circle, the Harp; the circle surmounted by the Crown. [For the field cap, plain gilt with the harp and crown within a wreath, in silver,—mounted.	In silver, an Escutcheon of the Arms of Nassau, with a silver scroll below, inscribed *Virtutis Namurcensis Præmium.*	In silver, on a scarlet ground, the Harp and Crown within a wreath of shamrock. On the universal scroll "The Royal Irish."	On a frosted gilt or gilding metal centre, badge as for helmet-plate. On the circle "The Royal Irish Regiment."	The Harp and Crown, in gold embroidery, on a blue cloth ground. The Crown on a crimson velvet cap.	In silver, the Harp and Crown with a scroll below inscribed "The Royal Irish Regiment."	54
61002 / 6367 / 61002 / Infantry / 137 — The Princess of Wales's Own (Yorkshire Regiment). 61002 / 6918	The Cypher of H.R.H. the Princess of Wales combined with a cross, and surmounted by the Coronet of the Princess. On the cross the figures 1875. On scroll below, "The Princess of Wales's Own." [For the field cap and mess dress, the Dagmar Cross is in silver,—mounted. The scroll is omitted.	The Cypher of H.R.H. the Princess of Wales, combined with a cross. The Cypher and Coronet in gold embroidery on a crimson velvet cap; the cross in silver embroidery.	On a black velvet ground, the Cypher of H.R.H. the Princess of Wales combined with a cross, and surmounted by the Coronet of the Princess. On the centre of the cross, the figures 1875. The Cypher and Coronet in gilt or gilding metal; the cross in silver. On the universal scroll "The Yorkshire Regiment."	On a frosted gilt or gilding metal centre, badge as for helmet-plate. On the circle "The Yorkshire Regiment."	As for helmet-plate, but in embroidery; the Princess's Cypher, the Coronet, and the figures 1875, in gold embroidery; the cross in silver embroidery, edged with crimson. Blue cloth ground.	In silver, an oak leaf wreath, upon the upper bend of the wreath a scroll inscribed "The Princess of Wales's Own," on the lower bend "Yorkshire." Within the wreath in gilt or gilding metal as for centre of helmet plate.	55
61002 / 6367 — The Lancashire Fusiliers.	Within a wreath of laurel, the Sphinx over Egypt, with the Crown above.	A grenade, in gold embroidery.	A grenade in gilt or gilding metal; on the ball, in silver, the Sphinx over Egypt within a laurel wreath.	On a frosted gilt or gilding metal centre, badge as for the grenade on the full dress head dress, but smaller. On the circle "The Lancashire Fusiliers."	A grenade in gold embroidery, with badge in silver, as for waist-plate.	In gilt or gilding metal, a grenade; on the ball, the Sphinx over "Egypt" within a laurel wreath. Below the grenade, a scroll in silver inscribed "The Lancashire Fusiliers."	55

Badges—Infantry.

Regiment.	On Buttons.	On Collar. See paragraph 567.	On Helmet-Plates; Ornaments for Bear or Racoon skin Caps and Highland Head-dress.	On the Waist Plate.	On the Forage Cap.	On the Field Cap (or Glengarry).	No. of Plate.
The Royal Scots Fusiliers. (61C02 / 6302 … Infantry 180)	The Thistle, surmounted by the Crown.	A grenade in silver embroidery; on the ball of the grenade, the Thistle, in silver metal. On the mess-jacket, gold embroidery with thistle in silver.	A grenade in gilt or gilding metal; on the ball of the grenade, the Royal Arms. Also worn on the Foreign Service Helmet.	Special pattern. In silver, on a frosted gilt rectangular plate, a wreath of thistles; within the wreath, the figure of St. Andrew with cross. On the wreath, at the bottom, a silver scroll, inscribed "Royal Scots Fusiliers."	Not worn. — On the shoulder belt. Burnished gilt rectangular plate. In silver, a thistle, within a circle, inscribed *Nemo me impune lacesset*, surmounted by a crown. The Maltese cross in the lower bend of the circle. Below the circle, a scroll inscribed "Royal Scots Fusiliers." Below the scroll "1678" in gilt metal.	As for Fusilier cap, but smaller. (Glengarry only.)	55
The Cheshire Regiment. (61002 / 6666)	On an eight-pointed star, a circle with acorn and oak-leaves in the centre. On the circle "The Cheshire Regiment."	Acorn with oak-leaves. The leaves and cup in dead gilt or gilding metal; the acorn in burnished silver.	In silver, on a black velvet ground, an eight-pointed star. Within a gilt or gilding metal circle on the star, the Prince of Wales's Plume on a burnished silver ground. The plume in silver, the coronet in gilt or gilding metal. On the universal scroll "The Cheshire Regiment."	On a frosted gilt or gilding metal centre, badge as for helmet-plate, but smaller. On the circle "Cheshire Regiment."	On the forage cap. — On a bright cut-silver eight-pointed star, a gilt or gilding metal circle with a gilt acorn and oak-leaves in the centre on a ground of silver-green enamel. On the circle "The Cheshire Regiment."	In silver, an eight-pointed star with a scroll below inscribed "Cheshire." On the star, in gilt or gilding metal, the acorn with oak-leaves.	55
The Royal Welsh Fusiliers. (61002 / Infantry 70 / 61002 / 6918)	The Prince of Wales's Plume within the designation "The Royal Welsh Fusiliers." For the field cap and mess waistcoat, a gilt-lined button with burnished edge, below the plume "R.W.F."	A grenade, in silver embroidery	A grenade in gilt or gilding metal; the Prince of Wales's Plume, in silver on the ball.	In silver, on a frosted gilt or gilding metal centre, the Prince of Wales's Plume. On the circle "Royal Welsh Fusiliers."	A grenade in gold embroidery. The Red Dragon in silver, on the ball.	A grenade in gilt or gilding metal; on the ball, in silver, a circle (frosted), inscribed "Royal Welsh Fusiliers." Within the circle, the Prince of Wales's plume, with gilt or gilding metal coronet.	55
The South Wales Borderers. (61002 / 5969 / 61002 / 6918)	The Welsh Dragon within a wreath of laurel. For the mess dress, the dragon in silver,—mounted on a plain gilt button.	The Sphinx over Egypt in dead gilt or gilding metal.	In silver, on a black velvet ground, the Welsh Dragon, within a laurel wreath. On the universal scroll "The South Wales Borderers."	On a frosted gilt or gilding metal centre, badge as for helmet-plate. On the circle "The South Wales Borderers."	In silver, within a gilt or gilding metal laurel wreath, the Welsh Dragon on a raised ground of black velvet. The Crown in gilt or gilding metal above the Dragon.	In silver, within a wreath of immortelles, the sphinx over Egypt. On the lower bend of the wreath the letters "S.W.B." in burnished silver.	55
The King's Own Scottish Borderers. (61002 / 6302 / 61002 / 5918)	The Royal Crest, within the designation "King's Own Scottish Borderers." For the mess dress, the Royal Crest over K.O.S.B. in silver,—mounted on a plain button.	On a dark blue cloth ground, the Castle of Edinburgh in silver embroidery. A flag in blue and crimson embroidery flies from each tower. The Castle rests on thistle leaves, etc., in gold embroidery. Beneath the gold embroidery a scroll, inscribed "The King's Own Scottish Borderers," on a ground of light blue silk.	In silver, a thistle wreath; within the wreath a circle pierced with the designation, "King's Own Scottish Borderers." Above the circle a scroll surmounted by the Royal Crest. The scroll pierced with the motto, *In veritate religionis confido*. Over the circle, the Cross of St. Andrew in burnished silver. On the cross, the Castle of Edinburgh. On the wreath at the bottom of the circle, a scroll with the motto in relief, *Nisi Dominus frustra*.	On a frosted gilt or gilding metal rectangular plate with bevelled edges burnished, the Cross of St. Andrew in burnished silver; on the cross, thistle wreath in silver; within the wreath and on the cross, the Castle of Edinburgh in silver.	Not worn.	As for centre of helmet plate.	55

Badges—Infantry.

Regiment.	On Buttons.	On Collar. See paragraph 567.	On Helmet-Plates: Ornaments for Bear or Racoon skin Caps and Highland Head-dress.	On the Waist Plate.	On the Forage Cap.	On the Field Cap (or Glengarry).	No. of Plate.
61002 / Infantry / 214 **The Cameronians (Scottish Rifles).**	Within a thistle wreath, a bugle with strings; above the bugle the Crown.	No badge.	On the chaco, in bronze, a bugle and strings; above the bugle a mullet on a black corded boss. On the puggaree, in silver, a mullet with a scroll below, inscribed "The Cameronians."	Special pattern. In silver, on a frosted silver rectangular plate with burnished edges, a thistle wreath. Within the wreath, in burnished silver, a mullet surmounted by a Crown. On the bottom of the wreath, a bugle with strings.	No badge. On the shoulder belt. In silver, a thistle wreath surmounted by a crown. Within the wreath, the mullet and bugle. On the lower bend of the wreath, a scroll inscribed "The Scottish Rifles." The ground of the plate frosted.	In silver, a mullet within a thistle wreath. On the lower bend of the wreath, a bugle and strings.	55
61002 / Infantry / 65 61002 / 6918 **The Royal Inniskilling Fusiliers.**	A castle with three turrets with St. George's colours flying, superscribed "Inniskilling.' For the field cap and mess dress the castle is in silver,—mounted on a plain gilt button.	A grenade in gold embroidery; the Castle, in silver, on the ball.	A grenade in gilt or gilding metal; the Castle, in silver, on the ball.	Special Pattern. In gilt or gilding metal, on a round burnished gilt plate, a deep laurel wreath intertwined with a silver scroll bearing the battles of the Regiment. Within the wreath, in silver, on a ground of gilt or gilding metal, the White Horse, with motto *Nec aspera terrent* on a scroll, in gilt or gilding metal below. Above the White Horse, a grenade, in gilt or gilding metal; on the ball of the grenade, in silver, the Castle of Inniskilling with scroll above, inscribed "Inniskilling." On the wreath, at the bottom, in gilt or gilding metal, the Sphinx over Egypt.	On the forage cap. A grenade in gold embroidery; the Castle, in silver, on the ball.	As for full dress head-dress. Below the Castle a scroll in silver inscribed "Inniskilling."	56
61002 / 5714 61002 / Infantry / 20 61002 / 6918 **The Gloucestershire Regiment.**	Within a laurel wreath of single leaves, inclining inwards, the Royal Crest above the monogram G.R. For the mess dress the wreath is omitted and the design is engraved.	In dead gilt or gilding metal, on two twigs of laurel, the Sphinx over Egypt. On collar of mess jacket, the badge is in embroidery.	In silver, on a black velvet ground, the Sphinx over Egypt. On the universal scroll, "The Gloucestershire Regiment." Badge for back of helmet— In dead gilt or gilding metal, the Sphinx over Egypt within a laurel wreath.	In silver, on a frosted gilt or gilding metal centre, the Sphinx over Egypt. On the circle, "Gloucestershire Regiment."	In gilt or gilding metal and red enamel, the Arms of the City of Gloucester surmounted by the Sphinx over Egypt on two twigs of laurel. Below the shield, a gilt or gilding metal scroll inscribed, in silver, "Gloucestershire Regiment."	In silver, within two twigs of laurel, the Sphinx over Egypt. On a scroll below, "Gloucestershire." Back badge as for helmet, but smaller.	56
61002 / 6081 61002 / 6918 **The Worcestershire Regiment.**	On an eight-pointed star, a circle surmounted by the Crown. The circle inscribed "The Worcestershire Regiment." Within the circle, a lion. Below the circle, a scroll, inscribed "Firm." For the mess dress the design is engraved.	On a silver eight-pointed star, in gilt or gilding metal, the Garter with motto; within the Garter, in silver, the Lion, pierced on a black velvet ground Below the Garter, in gilt or gilding metal, a scroll inscribed "Firm."	On a black velvet ground, a silver eight-pointed star. On the star, in gilt or gilding metal, the Garter with motto. Within the Garter, the Lion, in silver on a black velvet ground. Below the Garter, a scroll in gilt or gilding metal, inscribed "Firm." On the universal scroll, "The Worcestershire Regiment."	On a gilt or gilding metal frosted centre, a silver eight-pointed star. On the star, in gilt or gilding metal, the Garter with motto; within the Garter, in silver, the Lion pierced on a black velvet ground. Below the Garter, in gilt or gilding metal, a scroll inscribed "Firm." On the circle "The Worcestershire Regiment."	In gold embroidery, an eight-pointed star. The Garter, in gilt or gilding metal, raised on the star, and pierced with the motto *Honi soit qui mal y pense;* the ground of black velvet. Within the Garter, in silver, the Lion pierced on a black velvet ground. Below the star, a scroll, in gold embroidery, inscribed "Firm;" the ground of blue cloth.	As for centre of helmet plate, but with enamel substituted for velvet. Below the star, a scroll in gilt or gilding metal inscribed "Worcestershire."	56
61002 / 6351 **The East Lancashire Regiment.**	Within a circle inscribed "The East Lancashire Regiment," the Sphinx over Egypt; below the Sphinx, the Rose of Lancaster.	The Rose of Lancaster, in red and gold embroidery.	In silver, on a black velvet ground, the Sphinx over Egypt. On the universal scroll, "The East Lancashire Regiment."	In silver, on a frosted gilt or gilding metal centre, the Sphinx over Egypt; below the Sphinx, the Rose in gilt or gilding metal. On the circle "The East Lancashire Regiment."	In red and gold embroidery, the Rose; above the Rose, in silver metal, the Sphinx over Egypt.	In silver, a laurel wreath surmounted by a Crown. Within the wreath the Sphinx over "Egypt"; on the lower part of the wreath a scroll inscribed "East Lancashire." Below "Egypt," and within the wreath, the Rose in gilt or gilding metal.	56

Badges—Infantry.

Regiment.	On Buttons.	On Collar. See paragraph 567.	On Helmet-Plates; Ornaments for Bear or Racoon skin Caps and Highland Head-dress.	On the Waist Plate.	On the Forage Cap.	On the Field Cap (or Glengarry).	No of Plate.
61002 / 4904 / ... / Infantry / 132 — The East Surrey Regiment.	On an eight-pointed star, a circle surmounted by the Crown. The circle inscribed "East Surrey," with two twigs of laurel in the lower bend. Within the circle, the arms of Guildford.	On a bright cut-silver star, the arms of Guildford, in silver, on a shield in frosted gilt or gilding metal, with burnished edges, surmounted by a gilt or gilding metal Crown.	In silver, on a black velvet ground, an eight-pointed star; on the star, badge as for collar, but without the Crown. On the universal scroll, "The East Surrey Regiment."	On a frosted gilt or gilding metal centre, badge as for helmet-plate. On the circle, "East Surrey Regiment."	On a bright cut-silver eight-pointed star, a raised gilt or gilding metal circle surmounted by the Crown. The circle pierced with the words "East Surrey," with two twigs of laurel in the lower bend; the ground of blue velvet. On a ground of blue velvet, the arms of Guildford in silver on a gilt or gilding metal shield. The cap of the Crown is of crimson velvet.	As for collar, but with a scroll in gilt or gilding metal inscribed "East Surrey" below the star.	56
61002 / Infantry / 88 — The Duke of Cornwall's Light Infantry.	Within the designation "Duke of Cornwall's Light Infy.," a bugle with strings, surmounted by the Coronet of the Prince of Wales, as shown on His Royal Highness's Great Seal as Duke of Cornwall.	In black enamel set in gilt or gilding metal, the badge of the County of Cornwall, surmounted by the Coronet, in gilt or gilding metal, of the Prince of Wales, as shown on His Royal Highness's Great Seal as Duke of Cornwall. On a scroll the motto *One and All*, pierced in gilt or gilding metal letters on a ground of blue velvet.	In gilt or gilding metal, on a ground of dark green velvet, a bugle with strings. On the strings of the bugle two red feathers set in gilt or gilding metal. On the stems of the feathers, in silver, a turreted archway. On the universal scroll, "The Duke of Cornwall's Lt. Infy."	Oak-leaf ends. In silver, on a frosted gilt centre, a bugle with strings. Above the bugle, the Coronet of the Prince of Wales, as described for the Collar badge, but in silver. On the circle, "The Duke of Cornwall's Light Infantry."	Not worn.	In silver, a bugle with strings surmounted by the Coronet. Below the Coronet a scroll inscribed "Cornwall."	56
61002 / 5943 / 61002 / Infantry / 289 / 61002 / 6918 — The Duke of Wellington's (West Riding Regiment).	Within the designation "Duke of Wellington's West Riding Regt." the Elephant with howdah. For the field cap and mess dress the elephant and howdah in silver,—mounted on a plain gilt ground.	The Elephant in dead gilt or gilding metal, with howdah. On the mess jacket, the Duke of Wellington's Crest in gold embroidery. The flag in silver, within a gold edging. The Cross scarlet.	In silver, on a black velvet ground, the Crest of the Duke of Wellington, with motto on a scroll below, *Virtutis fortuna comes*. On the universal scroll "The West Riding Regiment."	On a frosted gilt or gilding metal centre, the Elephant with howdah, in silver. On the circle "The West Riding Regiment."	In gold embroidery, the Crest of the Duke of Wellington, with motto on scroll below. Blue cloth ground. The Cross in red silk.	In silver; badge as for helmet-plate. A gilt or gilding metal scroll below, inscribed "The West Riding."	56
61002 / 6496 / ... / Infantry / 152 / 61002 / 6918 — The Border Regiment.	The Dragon of China, with the word "China" above. In the 3rd and 4th Battalions the word "China" is omitted. For the field cap and mess dress the design is as for the Collar bagde, with the lions and scroll omitted, in silver,—mounted on a plain gilt ground.	In silver, a laurel wreath; on the wreath a Maltese Cross with a Lion between each division. On the divisions of the Cross, the battles of the Regiment. On the centre of the Cross, a raised circle inscribed *Arroyo dos Molinos*, "1811." Within the circle, on a ground of red enamel, the Dragon of China in silver and the word "China" on a silver ground. Below the wreath a scroll inscribed "The Border Regiment."	As for collar, but the Dragon and "China" in gold, and the upper part of the centre filled in with white enamel.	On a frosted gilt or gilding metal centre, the Garter in gilt or gilding metal on a silver eight-pointed star. The Garter pierced with the motto *Honi soit qui mal y pense;* the ground of blue enamel. Within the Garter, the Cross of St. George with the ground of red enamel. On the circle "The Border Regiment."	As for helmet-plate.	In silver, as for collar badge, on an eight-pointed diamond-cut star surmounted by a Crown.	56
61002 / Infantry / 83 / 61002 / Infantry / 301 / 61002 / 6918 — The Royal Sussex Regiment.	Within a circle inscribed "The Royal Sussex Regt.," a Maltese cross on a feather; on centre of cross a wreath; within the wreath, the Garter and motto; within the Garter, St. George's Cross. For the field cap and mess dress the buttons are mounted. The circle and titles are omitted.	A Maltese cross, in gilt or gilding metal, on a feather in silver; on the cross a wreath in silver and green enamel; on the wreath the Garter and motto in blue enamel set with silver. Within the circle the Cross of St. George in red enamel, set with silver, on a silver ground. On the mess jacket the feather in silver embroidery with the stem gilt. On the feather the star of the order of the Garter in gold embroidery. The centre of the star as above.	On a black velvet ground, badge as for collar. On the universal scroll "The Royal Sussex Regiment."	On a frosted gilt or gilding metal centre, badge as for the helmet-plate. On the circle "Royal Sussex Regiment."	In silver embroidery, an eight-pointed star on a feather; the stem of the feather in gold embroidery. On the star, the Garter in gilt or gilding metal, with the motto, pierced; the ground of silver blue enamel. Within the Garter, the Cross of St. George with the ground of silver red enamel. A blue silk and gold embroidered scroll, inscribed "Royal Sussex Regiment," the word "Regiment" being in the centre of the scroll. The upper part on a blue and the lower part on a red cloth ground.	As for the forage cap, but in silver; the stem of the feather gilt, the scroll inscribed, "The Royal Sussex Regiment." The Garter and cross filled in, and not pierced.	57

Badges—Infantry.

Regiment.	On Buttons.	On Collar. See paragraph 567.	On Helmet-Plates; Ornaments for Bear or Racoon-skin Caps and Highland Head-dress.	On the Waist Plate.	On the Forage Cap.	On the Field Cap (or Glengarry).	No. of Plate.
61002 Infantry 41 · 61002 6918 — **The Hampshire Regiment.**	Within a laurel wreath, the Royal Tiger; below the Tiger, the Hampshire Rose. For the field cap and mess dress the design is in silver,—mounted.	The Hampshire Rose, in gold and red and green embroidery.	On a black velvet ground, the Royal Tiger, in gilt or gilding metal, within a laurel wreath, in silver. On the universal scroll "The Hampshire Regt."	In silver, on a frosted gilt or gilding metal centre, the Royal Tiger within a laurel wreath; below the Tiger, the Hampshire Rose in silver gilt metal and red and green enamel. On the circle, "The Hampshire Regiment."	In gold embroidery an eight-pointed star. On the star, the Garter in blue silk, surmounted by the Crown, as represented in the Collar of the Order of the Star of India, in gold embroidery. The motto on the Garter embroidered in silver. Within the Garter, the Hampshire Rose, in red and gold embroidery.	In silver, the Tiger within a laurel wreath. In gilt or gilding metal, below the Tiger, the Rose; on the lower part of the wreath, a scroll inscribed "Hampshire."	57
61002 6174 — **The South Staffordshire Regiment.**	The Staffordshire Knot with Crown above.	The Staffordshire Knot, in gold embroidery.	In silver, on a black velvet ground, the Sphinx over Egypt. On the universal scroll, "The South Staffordshire Regiment."	Special pattern with oak-leaf ends. In silver, on a burnished gilt or gilding metal centre, a laurel wreath. Within the wreath, in silver, Windsor Castle with the Sphinx over Egypt above, and the Staffordshire Knot below. On the wreath, at the bottom, "The South Staffordshire Regiment."	On a black cloth ground, the Staffordshire Knot in gold embroidery; above the Knot the Sphinx over Egypt in gilt or gilding metal.	In silver, the Staffordshire Knot, surmounted by a Crown, with a scroll below in gilt or gilding metal, inscribed "South Staffordshire."	57
61002 6221 — **The Dorsetshire Regiment.**	The Castle and Key. Above the Castle, a scroll inscribed "Gibraltar," and one below, inscribed *Primus in Indis.* Above the top scroll, "The Dorsetshire Regiment": below the bottom scroll, the Sphinx on a tablet inscribed "Marabout."	The Sphinx in silver, on a gilt or gilding metal tablet. On the tablet "Marabout" in gilt or gilding metal letters on a ground of green enamel.	In silver, on a black velvet ground, the Castle and Key. A scroll above the Castle inscribed *Primus in Indis*, and one below, inscribed *Montis Insignia Calpe.* On the universal scroll "The Dorsetshire Regiment."	In silver, on a frosted gilt or gilding metal centre, the Castle and Key, with scroll above inscribed "Gibraltar." Below the Castle, the Sphinx on a tablet inscribed "Marabout." On the circle, "Dorsetshire Regiment."	The Castle and Key. Above the Castle the Sphinx resting on a tablet inscribed "Marabout." Below the Castle, a scroll, with the words *Primus in Indis.* The whole in silver.	In gilt or gilding metal, a laurel wreath. Above the wreath a scroll inscribed "Dorsetshire," the wreath and scroll forming a circle. Within the circle, in silver, the badge as for the forage cap, but smaller.	57
61002 650 · 61002 6918 — **The Prince of Wales's Volunteers (South Lancashire Regiment).**	Within a scroll inscribed "The Prince of Wales's Vols.," and a laurel branch issuing from either end, a circle surmounted by the Crown. On the circle, "The South Lancashire Regiment;" within, the Prince of Wales's Plume above the Sphinx over Egypt. For the field cap and mess dress the button is mounted. The plume in silver. The monogram P.W.V. in gilt metal below.	The Prince of Wales's Plume, in gold and silver embroidery, on a blue cloth ground; the scroll in blue silk, with the motto in silver embroidery.	In silver, on a black velvet ground, the Sphinx over Egypt. On the universal scroll "South Lancashire Regiment."	Special pattern; oak-leaf ends. In silver, on a burnished gilt or gilding metal centre, a laurel branch at either side; at the top, a scroll inscribed "South Lancashire Regt."; at the bottom, a scroll, inscribed "Prince of Wales's Vols." In silver, within the scrolls and laurel branches, the Prince of Wales's Plume above the Sphinx over Egypt.	In silver, on a raised ground of blue cloth, the Sphinx over Egypt. Above the Sphinx, in gold and silver embroidery, the Prince of Wales's Plume; the motto in silver embroidery on a blue silk ground. On each side a laurel branch, in gold embroidery. A blue silk gold embroidered scroll, inscribed "The Prince of Wales's Volunteers."	In silver, the Sphinx over "Egypt"; above the Sphinx, the Prince of Wales's plume and motto, the coronet in gilt or gilding metal. In gilt or gilding metal on either side, a spray of laurel; between the top ends of the spray a scroll inscribed "South Lancashire," between the bottom ends another scroll inscribed "Prince of Wales's Vols."	57
61002 Infantry 54 — **The Welsh Regiment.**	Within a laurel wreath, a circle surmounted by the Crown. On the circle, "The Welsh Regiment;" within, the Prince of Wales's Plume. For the field cap and mess dress the wreath is omitted, and the design is in silver,—mounted.	The Welsh Dragon, in gilt or gilding metal.	In silver, on a black velvet ground, the Prince of Wales's Plume, with scroll below inscribed *Gwell angau na Chywilydd.* The coronet in gilt or gilding metal. On the universal scroll "The Welsh Regiment."	Oak-leaf ends. The Welsh Dragon, in silver, on a frosted gilt or gilding metal centre. On the circle "The Welsh Regiment."	In gold and silver embroidery, on a blue cloth ground, the Prince of Wales's Plume; the scroll in blue silk; the motto in gold embroidery. 1st Bn.—In metal.	The Prince of Wales's Plume as for centre of helmet-plate. In gilt or gilding metal, a scroll inscribed "The Welsh." For the puggaree badge the regimental motto is added.	57

Badges—Infantry.

Regiment.	On Buttons.	On Collar. See paragraph 567.	On Helmet-Plates; Ornaments for Bear or Racoon skin Caps and Highland Head-dress.	On the Waist Plate.	On the Breast-plate.	On the Field Cap (or Glengarry).	No. of Plate.
$\frac{61002}{6302}$ $\frac{61002}{\text{Infantry}}$ 196 **The Black Watch (Royal Highlanders).**	Within the designation "The Royal Highlanders, Black Watch," the Star of the Order of the Thistle, indented. On the centre of the Star, a circle; within the circle, St. Andrew and Cross.	St. Andrew and Cross, in silver.	For Highland head-dress and white helmet. In silver, the Star of the Order of the Thistle; in gilt or gilding metal on the Star, a thistle wreath. Within the wreath, in gilt or gilding metal, an oval surmounted by the Crown. The oval inscribed, *Nemo me impune lacessit*. Within the oval, on a recessed seeded ground, St. Andrew and Cross, in silver. Below the wreath, the Sphinx, in gilt or gilding metal. In silver, a half scroll, to the left of the Crown, inscribed "The Royal"; another to the right inscribed "Highlanders." A half scroll to the left of the Sphinx, inscribed "Black"; another to the right, inscribed "Watch."	Special pattern. On a seeded gilt or gilding metal rectangular plate, with burnished edges, badge as for bonnet, but smaller.	Badge as for bonnet, but larger, on a gilt seeded rectangular plate with raised burnished edges. Brooch ornament. In silver, on an engraved burnished plate, a thistle wreath. Within the wreath, on an open centre, St. Andrew and Cross.	Glengarry—Badge as for Highland head-dress.	57
$\frac{61002}{\text{Infantry}}$ 21 $\frac{61002}{6918}$ **The Oxfordshire Light Infantry.**	Scalloped edge; within a laurel wreath a bugle with strings; below the bugle "Oxfordshire." For the mess dress the title is below the wreath.	Edgeless button; on the button, within a laurel wreath, a bugle with strings; above the bugle, the Crown; below the wreath "Oxfordshire." A piece of gold Russia braid 2½ inches long, attached to the button.	In silver, on a ground of black enamel, a bugle with strings. On the universal scroll, "The Oxfordshire Lt. Infy."	In silver, on a frosted gilt or gilding metal centre, a bugle with strings. On the circle "Oxfordshire Light Infantry."	On the Forage Cap. ——— Not worn.	In silver, a bugle and strings.	57
$\frac{61002}{\text{Infantry}}$ 104 ... 108 $\frac{61002}{6918}$ ... 199 ... 416 **The Essex Regiment.**	Within an oak-leaf wreath, the badge of the County of Essex, with the Sphinx over Egypt above, and the Castle and Key below. For the mess jacket the button is engraved, the county badge and wreath are omitted. For mess waistcoat, a gilt burnished button with the castle in silver.	The County Badge. The shield in gilt or gilding metal; the blades of the seaxes in silver. On the mess jacket, an Eagle on a plain tablet in gilt or gilding metal.	An oak-leaf wreath is substituted for the universal wreath. In silver, on a black velvet ground, the Castle and Key, with the Sphinx over Egypt above, and a scroll below, inscribed *Montis Insignia Calpe*. On the universal scroll "The Essex Regiment."	Special pattern with oak leaf ends. On a burnished gilt or gilding metal centre, an oak-leaf wreath, in silver. Within the wreath, a dead gilt or gilding metal circle, surmounted by the Crown, in silver. The circle inscribed, "The Essex Regiment." Within the circle, the County badge, on a silver shield filled in with red enamel. The seaxes inlaid in silver. The shield surmounted by the Sphinx over Egypt, in silver. On the wreath, at the bottom, the Castle and Key, in silver.	On a raised ground of blue cloth, a blue silk gold embroidered scroll inscribed "The Essex Regt." Within the scroll, the County badge surmounted by the Crown. The Crown and shield in gold embroidery; the seaxes in silver embroidery. The Crown on a crimson velvet cushion.	In silver, the Castle and Key within an oak-leaf wreath. The Sphinx over Egypt above the Castle, and scroll inscribed "The Essex Regt." on the wreath below the Castle.	57
$\frac{61002}{6349}$ **The Sherwood Foresters (Derbyshire Regiment).**	A Maltese cross surmounted by the Crown; within an oak-leaf wreath on the cross, a Stag lodged. A half-scroll on the left division of the cross, inscribed "Sherwood"; another on the right division, inscribed "Foresters." On the lower division, a scroll inscribed "Derbyshire."	A Maltese cross surmounted by the Crown, in silver. Wreath and scrolls, in gilt or gilding metal, as for buttons. Within the wreath, a Stag lodged, in silver, on a ground of silver blue enamel.	In the helmet-plate, the Garter, with motto, is omitted. Within the universal wreath, a Maltese cross, in silver. On the cross, in gilt or gilding metal, an oak-leaf wreath; within the wreath, on a ground of silver blue enamel, a Stag lodged, in silver. In gilt or gilding metal, on the left division of the cross, the word "The"; on the right division, "Regt.," and on a scroll on the lower division, "Derbyshire." A scroll of special pattern on the bottom of the universal wreath inscribed "Sherwood Foresters."	Special pattern: oak-leaf ends. On a burnished gilt plate, the badge as for collar, but larger.	As on Waist-plate.	In silver, badge as for forage cap, but with scroll inscribed "Derbyshire" in gilt or gilding metal below instead of on the cross.	58

Badges—Infantry.

Regiment.	On Buttons.	On Collar. See paragraph 567.	On Helmet-Plates; Ornaments for Bear or Racoon-skin Caps and Highland Head-dress.	On the Waist Plate.	On the Forage Cap.	On the Field Cap (or Glengarry).	No. of Plate.
61002 / 6416 — The Loyal North Lancashire Regiment.	Within a circle inscribed "Loyal North Lancashire Regiment," the Arms of the City of Lincoln, surmounted by the Royal Crest.	In embroidery, the Arms of the City of Lincoln. The ground of the shield in silver, the Cross of St. George in red silk on the shield; the *fleur-de-lis* in gold on the cross.	In silver, on a black velvet ground, the Royal Crest. Below the Crest, the Rose of Lancaster in silver gilt and red and green enamel. On the universal scroll, "Loyal North Lancashire Regiment."	On a frosted gilt or gilding metal centre, the badge as for helmet-plate. On the circle "Loyal North Lancashire Regiment."	In gold embroidery, the Royal Crest; below the Crest, the Rose of Lancaster.	In silver, the Royal Crest. In gilt or gilding metal, below the crown, the Rose of Lancaster; below the Rose, a scroll inscribed "Loyal North Lancashire."	58
61002 / Infantry / 53 — The Northamptonshire Regiment.	Within a scroll inscribed "The Northamptonshire Regiment," the Castle and Key with the Crown above.	In gilt or gilding metal, within a laurel wreath, a gilt or gilding metal circle pierced "Northamptonshire Regt."; the ground of silver blue enamel. In relief, within the circle, on a raised ground of silver blue enamel, the Cross of St. George, in silver. Below the cross, and on the circle, a horse-shoe in silver. The circle surmounted by a crown in gilt or gilding metal.	In silver, on a black velvet ground, the Castle and Key; on a scroll above, "Gibraltar," on a scroll below, "Talavera." On the universal scroll "The Northamptonshire Regiment."	In silver, on a frosted gilt or gilding metal centre, badge and scrolls as for helmet-plate. On the circle "Northamptonshire Regiment."	In gold embroidery, the Castle and Key. Above the Castle, a blue silk gold embroidered scroll, inscribed "Gibraltar," and a similar scroll, below, inscribed "Talavera."	In silver, within a laurel wreath, the Castle and key. Above the Castle a scroll inscribed "Gibraltar"; beneath a scroll inscribed "Talavera." On the lower bend of the wreath, in gilt or gilding metal, a scroll inscribed "Northamptonshire."	5
61002 / 6400 — Princess Charlotte of Wales's (Royal Berkshire Regiment). / 61002 / 6918	A circle inscribed "P⁵ Charlotte of Wales's"; within the circle, the Dragon of China; above the Dragon, the Crown; below, "R Berks." For the field cap and mess dress the Dragon and Crown are mounted on a plain gilt button.	The Dragon o China, in gold embroidery on a blue cloth ground.	In silver, on a scarlet cloth ground, a Stag under an oak. On the universal scroll "Royal Berkshire Regiment."	Oak-leaf ends. In silver on a frosted gilt or gilding metal centre, the Dragon of China. On the circle "Royal Berkshire Regiment."	In silver, chased, within a laurel wreath, the Dragon of China surmounted by a Crown. Beneath the Dragon the word "China." Above the Dragon, on a scroll, the words "Royal Berkshire Regiment."	In silver, the Dragon of China with a scroll below inscribed "Royal Berkshire."	5
61002 / Infantry / 91 — The Queen's Own (Royal West Kent Regiment).	The Royal Crest.	The Royal Crest, in gold embroidery.	In silver, on a black velvet ground, the White Horse of Kent on a scroll inscribed *Invicta*. Above the Horse, another scroll with motto *Quo fas et gloria ducunt*. On the universal scroll, "The Royal West Kent Regiment."	In silver, on a frosted gilt or gilding metal centre, the Royal Crest. On the circle "The Queen's Own Regiment."	In silver, the White Horse of Kent on a scroll, inscribed *Invicta*. Below, a blue silk gold embroidered scroll, inscribed "The Queen's Own Royal West Kent Regt."	In silver, the White Horse of Kent on a scroll, inscribed *Invicta*. On another scroll below, "Royal West Kent."	58
61002 / 6467 — The King's Own (Yorkshire Light Infantry).	A French horn surmounted by the Crown. In the centre of the horn the White Rose, in silver.	A French horn, in gold embroidery; in the centre of the horn, on a raised ground of dark green cloth, the White Rose, in silver metal.	In silver, on a black enamel ground, a French horn with the White Rose in the centre. On the universal scroll, "The King's Own Yorkshire Light Infantry."	In silver, on a frosted gilt or gilding metal centre, a French horn surmounted by the Crown. In the centre of the horn, the White Rose in silver. On the circle, "The Yorkshire Light Infantry."	Not worn.	In gilt or gilding metal, a French horn; within the horn, the White Rose in silver.	58
61002 / Infantry / 470 — The King's (Shropshire Light Infantry).	A circle surmounted by the Crown. On the circle, "Shropshire" with two twigs of laurel in the lower bend. Within the circle, the cypher K.L.I.	A bugle with strings, in gold embroidery, on a ground of dark blue cloth.	In silver, on a ground of dark green enamel, a bugle with strings. In gilt or gilding metal within the strings of the bugle, the cypher K.L.I. On the universal scroll, "King's Shropshire Lt. Infy."	In silver, on a frosted gilt or gilding metal centre, a bugle with strings. Within the strings, in gilt or gilding metal, the cypher K.L.I. On the circle, "Shropshire Light Infantry."	Not worn.	In silver, the bugle and strings. Within the strings, the letters "K.S.L.I.," in gilt or gilding metal. The field cap badge is half the size of the puggaree badge.	58

Badges—Infantry.

Regiment.	On Buttons.	On Collar. See paragraph 567.	On Helmet-Plates; Ornaments for Bear or Racoon-skin Caps, and Highland Head-dress.	On the Waist Plate.	On the Forage Cap.	On the Field Cap (or Glengarry).	No. of Plate.
61002 / 5760 ••• / 5630 ••• / 6918 — The Duke of Cambridge's Own (Middlesex Regiment).	Within a wreath of laurel, the Prince of Wales's Plume; on the bottom of the wreath, a scroll inscribed "Albuhera." For the field cap the design is in silver,—mounted.	In silver, a laurel wreath; within the wreath, the Prince of Wales's Plume; below the Plume, the Coronet and Cypher of H.R.H. the Duke of Cambridge; on the lower bend of the wreath, "Albuhera."	In silver, on a black velvet ground, a laurel wreath; within the wreath, the Prince of Wales's Plume; below the Plume, the Coronet and Cypher of H.R.H. the Duke of Cambridge. On the bottom of the wreath a scroll inscribed "Albuhera." On the universal scroll "The Middlesex Regt."	In silver, on a frosted gilt or gilding metal centre, a laurel wreath; within the wreath the Prince of Wales's Plume; below the Plume, the badge of the County of Middlesex. A scroll on the bottom of the wreath, inscribed "Albuhera." On the circle "The Duke of Cambridge's Own."	In gold embroidery on a raised blue cloth ground, a laurel wreath; within the wreath, the Prince of Wales's Plume in silver, the motto embroidered in silver on a ground of blue silk; below the Plume, in gold embroidery, the Coronet and Cypher of H.R.H. the Duke of Cambridge. On the bottom of the wreath, a light blue silk scroll, inscribed "Albuhera," in gold embroidery.	In silver, as for collar, with scroll below inscribed "Middlesex Regiment."	58
61002 / 6436 — The King's Royal Rifle Corps.	Within a laurel wreath, a bugle with strings; above the bugle, the Crown.	No badge.	On the Busby:—In bronze, a Maltese cross surmounted by a tablet, inscribed *Celer et Audax*. On the Cross a circle, inscribed "The King's Royal Rifle Corps"; within the circle, a bugle with strings. On each division of the cross, the battles of the Regiment. On the White Helmet:—As for busby badge, but surmounted by a Crown, and with a scarlet cloth ground in the centre. The dimensions are:—From the top of the Crown to the bottom of the plate, back measurement, 4 inches; extreme width 2½ inches.	No badge. A snake hook in silver is worn with the frock coat by officers serving on the staff. ___ On the shoulder belt. ___ As for white helmet, but in silver throughout.	No badge.	On the Field Cap only:—In silver, the bugle and strings on a scarlet cord boss.	58
61002 / 5139 ••• / 5758 — The Duke of Edinburgh's (Wiltshire Regiment).	The Cypher of H.R.H. the Duke of Edinburgh, with Coronet above, and "Wiltshire Regiment" below. For the field cap and mess dress the design is in silver,—mounted; the title is omitted.	A Maltese cross in lined silver, with burnished edges. On the cross, a round convex plate, in burnished silver. On the plate, in gilt or gilding metal, the Coronet within the Cypher.	On a black velvet ground, the Maltese cross in lined gilt or gilding metal, with burnished edges. On the cross, a round convex burnished plate. On the plate, in silver, the Cypher surmounted by the Coronet. On the universal scroll, "The Wiltshire Regiment."	On the waist plate. ___ On a frosted gilt or gilding metal centre, badge as for helmet-plate. On the circle "The Wiltshire Regiment."	As for centre of helmet plate, with Coronet above in dead gilt or gilding metal, and scroll beneath inscribed "The Wiltshire Regiment."	As for forage cap, but with Cypher and Coronet in gilt or gilding metal.	59
61002 / 6667 — The Manchester Regiment.	The Garter, with motto, *Honi soit qui mal y pense*. Within the Garter, the Sphinx over Egypt with the Crown above.	The Sphinx over Egypt in gold embroidery; the word "Egypt" embroidered in silver.	In silver, on a black velvet ground, the Arms with motto of the City of Manchester. On the universal scroll, "The Manchester Regiment."	In silver, on a frosted gilt or gilding metal centre, an eight-pointed star; on the star, in dead gilt or gilding metal, the Sphinx over Egypt. On the circle "The Manchester Regiment."	The Sphinx over Egypt in gold embroidery; the word "Egypt" in silver embroidery. Below, on a blue cloth gold embroidered scroll, "Manchester Regiment."	In silver, the Arms and motto of the City of Manchester above a scroll in gilt or gilding metal inscribed "Manchester."	59
61002 / 5941 ... 61002 / 6918 — The Prince of Wales's (North Staffordshire Regiment.)	Within a scroll inscribed "Prince of Wales's" and a laurel branch issuing from either end, a circle inscribed "The North Staffordshire Regiment"; within the circle, the Staffordshire Knot; above the circle, the Prince of Wales's Plume. For the field cap and mess dress the button is mounted and the Knot and Crown are in silver.	The Staffordshire Knot in gold embroidery.	In silver, on a black velvet ground, the Prince of Wales's Plume. On the universal scroll, "The North Staffordshire Regiment."	On a frosted gilt or gilding metal centre, badge as for helmet-plate. On the circle, "North Staffordshire Regiment."	On a blue cloth ground, the Staffordshire Knot in gold embroidery, surmounted by the Prince of Wales's plume in gold and silver embroidery. The motto in silver embroidery on a gold embroidered scroll.	As for forage cap, but with the Knot and Coronet in gilt or gilding metal; the plume and scroll in silver. Below the knot, in silver, a scroll inscribed "North Stafford."	59

APPENDIX I—continued.

Badges—Infantry.

Regiment.	On Buttons.	On Collar. See paragraph 567.	On Helmet-Plates; Ornaments for Bear or Racoon-skin Caps and Highland Head-dress.	On the Waist Plate.	On the Forage Cap.	On the Field Cap (or Glengarry).	No. of Plate.
61002 / Infantry / 256 — 61002 / 6918 **The York and Lancaster Regiment.**	A scroll inscribed "The York and Lancaster Regiment;" within the scroll, a laurel wreath; within the wreath the Royal Tiger; above the Tiger, a Coronet. On the wreath at the bottom, the Union Rose. For the field cap and mess dress the tiger and rose are in silver,—mounted on a plain gilt button.	The Royal Tiger, in dead gilt or gilding metal, the rose above in gilt or gilding metal and silver.	In silver and gilt or gilding metal, on a black velvet ground, the Union Rose. On the universal scroll, "The York & Lancaster Regiment."	On a frosted gilt or gilding metal centre, the Union Rose in gilt or gilding metal and silver. Below the Rose, the Royal Tiger, in silver. On the circle "York & Lancaster Regiment."	On a blue cloth ground, in gold embroidery, the Union Rose. Below the Rose, the Royal Tiger.	In gilt or gilding metal, the Tiger within a scroll inscribed "York and Lancaster" upon a laurel wreath. Between the ends of the wreath a coronet in silver; below the coronet, the Union Rose in gilt or gilding metal and silver.	59
61002 / Infantry / 27 — ... / 328 **The Durham Light Infantry.**	Bugle, with the Crown on the strings. For the mess jacket "D.L.I." in cypher with the Crown above.	Bugle with strings, in gold embroidery on a white cloth ground.	In silver, on a black velvet ground, a bugle with strings. On the universal scroll, "The Durham Light Infantry."	On a frosted gilt or gilding metal centre, badge as for helmet-plate. Below the Bugle, "Durham Light Infantry."	Not worn.	In silver, a bugle ornamented with laurel leaves. Upon the strings a crown. Within the strings "D.L.I."	59
61002 / 6302 — 61002 / 6918 **The Highland Light Infantry.**	Star of the Order of the Thistle. On the star, a horn; in the centre of the horn, the monogram H.L.I. Above the horn, the Crown as represented in the collar of the Order of the Star of India; below the horn a scroll, inscribed "Assaye"; under the scroll, the Elephant. For the mess dress a mounted button, the monogram H.L.I. with the crown above.	In silver, the Star of the Order of the Thistle. On the star a silver horn. In the centre of the horn, the monogram H.L.I. in gilt or gilding metal. Above the horn, in gilt or gilding metal, the Crown as represented in the collar of the Order of the Star of India; below the horn, a scroll, in gilt or gilding metal, inscribed "Assaye"; under the scroll, in gilt or gilding metal, the Elephant.	For chaco. As for collar badge, except that the cap of the Crown is of crimson velvet. The scroll is detached from the Elephant, and the badge is larger.	Special pattern. Burnished gilt or gilding metal rectangular plate, with badge as for chaco, mounted.	Not worn. — On the shoulder belt. — As for waist plate, but larger.	As for chaco.	59
61002 / 6302 — ... / 6485 — ... / Infantry / 196 **Seaforth Highlanders (Ross-shire Buffs, the Duke of Albany's).**	Raised edge, a stag's head, with the Cypher of H.R.H. the Duke of Albany above. A scroll below, inscribed "Seaforth Highlanders."	Two badges in gilt metal— I. The Cypher of H.R.H. the late Duke of York with scroll inscribed "Caber Feidh." II. The Elephant. Both badges to be worn on each side of the collar, the Cypher of the late Duke of York next the hooks and eyes.	For Highland head-dress and white helmet. In silver, a stag's head; above, the Coronet and Cypher of H.R.H. the Duke of Albany; below, a scroll inscribed "Cuidich'n Righ."	Special pattern. Burnished gilt or gilding metal rectangular plate. Badge as for Highland head-dress, except that it is smaller, and that the motto on scroll is *Tulloch Ard.*	On the Breast-plate. — Plain rectangular waist plate. In silver, the coronet, the Cypher of H.R.H. the late Duke of York, the Elephant, the stag's head, and scroll inscribed "Seaforth Highlanders." — Brooch Ornament. — In silver, a thistle wreath intertwined with a scroll bearing the honours of the regiment. Within the wreath badges as for head-dresses, without the scroll.	As for Highland head-dress.	59
61002 / 6302 — 61002 / Infantry / 196 **The Gordon Highlanders.**	The Cross of St. Andrew; on the cross a thistle wreath joined to a scroll let into the upper divisions of the cross, and inscribed "Gordon Highlanders." Within the scroll, on the upper divisions of the cross, the Sphinx over Egypt; within the wreath on the lower divisions of the cross, the Royal Tiger over India.	The Royal Tiger, in gold embroidery.	For Highland head-dress and White Helmet. In silver, the Crest of the Marquis of Huntly within an ivy wreath. On the bottom of the wreath, *Bydand.*	Special pattern. Burnished gilt or gilding metal rectangular plate. In silver, badge as on buttons, but larger.	On the Breast plate. — On a burnished gilt rectangular plate in silver, the star of the Order of St. Andrew. On the top of the star the Sphinx over Egypt; on the lower part of the star the Tiger over India; on the centre the Crest of the Marquis of Huntly, above a spray of thistles; above the crest a scroll inscribed "Gordon Highlanders."	As for Highland head-dress.	59

Badges—Infantry.

Regiment.	On Buttons.	On Collar. See paragraph 567.	On Helmet-Plates; Ornaments for Bear or Racoon-skin Caps and Highland Head-dress.	On the Waist Plate.	Brooch Ornament.	On the Field Cap (or Glengarry).	No. of Plate.
The Gordon Highlanders— *(continued).*					In burnished silver a plate with a scroll inscribed "Peninsula," "Egypt" on the right; "Waterloo," "India" on the left, and on the lower bend " Gordon Highlanders." On an open centre, badge as for Head-dresses.		
61002 / 5989 — 61002 / Infantry / 196 — **The Queen's Own Cameron Highlanders.**	Within the designation "The Queen's Own Cameron Highlanders," the Thistle surmounted by the Crown.	The Thistle surmounted by the Crown on a crimson velvet cushion, in silver embroidery, on a blue cloth ground.	For Highland head-dress and Puggaree. In silver, a thistle wreath; within the wreath the figure of St. Andrew with Cross, but with a scroll on the lower bend of the wreath inscribed "Cameron."	Special pattern. Burnished gilt or gilding metal rectangular plate. In silver on the plate, a thistle wreath; within the wreath St. Andrew with Cross.	On the Breast-plate. —— On a gilt seeded rectangular plate with raised burnished edges, the Cross of St. Andrew in cut bright silver with raised edges. On the Cross a gilt oval collar inscribed "Queen's Own Cameron Highlanders," surmounted by a Crown. Within the collar, on a burnished ground, the thistle and Crown in silver. Below the collar the Sphinx over Egypt in silver. —— Brooch Ornament. —— In silver, a thistle wreath. Within the wreath the Sphinx over Egypt. Above the Sphinx a scroll inscribed "Peninsula," below a scroll inscribed "Waterloo."	As for Highland head-dress.	59
61002 / Infantry / 312 — **The Royal Irish Rifles.**	Scalloped edge; within a scroll and the shamrock leaves issuing from either end, the Harp and Crown. On scroll, "Royal Irish Rifles."	No badge	In bronze, the Harp and Crown; below the Harp, a scroll, inscribed *Quis separabit;* on the boss, the Sphinx over Egypt; below the Sphinx, a bugle with strings. On the puggaree badge as for busby.	No badge	On the Forage Cap. —— No badge... ... —— On the Shoulder Belt. —— In silver, a shamrock wreath intertwined with a scroll, bearing the battles of the regiment; within the wreath the Harp and Crown; above the Harp a scroll inscribed *Quis separabit;* below the Harp the Sphinx over Egypt; below the Sphinx a bugle with the strings. Over the strings of the bugle a scroll, inscribed "Royal Irish Rifles."	In silver, the Harp surmounted by a Crown; across the Harp, a scroll, inscribed "Royal Irish Rifles."	59 60
61002 / 5879 — 61002 / 5873 — ... — 6918 — **Princess Victoria's (Royal Irish Fusiliers).**	Scalloped edge; an Eagle with a wreath of laurel; below the Eagle a small tablet inscribed with the figure 8. For the field cap and mess dress, plain edge with the eagle and tablet in silver,—mounted.	A grenade in gold embroidery, with badge on ball as for buttons, but in silver. 2nd Badge—Coronet of H.R.H. the Princess Victoria in silver, worn next the hooks and eyes.	A grenade in gilt or gilding metal. In silver on the ball, the Eagle with a wreath of laurel. Below the Eagle a small tablet inscribed with the figure 8.	Special pattern; shamrock ends with harp. In gilt or gilding metal, on a frosted gilt or gilding metal centre, a grenade, with badge in silver, as for the Fusilier cap, but smaller. On the circle, a laurel wreath with the Crown at the top; on the wreath at the bottom, a scroll, inscribed "Royal Irish Fusiliers."	On the Forage Cap. —— In gold embroidery, a grenade; above the grenade, the Coronet of H.R.H. the Princess Victoria on a silver cushion. In silver, on the ball of grenade, the Prince of Wales's Plume over the Harp.	1st Badge:—The coronet of H.R.H. the Princess Victoria. 2nd Badge:—As for Racoon-skin cap, but smaller.	60

Badges—Infantry.

	Regiment.	On Buttons.	On Collar. See paragraph 567.	On Helmet-Plates; Ornaments for Bear or Racoon skin Caps and Highland Head-dress.	On the Waist Plate.	On the Forage Cap.	On the Field Cap (or Glengarry).	No. of Plate.
61002 / Infantry / 21	The Connaught Rangers.	Scalloped edge. Within a wreath of shamrock, the Harp surmounted by a Crown; on the lower part of the wreath a scroll inscribed *Quis separabit.*	The Elephant, in silver.	In silver, on a dark green velvet ground, the Harp, with scroll, inscribed *Quis separabit.* A sprig of laurel issues from either end of the scroll. On the universal scroll, " The Connaught Rangers."	In silver, on a frosted gilt or gilding metal centre, the Elephant with the Crown above. On the circle, " Connaught Rangers."	In gold embroidery, on a blue cloth ground, the Harp and Crown. The Crown on a crimson velvet cushion.	[In silver, the Harp and Crown; below the Harp a scroll inscribed " Connaught Rangers."	60
61002 / 6302 / 61002 / Infantry / 136	Princess Louise's (Argyll and Sutherland Highlanders)	A myrtle wreath interlaced with a wreath of butcher's broom. Within the myrtle wreath, a Boar's head on scroll inscribed, *Ne obliviscaris;* within the wreath of butcher's broom, a Cat on scroll, inscribed *Sans peur.* A label of three points above the Boar's head and the Cat. Above the wreaths, the Coronet of H.R.H. the Princess Louise.	In frosted silver, a myrtle wreath interlaced with a wreath of butcher's broom. In gilt or gilding metal, within the myrtle wreath, the Boar's head on scroll, inscribed *Ne obliviscaris;* within the wreath of butcher's broom, the Cat on scroll, inscribed *Sans peur.* A label of three points in silver above the Boar's head and the Cat.	For Highland head-dress and White Helmet. In silver a thistle wreath; within the wreath, a circle, inscribed " Argyll and Sutherland." Within the circle, the double Cypher of H.R.H. the Princess Louise. To the left of the Cypher, the Boar's head; to the right the Cat. Above the Cypher, and on the circle, the Coronet of the Princess.	Burnished gilt or gilding metal rectangular plate. Devices as for collar badge, but *all* in silver; above the wreaths, in frosted silver, a scroll surmounted by the Coronet of the Princess. The scroll inscribed " Princess Louise's"; below the wreath a silver scroll, inscribed " Argyll and Sutherland Highlanders."	Not worn. ——— On the Breast-plate. ——— Brooch Ornament. Silver circular brooch with open centre. On the left, the boar's head and motto; on the right, the cat and motto. Above the opening the Cypher and Coronet; below the opening a scroll inscribed " Argyll and Sutherland Highlanders."	Badge as for Highland head-dress.	60
61002 / 5942 / 61002 / 6918	The Prince of Wales's Leinster Regiment (Royal Canadians).	A Circle, inscribed " Prince of Wales's Leinster Regiment"; within the circle, the Prince of Wales's Plume. [For the field cap and mess dress the plume is in silver,—mounted, on a plain gilt button.	The Prince of Wales's Plume, in silver; the Coronet in gilt or gilding metal.	In silver, on a black velvet ground, the Prince of Wales's Plume over two maple leaves. On a scroll, beneath the leaves, " Central India." On the universal scroll, " Prince of Wales's Leinster Regiment." The Coronet in gilt or gilding metal.	Special pattern, maple-leaf ends. In silver, on a burnished gilt or gilding metal centre, a maple and laurel wreath. Within the wreath, a circle inscribed, " The Leinster Regt." Above the circle, the Crown; within, the Prince of Wales's Plume; below, in dead gilt or gilding metal on the maple and laurel wreath, a scroll, inscribed " Central India." The Coronet in gilt or gilding metal.	On the Forage Cap. ——— In silver, the Prince of Wales's Plume, the scroll with motto, and the Coronet in gilt or gilding metal. Below the Coronet a scroll, in gilt or gilding metal, inscribed " The Leinster."	As for the forage cap, but with the scroll with motto, *Ich Dien,* in silver.	60
61002 / 6721 / .. / 6918	The Royal Munster Fusiliers.	Within the designation, " Royal Munster Fusiliers," a grenade, with the Royal Tiger on the ball. [For the field cap and mess dress the Royal Tiger, in silver,—mounted, on a plain gilt button.	A grenade in gold embroidery, with the Royal Tiger, in silver, on the ball.	A grenade, in gilt or gilding metal. On the ball a deep wreath of laurel intertwined with a scroll bearing the battles of the Regiment. Within the wreath, the Heraldic device for the Province of Munster, the Crowns in gilt or gilding metal, the shield in silver. On the bottom of the wreath, a scroll, in silver, inscribed " Royal Munster."	Special pattern; oak-leaf ends. On a burnished gilt or gilding metal centre, a deep laurel wreath intertwined with a silver scroll, bearing the battles of the Regiment. Within the wreath, a grenade, in gilt or gilding metal, with the Royal Tiger, in silver, on the ball. On the wreath at the bottom, a scroll, in silver, inscribed " Royal Munster."	A grenade, in gold embroidery, with the Royal Tiger, in silver metal, on the ball.	In gilt or gilding metal, a grenade. On the ball, in silver, the Tiger and scroll inscribed " Royal Munster."	60

Badges—Infantry.

Regiment.	On Buttons.	On Collar. See paragraph 567.	On Helmet-Plates: Ornaments for Bear or Racoon skin Caps and Highland Head-dress.	On the Waist Plate.	On the Forage Cap.	On the Field Cap (or Glengarry).	No. of Plate.
61002 / 6510 **The Royal Dublin Fusiliers.**	Within the designation "Royal Dublin Fusiliers," a grenade; on the ball of the grenade, the Crown.	A grenade in gold embroidery; in silver, on the ball, the Royal Tiger; below the Tiger, the Elephant.	A grenade in gilt or gilding metal: on the ball, in silver, the Arms of the City of Dublin; below the shield—to the right, the Royal Tiger, on a silver tablet inscribed "Plassey," to the left, the Elephant, on a silver tablet inscribed "Mysore." Below the tablets a silver scroll inscribed *Spectamur agendo*. In silver on either side of the shield, a rich mounting of shamrock leaves.	Special pattern; shamrock ends, with the Harp. In gilt or gilding metal, on a round burnished gilt or gilding metal plate, a grenade; in silver, on the ball, a circle inscribed "Royal Dublin Fusiliers"; within the circle, the Harp. Below the ball, in gilt or gilding metal, a scroll inscribed *Spectamur agendo*. Below the scroll, in gilt or gilding metal — to the right, the Royal Tiger on a scroll inscribed "Plassey," to the left, the Elephant on a scroll inscribed "Mysore." On either side of the grenade, a rich mounting of shamrock leaves, in gilt or gilding metal.	A grenade, in gold embroidery; in silver, on the ball, the Royal Tiger; below the Tiger, the Elephant. Below, and detached from the grenade, a gilt or gilding metal scroll pierced "Royal Dublin Fusiliers"; the ground of silver blue enamel.	In gilt or gilding metal, a grenade. On the ball, in silver, the Tiger; below the Tiger, the Elephant. Below the grenade, a scroll in silver inscribed "Royal Dublin Fusiliers."	60
61002 / 6436 61002 Infantry / 205 **The Rifle Brigade (The Prince Consort's Own).**	Within a laurel wreath, and the designation Rifle Brigade, a bugle with strings; above the bugle, the Crown.	.. .. … …	On the busby, a bugle in bronze relieved. On the white helmet:— In silver, a wreath of laurel intertwined with a scroll, bearing some of the battles of the Brigade. Within the wreath, a Maltese cross, with a Lion between each division. On each division, other battles of the Brigade. On the centre of the cross, a circle inscribed "Rifle Brigade"; within the circle, a bugle with strings, surmounted by the Crown. Above the Cross, a Crown on a tablet, inscribed "Waterloo"; below the cross, a scroll, inscribed "Peninsula."	No badge … … ⎯⎯ On the Shoulder Belt. ⎯⎯ As for white helmet, but 4 inches in height, and a scroll on the lower part of the wreath. inscribed "The Prince Consort's Own."	No badge …	On the Field Cap only:—In silver, the bugle and strings on a black cord boss.	60
61002 Infantry / 169 **The West India Regiment.**	A wreath of laurel and palm leaves. Within the wreath, the cypher "W.I.R."	No badge … …	A wreath of laurel and palm leaves in gilt or gilding metal. Within the wreath, the Garter, with motto. Within the Garter, on a burnished ground, the cypher "W.I.R." The battles of the Regiment on the larger rays of the star.	On the Waist Plate. ⎯⎯ Special pattern. Oak-leaf ends. Badge as on helmet-plate, but smaller.	In gold embroidery, on a blue cloth ground, the wreath as on helmet-plate. Within the wreath, the Garter, with motto on a blue silk ground. Within the Garter, the cypher "W.I.R."	The wreath and garter as for the helmet-plate. The motto pierced on a silver blue enamel ground. Within the Garter, in silver, the cypher "W.I."	60
The West African Regiment.	… … …	… … …	… … …	… … …	… … …	… … …	
The Chinese Regiment.	… … … …	… … …	… … …	… … …	… … …	… … .. …	
61002 / 6298 **Royal Jersey Militia.**	The Royal Crest.	In gilt or gilding metal, the Cross of St. Patrick; on the Cross a shield surmounted by a Crown. The shield charged with three lion-leopardés, in silver.	On the universal plate a circle inscribed "Royal Jersey Light Infantry" is substituted for the Garter. In the centre, in gilt or gilding metal, the bugle and strings; within the strings the number of the regiment.	In silver, on a frosted gilt or gilding metal centre, the bugle and strings. Within the strings the number of the regiment.	In gold embroidery, on a blue cloth ground, a bugle with strings, surmounted by the Royal Crest. The number of the regiment within the strings of the bugle. A sprig of laurel on each side of the bugle; below, a crimson velvet scroll, inscribed "Royal Jersey." The bugle is of special pattern.	As for collar badge.	

Badges—Infantry.

Regiment.	On Buttons.	On Collar. See paragraph 567.	On Helmet-Plates; Ornaments for Bear or Racoon skin Caps and Highland Head-dress.	On the Waist Plate.	On the Forage Cap.	On the Field Cap (or Glengarry).	No. of Plate.
$\frac{61002}{6320}$ **Royal Guernsey Militia.**	Bugle with strings, surmounted by a sprig of laurel. Within the strings the number of the regiment.	In gold embroidery a lion-leopardé.	The universal plate, with the Garter inscribed *Pro aris, rege et focis.* In silver within the Garter, on a black velvet ground, a shield charged with three lion-leopardés, surmounted by a sprig of laurel; above the Garter, a scroll inscribed *Diex Aie;* below the shield, a bugle with strings. Within the strings, the number of the regiment. On universal wreath at the bottom, a scroll inscribed "Royal Guernsey Militia."	In silver, on a frosted gilt or gilding metal centre, a bugle of special pattern with strings, surmounted by a sprig of laurel. Within the strings the number of the regiment. On the circle, "Royal Guernsey Militia."	In gold embroidery, on a blue cloth ground, device as for waist-plate. A crimson velvet scroll below, inscribed "Royal Guernsey."	In gilt or gilding metal, device as for forage cap.	61
$\frac{61002}{\text{Infantry}}$ $\frac{}{303}$ **Royal Malta Regiment of Militia.**	Within a Garter inscribed "Royal Malta Militia," and surmounted by the Crown, a Maltese Cross.	On collar of tunic, a Maltese Cross in burnished silver; on the centre of the Cross, the Crown in gilt or gilding metal.	On helmet-plate, a Maltese Cross in gilt or gilding metal, surmounted by the Crown. On the cross, a scroll in silver, inscribed "Royal Malta Militia, MDCCC."	In silver, on a frosted gilt or gilding metal centre, a laurel wreath with the Crown above; a Maltese Cross in silver within the wreath. On the circle, "Royal Malta Militia, MDCCC."	In gold embroidery, on a scarlet ground, a wreath; within the wreath, a Garter inscribed "Royal Malta Militia" on a blue silk ground; within the Garter, a Maltese Cross in burnished silver on a ground of which the left half is in white lined silk, and the other in scarlet lined silk. The Garter is surmounted by the Crown on a blue velvet ground. Below the Garter a scroll, inscribed "MDCCC."	The Maltese Cross in silver, on the front of the cap.	61
$\frac{20}{\text{Hong Kong Regt.}}$ $\frac{}{41}$ **The Hong Kong Regiment.**	Within a laurel wreath a circle inscribed "The Hong Kong Regt." Upon the upper bend of the circle a Crown. Within the circle the Dragon of China.	... ...	... ...	Oak leaf ends. Centre of plate as for buttons, without the wreath. Title and Dragon in silver, the remainder in gilt or gilding metal.	As for waist-plate.	... ...	

Badges—Corps, Departments and Miscellaneous.

	Branch of Service.	On Buttons.	On Collar.	On the Helmet.	On the Waist Plate.	On the Pouch.	On the Staff Forage, or Field Cap.	No. of Plate.
61002 Staff 59								
61002 6205	Army Service Corps.	Within a circle inscribed "Army Service Corps," the Royal Cypher. Above the circle a Crown.	On the tunic:—In silver an eight-pointed star, surmounted by a Crown. On the star in gilt or gilding metal, a laurel wreath. Within the wreath, filled in with white enamel, the Garter and motto. Within the Garter the initials of the corps in monogram. Not worn on mess jacket.	In silver, the letters "A.S.C." in monogram.	On a gilt or gilding metal rectangular plate in silver, the Royal Cypher and Crown within a laurel wreath. Below the wreath a scroll inscribed *Dieu et mon droit*.	The Royal Cypher and Crown in gilt or gilding metal.	In silver, as for the collar badge, but with the corps monogram on a ground of black enamel.	61
61002 6268	Army Medical Staff.	On an eight pointed star, a Garter inscribed "Army Medical Staff," surmounted by the Crown. Within the Garter, the Royal Cypher, the edge of the button raised and burnished.	... ...	... ...	Round gilt or gilding metal chased clasp, with the Royal Crest in silver on the centrepiece. A laurel wreath on the outer circle.	A gilt or gilding metal chased Royal Cypher and Crown.	As for General officer.	46
61002 Departments. 8 / 61002 6925	Royal Army Medical Corps.	Gilt, with burnished edges. Within a laurel wreath, surmounted by a Crown, the rod of Esculapius with a serpent entwined. Around the wreath, "Royal Army Medical Corps." For the Field Cap buttons, the design is in silver and the title is omitted.	As for the buttons, but the serpent and the title on a scroll below, in silver.	The Royal Arms, with a scroll below, inscribed "Royal Army Medical Corps."	As for Army Medical Staff.	As for Army Medical Staff.	As for collar, but larger.	61
	Army Chaplains' Department.	Plain black silk buttons.	A Maltese Cross in black and gold embroidery.	Not worn.	Not worn.	Not worn.	A Maltese Cross in black and gold embroidery.	61
61002 626	Army Ordnance Department and Corps.	The Ordnance Arms within the Garter, with motto; above the shield, and upon the Garter, a Crown on a frosted centre, with burnished edge.	In gilt or gilding metal, the Ordnance Arms. (Worn on all garments.)	The Ordnance Arms in silver, on a black velvet ground.	Oak-leaf ends, round burnished gilt or gilding metal clasp with the Ordnance Arms in silver. On the circle "Ordnance," in the upper, and two twigs of laurel in the lower bend.	The Royal Cypher and Crown in gilt or gilding metal.	In gilt or gilding metal the Ordnance Arms, with a scroll below inscribed "Ordnance." [The height is 1¼ instead of 1⅝ inches.	61
61002 6297	Army Pay Department.	The Royal Crest in the centre, and the words "Army Pay Department" round the edge.	... ...	... ...	Round gilt or gilding metal clasp, with the Royal Crest, in silver, on the centre-piece; on the outer circle the words "Army Pay Department," with two twigs of laurel on the lower bend.	The Royal Cypher and Crown in gilt or gilding metal.	The Royal Crest in gold embroidery.	61
61002 6295	Army Veterinary Department.	Indented. On an eight-pointed star a circle, inscribed "Army Veterinary Department," surmounted by a Crown; within the circle the Royal Cypher on a burnished ground.	... ...	Helmet-plate:— In silver, on a ground of black enamel, the letters "A.V.D." in monogram.	Full Dress:— On a gilt or gilding metal frosted rectangular plate with bevelled edges, in silver, the Royal Cypher and Crown encircled with oak leaves; on the bottom of the wreath a scroll inscribed *Dieu et mon droit*. Undress:— A gilt snake clasp.	In gold embroidery, within an oak-leaf wreath, the Royal Cypher and Crown.	The Royal Crest in gold embroidery.	61
	Provost Marshal and Officers of Military Police.	Frosted, with Royal Cypher and Crown.	None worn.	None worn.	Gilt rectangular burnished plate. In silver, the Royal Cypher and Crown within an oak-leaf wreath; on the lower part of the wreath, a scroll inscribed *Dieu et mon droit*.	None worn.	The Royal Crest, in gold embroidery.	46

APPENDIX I—continued.

Badges—Miscellaneous.

	Branch of Service.	On Buttons.	On Collar.	On Full Dress Head-dress.	On the Waist Plate.	On the Forage Cap.	On the Field Cap.	No. of Plate.
	Governors of Military Prisons.	Frosted, with Royal Cypher and Crown.	... ...	The Royal Arms.	Round gilt or gilding metal clasp with Royal Cypher and Crown.	... ...	No badge.	
61002/6140	Inspectors of Army Schools.	A Crown, on the large and small buttons, within a scalloped edge. On the gorget buttons the edge is plain.	No badge.	As for infantry; in the centre "V.R.," in silver, on a light blue ground of copper enamel. No scroll.	On a frosted gilt or gilding metal centre, a Crown in silver. On the circle a laurel wreath. Ends of special pattern.	On the Pouch. ——— The Royal Cypher and Crown, in gilt or gilding metal.	On a blue cloth ground in gold embroidery, the Royal Cypher with a crown above on a crimson velvet cap.	61
61002/6791	Officers of the Royal Military College, Sandhurst.	Frosted, with burnished laurel round the edge.	None worn.	None worn.*	In gilt or gilding metal, the Royal Cypher and Crown.	On the Forage Cap. ——— None worn.	In gilt or gilding metal a circle, inscribed *Nec aspera terrent*, surmounted by a Crown; within the circle the Royal Cypher.	61
	Officers of the Royal Hospitals at Chelsea and Kilmainham.	Badges of their rank, or their late regiment.						
	Captains of Invalids.	Windsor pattern.	... ...	... ...	The Royal Cypher and Crown.	... ...	... ...	
	Officers of the Royal Military Schools.	The badges forming part of their uniform.						
	Military Knights of Windsor.	Gilt, half dome, Garter, Star, and Crown above.	None worn.	None worn.	Gilt clasp with Garter, Star, and Crown above, encircled by a laurel wreath.	In embroidery, St. George's Cross.	... .	
	Army Post Office Corps (on mobilisation).	A Crown, with "P.O.C." below.	... ...	In bronze, a circle, inscribed "Middlesex Rifle Volunteers," within a laurel wreath, and surmounted by a Crown. Within the circle "24."	... ...	... .	As for full dress head-dress.	

* The Quartermaster wears a badge as for the Field Cap.

APPENDIX II.

I,—CARE AND PRESERVATION OF UNIFORM.

Care and preservation of uniform and of gold lace.

61002
5763

Articles of Uniform liable to be moth-eaten should be unfolded at intervals and well beaten and brushed in the open air. Russia leather parings, powdered camphor, naphthaline, carbolised paper, or turpentine sprinkled on brown paper, or on the garments, are good for the prevention of moth, and one or another of these preventives should be placed amongst articles of uniform which are to be packed away for any time.

Before being packed away, gold lace, braid, cord, or buttons on garments should be covered with tissue paper, and hen placed in tin-lined air-tight cases. Care must be taken to use paper that is thoroughly dry. For the prevention of moth, the garments should be well aired and brushed before being packed.

Gold trimmings and gold lace that have become slightly tarnished can be cleaned with a mixture of cream of tartar and dry bread rubbed up very fine, applied in a dry state, and brushed lightly with a clean soft brush.

Removing stains from scarlet tunics or frocks.

In many cases stains may be removed by the part affected being rubbed with dry pipeclay and then well brushed with a clean brush. Should this fail to remove them the following mixture may be tried :—

$\frac{1}{3}$ ounce of salts of sorrel to $\frac{1}{2}$ a pint of boiling water.
$\frac{1}{3}$ ounce of cream of tartar to $\frac{1}{2}$ a pint of cold water.

Each solution should be kept in a separate flat vessel.

These quantities will be sufficient to clean 2 or 3 garments.

The garment which requires cleaning should be first well beaten and brushed, and a perfectly clean hard brush should be used in applying the solutions.

The solutions should be applied alternately commencing with the salts of sorrel, until the garment has been washed all over, and all the stains removed.

If the weather permit, the cleaned garments should be hung up in the sun to dry ; if not, they should be hung up in a dry place, but not near fires or stoves.

APPENDIX III.

BUTTONS AND LACE.

61002
181

Buttons—Buttons are of the following sizes :—

Large	....	35 to 40 lines (Hussars 32 lines).
Medium	....	30 ,, 34 ,,
Small	....	24 ,, 29 ,,
Gorget	....	20 lines.

A.O. 180
1894

Lace, Quality of—The standard quality recommended for gold lace is as follows .

Gold .... 3·500 ⎫
Silver .... 87·334 ⎬ per cent.
Alloy .... 9·166 ⎭

The lace should be fire-gilt.

For laces more than $\frac{1}{2}$ inch wide, the thread should be 4-drachm, and wire "20 fine." For narrower laces, the thread should be $3\frac{1}{2}$-drachm, and wire "20 extra fine."

APPENDIX IV.

DESCRIPTION OF THE LATEST PATTERN OF SERVICE REVOLVER: "PISTOL, WEBLEY, MARK IV." See paragraph 30.

(Plate 65.)

This Pistol belongs to the class of extracting revolvers. The calibre is ·441 inch. The principal parts are the barrel (a), the cylinder (b), and the body (c).

The barrel is jointed to the body at (d), and held in position for firing by the rib (e) extending back on to the body, and is firmly secured by the barrel catch (f).

The cylinder is chambered to hold 6 cartridges, and is mounted to the barrel on a fixed axis, and held in position at the time of extracting by the cam (g).

The stem of the extractor lies in the fixed axis, surrounded by a spiral spring which returns the extractor after ejecting the cartridge cases ; the extractor is forced out by a small lever in the joint as the barrel is being rotated on the joint pin.

When it is necessary to remove the cylinder for cleaning, the fixing screw (j) must be unscrewed, and the pistol opened to its fullest extent ; then, by pressing the lever (h) against the cam (g), the cylinder will be free ; in no other position can the cylinder be taken off the axis.

The body is fitted with a shield plate (i) of hardened steel, to prevent wear of firing hole, and to support base of cartridge.

Weight of pistol about 2 lbs. 3 ozs.

The latest pattern of cartridge for this pistol is shown on plate 65.

Charge, about $7\frac{1}{2}$ grains of cordite. Bullet, about 265 grains.

APPENDIX V.

DESCRIPTION OF SABRETACHES :—

1. FOR OFFICERS WEARING THE UNIFORM OF " COLONEL ON THE STAFF."
2. ALL MOUNTED OFFICERS EXCEPT AS ABOVE.* (ROYAL ARTILLERY AND HUSSARS FOR UNDRESS ONLY.)

Dimensions are subject to reasonable manufacturing toleration.

(1) OFFICERS WEARING UNIFORM OF COLONEL ON THE STAFF.

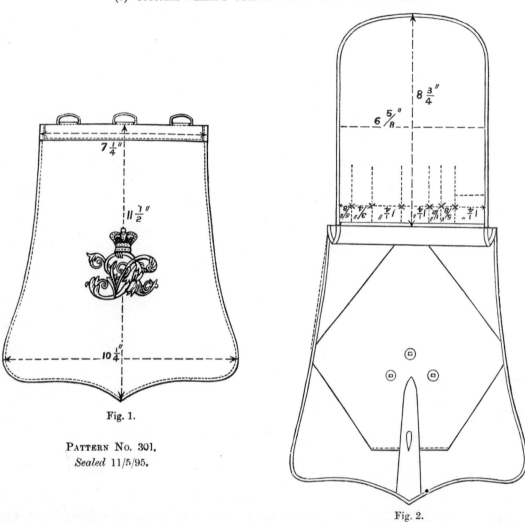

Fig. 1.

PATTERN No. 301.
Sealed 11/5/95.

Fig. 2.

Flap.—Front, as in Fig. 1, made of millboard, covered back and front with red Russia leather. The front part is turned over the edge so as to form a binding, and is sewn all round with silk to match. Three gilt metal dees ¾ inch wide are attached to the flap at top by means of leather chapes sewn on to the back. The centre part of the pocket comes over the top, forming a binding through which the chapes for the dees pass.

Ornament.—Gilding metal, " V.R." and Crown above. It is fastened through the flap by means of fixed screws and small nuts.

The back of the flap is covered with red Russia leather, having extra pieces on the corners, as in Fig. 2, which shows the sabretache opened. A tab is fitted at the bottom to fasten the pocket down.

Pocket.—The pocket is double, one compartment being on either side of the centre piece. This, as above stated, passes over the top of the flap and forms a binding.

The gussets are made in one piece for each of the two compartments, and are sewn on to the centre piece; each gusset is 1⅜ inches wide when made up.

The inner compartment is shown in Fig. 2. It is a plain pocket without flap, bound all round. Inside the top on the front part is attached a piece of elastic webbing 1½ inches wide, sewn down at intervals to form loops for pens &c. In the centre is a small leather inner pocket for safety ink bottle, 1½ inches wide, and 2 inches deep.

---

* Regiments of Cavalry having special regimental patterns are allowed to retain them.

Both compartments, except the gussets, are lined with red skiver.

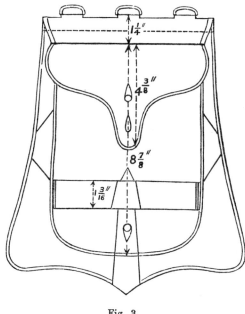

Fig. 3.

Fig. 3 shows the back of the pocket when closed. There is a sword loop across the bottom of the pocket $1\frac{3}{16}$ inches wide, with a loop in the centre for the tab to pass through. The pocket and flap thereof are bound all round. The flap is sewn on from the inside and is turned over. Two studs are sewn in as shown.

The centre piece is bound on each side above the pockets.

(2) Pattern for Mounted Officers except those wearing (1).

This is the same as Fig. 1, in shape, make, and size, with the following exceptions :—

The front is of solid black patent leather. It is unlined, but has corner-pieces at the back (as shown in Fig. 2), and is not bound, but is stitched round the edge.

The pocket is made as in pattern (1), except that it is of black enamelled horse hide, lined with black roan and the gussets are of black roan.

No ornament is worn on it by Mounted Officers of Infantry except in Rifle Regiments.

Departmental Officers wear the same device as shown in Fig. 1.

In other branches regimental devices are worn as authorized.

APPENDIX VI

DESCRIPTION OF SADDLERY.

(1) FIELD MARSHALS AND GENERAL OFFICERS.

Head Collar.—Bridle leather.

The *head* is $1\frac{1}{8}$ inches, and the throat lash $\frac{7}{8}$ inch in width ; each is fitted with a chased gilt double buckle.

The noseband and backstay are $1\frac{1}{8}$ inches in width, and are fitted with two $1\frac{3}{8}$-inch by $1\frac{1}{8}$-inch gilt squares.

The jowl piece is $\frac{7}{8}$ inch in width, and is fitted with two gilt rings, the lower $1\frac{3}{8}$ inches, and the upper $1\frac{1}{8}$ inches, internal diameter.

The browband is covered with blue enamelled leather. It is 1 inch in width, and has two loops formed at each end, the larger one for the head piece, and the smaller one for the throat lash. A tab, to close with a gilt stud, is sewn on each end. The ends are each fitted with a rosette of blue enamelled leather, $2\frac{1}{4}$ inches in diameter, $1\frac{3}{8}$ inches in height.

Bit, Portmouth.—Of steel, with medium port, bent branch, pads, and bottom bar ; cheeks of shell pattern having open tails with bolts and rings ; it is fitted with two steel curb hooks, and a graduated double link curb chain. The bosses are gilt, and are secured to the bits by copper shanks. Royal Cypher in the centre, with crossed batons under for Field Marshals, baton and sword for General Officers, encircled with laurel and surmounted by a Crown.

Bit Head.—Of bridle leather, $\frac{3}{4}$ inch wide, fitted with a $\frac{3}{4}$-inch chased gilt double buckle, and sewn on to bit.

Bit Reins.—Of bridle leather, $\frac{7}{8}$ inch in width, fitted with billets, and $\frac{7}{8}$-inch chased gilt double buckles. A leather slide loop is fitted to the reins, and the hand part is made up with a wedge.

Bridoon Bit.—Of wrought iron, with plain mouthpiece, 6 inches in width ; rings $1\frac{3}{4}$ inches in diameter, and tees $5\frac{1}{4}$ inches in length.

Bridoon Reins.—Of bridle leather, $\frac{3}{4}$ inch in width, sewn on to the bridoon ; the hand part to overlap, and neatly sewn.

The reins for Field Marshals are fitted with billets, and $\frac{3}{4}$-inch chased gilt double buckles, to buckle over bits. The reins for "review order" for Field Marshals are covered with 1-inch gold lace and lined with red morocco.

Breastplate.—Of bridle leather.

The body is $2\frac{1}{4}$ inches in width at top, and is shaped to 1 inch, and fitted with a 1-inch brass roller single buckle. The ends of the top piece are crossed over the top of the body, and a boss is fitted over the junction.

The buckling pieces are $\frac{7}{8}$ inch in width, and are fitted with $\frac{5}{16}$-inch slide loops, $\frac{7}{8}$-inch chased gilt double buckles, and two leather safes.

The neck straps are $\frac{7}{8}$ inch in width, and are fitted with 1-inch gilt rings, and joined by a connecting piece $1\frac{1}{4}$ inches in width, shaped, and furnished with two detachable attachment straps, $\frac{3}{4}$ inch in width, which are fitted with buckles.

Case, Horse-shoe.—Of blocked bridle leather, horse-shoe shape, $6\frac{1}{4}$ inches in width by 6 inches in depth ; fitted with a nail pocket of hogskin.

It is buckled under the near flap of the saddle.

Girths.—Of dark blue woollen web.

The undergirth is 5 inches in width ; the overgirth is $2\frac{3}{4}$ inches in width ; each being bound with hogskin, fitted with solid nickel silver buckles, and having chapes of bridle leather.

Head Rope.—Universal pattern, $1\frac{1}{4}$-inch white cotton rope, fitted at one end with a brown leather billet, but having a chased gilt double buckle. The other end whipped.

Runners, Stirrup leather.—Of brass, $1\frac{7}{16}$ inches by $\frac{1}{2}$ inch by $\frac{7}{8}$ inch, internal measurement ; the outside edges are bevelled, and inside rounded.

Saddle.—Hunting pattern, but with fans and front points to the side bars.

The seat is covered with hogskin.

The flaps are plain, of printed skirt leather.

The pannels are lined, and have pockets of bridle leather, and facings and welts of hogskin, and are stuffed with white wool flock. The near side pannel is fitted with a strap for the carriage of the shoe case.

Stirrup Leathers.—Of stirrup butt leather, $1\frac{3}{8}$ inches in width, fitted with a $1\frac{3}{8}$-inch barred end curved solid nickel silver buckle.

Stirrup Irons.—Of wrought iron, hollow tread pattern. The tread is $4\frac{1}{2}$ inches by $2\frac{1}{4}$ inches, internal measurements ; the height of the iron $4\frac{3}{4}$ inches.

Straps.—Of bridle leather.

Cape centre	$25\frac{1}{2}$ inches by $\frac{3}{4}$ inch.
Cape and Wallet	$40\frac{1}{2}$,, ,, $\frac{3}{4}$,,
Baggage or Cloak	$25\frac{1}{2}$,, ,, $\frac{3}{4}$,,

Each strap is fitted with $\frac{3}{4}$-inch brass roller double buckles.

Wallets.—The backs are of crop butt leather ; the connecting band of collar back ; the fronts, covers, gussets, pocket, and inside loop, of bag-hide.

The wallets are 12 inches in length by $5\frac{1}{2}$ inches in width. They are lined with check waterproof material.

An ammunition pocket is fitted inside the "near" wallet, and a loop for pistol inside the "off" one.

The back of each wallet is furnished with two loops.

(2) Mounted Services below the rank of General Officer, except Artillery.

Differences from the general patterns are allowed in some regiments. These are mentioned in the text of the Regulations.

Head Collar.—Bridle leather.

The head is $1\frac{1}{8}$ inches, and the throat lash $\frac{7}{8}$ inch in width; each is fitted with a brass roller double buckle.

The noseband and backstay are each 1 inch in width, and are fitted with two $1\frac{3}{8}$-inch by $1\frac{1}{8}$-inch brass squares.

The jowl piece is $\frac{7}{8}$ inch in width. It is fitted with two brass rings, the lower $1\frac{3}{8}$ inches, and the upper $1\frac{1}{8}$ inches, internal diameter.

The browband is 1 inch in width, and has two loops formed at each end, the larger one for the head piece, and the smaller one for the throat lash; a tab, to close with a brass stud, is sewn on each end. The ends are each fitted with a brass ear rosette $2\frac{1}{4}$ inches by 2 inches, mounted on leather.

Bit, Portmouth.—Of steel, medium port, with bent branch, pads, bottom bar, and fitted with two steel curb hooks, and a graduated double link curb chain.

The bosses are of brass, and have the Royal Cypher shown within a Garter bearing the words HONI. SOIT. QUI. MAL. Y. PENSE, and surmounted by a crown, or are of other authorized regimental patterns.

Bit Head.—Of bridle leather, $\frac{3}{4}$ inch wide; sewn to the bit.

Bit Reins.—As for General Officers, except that they are fitted with brass roller double buckles.

Bridoon Bit.—As for General Officers.

Bridoon Reins.—As for General Officers.

Breastplate.—Bridle leather. The body is $1\frac{5}{8}$ inches in width at the top end, and is shaped to $1\frac{1}{8}$ inches. Where the top straps join the body, the junction is covered with a "heart," on which is fitted a boss similar to that on the bit. The buckling pieces have brass roller double buckles, and the neck strap is fitted with brass rings and studs.

Case, Horse-shoe.—Of bridle leather, $5\frac{1}{4}$ inches in depth by $6\frac{3}{8}$ inches in width; back and flap cut in one piece. The inside is fitted with a nail pocket.

Two suspending straps, $7\frac{1}{2}$ inches in length by $\frac{3}{4}$ inch in width, fitted with two $\frac{3}{4}$-inch brass roller double buckles, are sewn on.

Girths.—As for General Officers.

Head Rope.—Universal pattern; $1\frac{1}{4}$-inch 3-strand twisted white cotton rope, fitted at one end with a brown leather billet and a 1-inch brass roller double buckle; the other end whipped.

Runners, Stirrup leather.—As for General Officers.*

Saddle.—Cavalry pattern, with pommel and cantle bound with brass.

The seat is covered with hogskin. The flaps are plain, of printed skirt leather.

The pannels are lined with wool serge. They have pockets of bridle leather, and facings and welts of hogskin, and are stuffed with white wool flock.

Stirrup Leathers.—As for General Officers.

Stirrup Irons.—As for General Officers.

Surcingle.—Of bridle leather; body $1\frac{7}{8}$ inches in width.

Straps.—As for General Officers.

Wallets.—As for General Officers.

Lambskin.—Front and rear portions of black lambskin, connected by a central piece, forming the seat, of black bag hide. Two holes in front portion, to give access to wallets, bound round the edges with black leather, and covered by a flap. Hole in rear portion for cantle, bound round edges with black leather. Lambskin points edged with scarlet cloth, scalloped, showing about $1\frac{1}{2}$ inches. The whole lined with moleskin.

Extreme length	3 feet 2 inches.
Extreme width of front portion	2 ,, 11 ,,
Width of rear portion immediately behind leather	1 ,, $8\frac{1}{2}$,,
Width of leather seat at middle (hollowed out)	1 ,,

(3) Royal Horse Artillery.

As for mounted services, except :—

Case, Horse-shoe.—The same pattern, but adjusted for attachment to form of tree.

Girths.—Both $3\frac{1}{4}$ inches wide, one being fitted with loops for surcingle.

Saddle.—Regimental pattern of tree, showing wooden cantle bound with brass. Seat, solid blocked leather, covered with hogskin.

Wallets.—The same pattern, but adjusted for attachment to form of tree.

(4) Dismounted Services and Staff Officers below the rank of General Officer.

The same as for mounted services, except :—

Head Collar.—The brow band is covered with enamelled leather, colour according to branch of Service.

Case, Horse-shoe.—As for General Officers.

Saddle.—As for General Officers.

NOTE.—Rifle Battalions have special patterns as to colour of head rope.

Saddle Bag for Manœuvres or Active Service.—Brown bag hide leather, lined with check waterproof material, fitted with a shaped flat cap $6\frac{1}{2}$ inches deep and 9 inches wide. A strap and buckle in front to secure the bag when closed. Two straps and buckles at the back of the bag to attach it to the dees on the off-side of the saddle. A dee with steadying strap at the side to connect the bag with the girth.

The dimensions of the bag are as follows :—

Depth 10 inches, width 7 inches at the top, and 11 inches at the bottom. Gusset, 3 inches at the bottom, gradually narrowing to $2\frac{1}{2}$ inches at the top, with pieces of the leather left on to turn in and fasten with a strap and buckle.

NOTE.—The provision of this saddle bag is optional.

---

* Regimental pattern in the 7th Dragoon Guards, and 2nd Dragoons.

APPENDIX VII.

SWORDS AND SCABBARDS.

(1) FIELD MARSHALS AND GENERAL OFFICERS. (Approved, 27th July, 1896.)

(*Plate* 66.)

Sword.—The blade is of the shape shown in the annexed plate. The mounting is metal gilt, and consists of crosspiece, strap, two studs and screws, and sword-knot bushes (all ornamented). The grips are of ivory, fastened on the tang with the above-mentioned studs and screws.

61002 / 6432

The blade may be plain, or ornamentally embossed.

The blade recovers straightness after being subjected to a weight of 10 lbs. vertically with 1 inch depression.

Scabbard.—The scabbard is of steel, and is fitted with an iron sputcheon with brass mouthpiece, brazed on and fixed in scabbard with two screws. Two bands with loose rings are fixed on with two screws 3 inches and 12 inches respectively from the top of the mouthpiece.

The lining consists of two strips of wood held in position by the sputcheon.

Length of Sword	....	....	....	....	....	....	....	2 feet 11½ inches
,, ,, Scabbard	....	....	....	....	....	....	....	2 ,, 7 ,,
,, ,, Blade from shoulder to point	....	.. ..	....	....	2 ,, 6 ,,
,, ,, Sword and Scabbard	....	....	....	.. ..	3 ,, 0 ,,
Balance from hilt	....	....	....	....	....	....	0 ,, 4¼ ,,
Weight of Sword	....	....	....	....	about....	1 lb. 10½ ozs.
Weight of Scabbard complete	....	....	,, ...	1 lb. 1 oz.

---

(2) OFFICERS OF CAVALRY OF THE LINE. (Approved, 11th September, 1896.)

(*Plate* 67.)

Sword.—The blade is slightly curved, and tapers gradually from shoulder to point. It is fullered on both sides to a thickness of not less than ·05 inch, commencing at 1½ inches from the shoulder to 11 inches from the point.

The mounting consists of guard, grip, strap, ferrule, and nut.

The guard, grip, and ferrule are held in position by a nut screwed on the tang; the strap is held in position by the ferrule, and by the tang being riveted over the top of the strap.

The guard is of steel, and is pierced by an ornamental device. The grip is of wood, covered with fish skin, and bound with silver wire. It must be from 5 inches to 5¾ inches long, variation being allowed according to size of hand.

The blade may be plain, or ornamentally embossed. In the latter case, while it is not necessary that a uniform pattern of ornamentation should be followed, the design should not include any badge or device beyond the Royal Monogram and Crown, and the usual manufacturer's name or trade mark.

Swords of this pattern should stand the following tests :—

Blade, in set and stiffened stage.— Struck back and edge, and on both flats, on an oak block by hand.

With a weight of 30 lbs. in the vertical testing machine, the blade should recover straightness after not less than 1 inch depression; in the same machine it should be shortened 4 inches.

Hilt assembled.—Struck a moderate blow on an oak block, back and edge, to test the soundness of hilting.

Sword complete.—With a weight of 28 lbs. in the vertical testing machine, the sword should recover straightness after not less than 1 inch depression.

Scabbard.—The scabbard is of steel, and is fitted with a German silver mouthpiece with sputcheon brazed on, fixed to the scabbard by two screws. Two bands with loose rings are brazed on the scabbard, 2 5/16 inches and 10⅝ inches respectively from the top of the mouthpiece.

The lining is of leather, blocked flesh side out, turned, butted, and herring-bone stitched with fine waxed thread on the right side of lining, and held in position by the sputcheon.

Length of Sword....	....	....	....	....	.. .	.... about	3 ft. 5 inches.*
,, ,, Scabbard	....	....	....	....	....	....	3 ,, 0 ,,
,, ,, Blade from shoulder to point	....	....	....	....	2 ,, 11 1/16 ,,
,, ,, Sword and Scabbard	....	....	. ....	.... about	3 ,, 6 ,, *
Balance from hilt	....	....	....	....	....	.... ,,	6½ ,, *
Weight of Sword	....	....	....	....	....	,,	2 lbs. 1 ounce.*
,, ,, Scabbard complete ...	....	....	....	....	,,	1 lb. 3½ ounces.
,, ,, ,, lining	....	....	....	....	....	,,	2 ,,

---

* These particulars will vary slightly according to the length of grip.

(3) OFFICERS OF ROYAL ENGINEERS; INFANTRY OF THE LINE, EXCLUDING HIGHLAND AND SCOTTISH REGIMENTS; ARMY PAY DEPARTMENT; ARMY ORDNANCE DEPARTMENT. (Approved 13th December, 1897.)

(Plate 68.)

Sword.—The blade is straight, tapers gradually, is $32\frac{9}{16}$ inches long from shoulder to point, and is fullered on both sides to a thickness of not less than ·05 inch.

The mountings consist of guard, grip, strap, ferrule, nut, and washer.

The guard, grip, and ferrule are held in position by a nut screwed on the tang; the strap is held in position by a ferrule and washer, the tang being riveted over the washer.

The guard is of steel, and is pierced with an ornamental device. The size of the perforations, is important. They are so arranged as not to permit of a sword point passing through, so as to injure the hand.

The grip is of wood covered with fish skin, and bound with silver wire.

The length of the grip must be from 5 to $5\frac{3}{4}$ inches, variation being allowed to suit the size of the hand.

The blade may be plain, or ornamentally embossed. In the latter case, while it is not necessary that a uniform pattern of ornamentation should be followed, the design should not include any badge or device beyond the Royal Monogram and Crown, and the usual manufacturer's name or trade-mark.

Swords of this pattern should withstand the following tests :—

Blade.—In set and stiffened stage :—Struck on back and edge and on both flat sides, on an oak block by hand.

With a weight of 34 lbs., in the vertical testing machine, the blade should recover straightness after not less than 1 inch depression. In the same machine the blade should be shortened 4 inches by bending from right to left, and then from left to right.

Hilt assembled.—Struck a moderate blow on an oak block, back and edge, to test the soundness of hilting.

Sword complete.—With a weight of 32 lbs. in the vertical testing machine, it should recover straightness after not less than 1 inch depression.

Scabbard.—The scabbard is of steel. It is fitted with a German silver mouthpiece with the sputcheon brazed on, fixed to the scabbard by two screws. Two bands with loose rings are brazed on to the scabbard $2\frac{1}{8}$ inches and $10\frac{3}{8}$ inches respectively from the top of the mouthpiece.

The lining is of leather, blocked flesh side out, turned, butted, and herring-bone stitched with fine waxed thread on the right side of lining, and held in position by the sputcheon.

Length of Sword			3 feet $2\frac{1}{2}$ inches. *
„ „ Scabbard			2 „ $9\frac{3}{4}$ „
„ „ Blade from shoulder to point			2 „ $8\frac{1}{2}$ „
„ „ Sword and Scabbard....			3 „ $3\frac{3}{8}$ „ *
Balance from hilt		about	$4\frac{1}{2}$ „ *
Weight of Sword		„	2 lbs. 0 ounces.*
„ „ Scabbard		„	$15\frac{1}{4}$ „
„ „ „ Lining		„	$1\frac{1}{2}$ „

61002
6815

(4) DESCRIPTION OF SCABBARD FOR USE WITH "SAM BROWNE" BELTS.

PATTERN NOS. 398, 399. *Sealed 4th January,* 1900.

(Plate 69.)

A.O.
151
1899

The scabbard is built up with two strips of wood, grooved to receive blade of sword; they are butted and glued together.

The strips of wood are covered with brown leather, sewn down one side. A raised rib is formed $2\frac{5}{8}$ inches from the top of the locket by a piece of packing between wood and leather.

The scabbard is mounted with steel locket and chape, fastened with wire lace, on the sewn side.

A scabbard supporter accompanies the scabbard (see drawing). The body is made of bridle leather, and the tab of hogskin or other suitable leather. The supporter slides on the scabbard to hold it at a proper height in the frog, the tab being buttoned on to the front stud of the latter.

Length overall		2 feet 10 inches.
„ of locket		$1\frac{3}{4}$ inches.
„ of chape		9 inches.
Weight of scabbard complete....		$10\frac{1}{2}$ ounces.

The pattern scabbard is to be regarded as typical only, as shape and dimensions may require to be varied according to the sword to be carried.

---

* These particulars will vary slightly according to the length of grip.

APPENDIX VIII

BELTS AND SWORD KNOT (UNIVERSAL PATTERN).

---

(1) THE "SAM BROWNE" BELTS.

Pattern No. 397.   Sealed 4th January, 1900.

(Plate 70.)

(Worn by officers of all branches of the service.   See paragraph 28).

A.O.
151

1899

The belts, complete, consist of a waist-belt, two shoulder-belts, a sword-frog, an ammunition-pouch, and a pistol-case ; the whole made of brown bridle leather.

The waist-belt is 2⅜ inches wide, and of a length to suit the wearer.   It is fitted with a double-tongued brass buckle, and has four brass dees for the shoulder-belts (two at the back, and one on each side), a running loop for the free end of the belt, two brass rings for attachment of the frog, and a hook for hooking it up.   The waist-belt is lined with faced basil.

The shoulder-belts are plain straps (crossed at the back through a loop).   They are 1½ inches wide.   The patterns are about 35 inches long over all, without chapes.   The length however may be varied to suit the wearer.   They are fitted with studs for attachment to the dees at the back of the waist-belt.   A chape, with stud and a buckle, is provided for each, for attachment to the dees at the sides of the belt.

In mounted services the strap over the left shoulder need not be worn, except when it is required to support the revolver.

The frog is fitted with two straps, which are to be passed through the rings on the lower part of the belt.   Each strap is secured by a stud.   The frog has a small brass dee on the top, to go over the hook on the belt when "hooking up."   A small strap passes through the front and back for securing the sword scabbard.   A stud is fitted on the front of the frog, upon which the tab of the scabbard supporter may be fastened.   (See description of leather scabbard.)

A small strap for steadying the sword hilt is attached to the rear ring for the frog, holes being made in the strap to pass over a stud on the belt above the front ring.

The ammunition-pouch and pistol-case are fitted with loops on the back for attachment to the waist-belt ; also with stud and tab fastenings.   The loop on the pistol-case is furnished with a small brass hook, which should pass through a hole to be made for the purpose in the belt to suit the wearer in order to secure the case and keep it in position.

The pattern pistol-case is to be regarded as typical only, as its dimensions must suit the particular pattern of pistol carried.

The "furniture" should be of the best yellow brass.

(2) WEB SWORD BELT.

(See paragraph 28.)

This consists of a waist belt and a shoulder suspender of worsted web, strengthened at various parts with black Morocco leather.   It is furnished with loops, chapes, and dees, as shown in the drawing annexed.   The loops and chapes are of Morocco leather, and the furniture of gilding metal.

The suspender is fitted with hooks so that it can be removed by officers wearing the web belt under the sash, outside the frock coat.

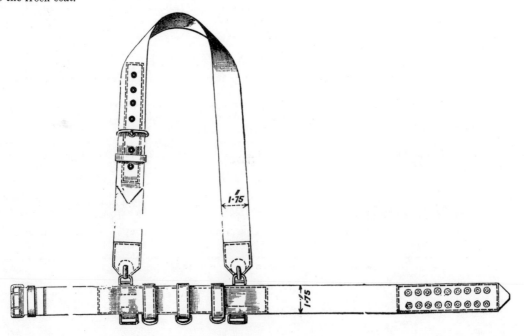

(3) WEB BELT AND BUFF STRAPS FOR CARRYING GREAT-COAT, see paragraph 14.

The belt is made from 2⅛-inch worsted web, and is strengthened at the eyelet holes by a light piece of leather. The coat straps are made from buff leather, and the furniture of gilding metal.
For Rifle Regiments the web and leather are black.

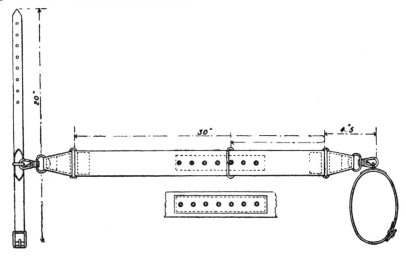

(4) SWORD-KNOT (UNIVERSAL PATTERN), UNDRESS

A.O. 151
——
1899

The sword-knot to be used with the "Sam Browne" belt is the universal pattern of brown leather. It is a plain strap made of pigskin, best bridle leather, or calf, the ends being secured into an "acorn" having plaited leather covering. It is furnished with a sliding keeper.
Length of strap in the double, 15 inches; width of strap, ⅝ inch; length of acorn, 2½ inches.

APPENDIX IX.

WATER BOTTLE.

DESCRIPTION OF THE PATTERN WITH WHICH OFFICERS ARE RECOMMENDED TO PROVIDE THEMSELVES.

The bottle is made of pure aluminium, of the form and dimensions shown in the accompanying drawings :—

Bottle complete, with cover and sling.

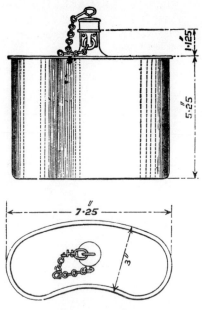

Bottle uncovered.

It has a cork stopper attached by a short chain. The cork is held on a stem, tapped at the end to receive a small nut, so that the cork, which is of the size generally used for wine bottles, &c., may be readily renewed when necessary.

The bottle is covered with felt, and has a strap fixed around it, passing through four loops sewn on to the felt. The extremities of this strap, which are at the shoulders of the bottle, are provided with brass loops, through which the ends of the sling or carrier are passed. The sling is $\frac{5}{8}$ inch wide, and of suitable length for the wearer. It has a brass stud fixed near each end and a hole at the end to button on to the stud. The sling may therefore be worn under belts, so as to carry the bottle steadily, and the latter may be removed without disturbing the sling. The leather is all brown "best bridle."

Weight complete, about 14 ozs.

Capacity of bottle, $2\frac{1}{4}$ pints.

APPENDIX X.

SHOULDER-CHAINS FOR OFFICERS OF CAVALRY AND ROYAL HORSE ARTILLERY.

EXTRACTS FROM OFFICIAL SPECIFICATION.

(Plate 63.)

"The rings must be made of the best hard-drawn steel wire, which when faced together will make a diameter "of ·065 inch. The external diameter of the rings to be ·400 inch.

"The chains are to contain 319 links, and weigh from 4 to $4\frac{1}{2}$ ozs.; they must be perfectly sound, well finished, "and in all respects equal to the sealed pattern.

"The chains must resist a tensile strain of not less than 160 lbs., and the permanent elongation after such strain "must not exceed $\frac{1}{16}$ inch over the full length of the shoulder-chain. The breaking strain must be not "less than 224 lbs., applied over the uniform width of 11 links, with attachments to 5 links, so that the "weight is applied from end to end of the shoulder-chain."

APPENDIX XI.

List of Materials, &c., which can be obtained on repayment from the Royal Army Clothing Department (see paragraph 33) :—

Material.

Pattern No. 1. Tartan, No. 1, Black Rifle.
,, ,, 2. ,, blue, Warrant Officers.
,, ,, 3. ,, red, new pattern.
,, ,, 4. ,, blue, ,, ,,
,, ,, 5. Cloth, scarlet, Warrant Officers.
,, ,, 6. ,, blue, ,, ,,
,, ,, 7. ,, ,, No. 3, Serjeants R.A., &c.
,, ,, 8. ,, ,, pantaloon, Warrant Officers.
,, ,, 9. ,, grey, great coat, No. 1, Serjeants.
,, ,, 10. Tweed, blue, Warrant Officer's trousers.
,, ,, 11. Khaki, drill
,, ,, 12. Bedford cord.
,, ,, 13. Serge blue, Warrant Officers.
,, ,, 14. ,, scarlet, ,, ,,
,, ,, 15. ,, blue, privates, thin.
,, ,, 16. Puttees, khaki.
,, ,, 17. ,, blue.
,, ,, 18. Cap, field, Warrant Officers and Staff Serjeants.
,, ,, 19. Field dressing.
,, ,, 20. Jersey, woollen, blue, No. 2.
,, ,, 21. Shoes, canvas.

Prices are published in the Price List of clothing, &c., issued with Army Orders.

APPENDIX XII.

ILLUSTRATIONS.

INDEX.

INDEX TO LACE DESIGNS.

	Forage Cap.	Tunic.	Mess Jacket.	Trousers.	Levée Trousers.	Shoulder Belt.	Slings.	Girdle.
Field Marshal and General Officer	—	—	1	1	—	—	—	—
Colonel on the Staff	—	2	2	2	—	—	—	—
1st Life Guards	—	—	1	1	—	—	1	—
2nd „	—	—	1	1	—	—	1	—
Royal Horse Guards	—	—	3	3	—	—	3	—
1st Dragoon Guards...	4	5	6	7	—	4	4	4
2nd „ „	8	9	9	—	—	10	10	10
3rd „ „	11	12	13	11	—	11	14	11
4th „ „	15	16	16	15	—	15	15	15
5th „ „	11	17	18	11	—	11	19	11
6th „ „	20	21	22	—	—	1	1	1
7th „ „	11	5	9	11	—	10	10	10
1st Dragoons	23	24	24	23	—	25	25	25
2nd „	26	28	6	27	—	29	30	30
3rd Hussars	31	32	—	32	33	34	34	—
4th „	35	36	—	36	37	34	34	—
5th Lancers	38	38	38	38	—	39	39	40
6th Dragoons...	41	42	43	41	—	44	41	41
7th Hussars	45	45	—	45	—	46	46	—
8th „	45	45	—	45	—	47	16	—
9th Lancers	38	38	38	38	—	48	49	40
10th Hussars	45	45	—	45	—	45	45	—
11th „	20	21	—	21	—	50	51	—
12th Lancers	52	52	52	52	—	39	39	40
13th Hussars	45	36	—	36	37	53	53	—
14th „	54	55	—	54	55	53	53	—
15th „	56	56	—	56	—	57	58	—
16th Lancers	59	59	59	60	—	39	58	40
17th „	38	38	38	—	—	61	{ 61 (sword) 62 (tache) }	40
18th Hussars...	45	45	—	45	—	63	45	—
19th „	64	36	—	36	37	45	45	—
20th „	64	36	—	36	—	34	34	—
21st Lancers	64	37	37	36	—	53	53	40
Royal Artillery	65	66	65	65	—	65	65	65
„ Engineers	67	67	67	67	—	—	67	—

								Sword Belt.
Brigade of Guards	—	—	—	—	68	—	68	68
Infantry	—	69, 70, 71	—	—	72	—	72	72
West India Regiment	—	73	—	—	72	—	72	72
Army Service Corps...	74	2	2	74	—	74	74	74
„ Medical Service	75	2	2	75	—	—	—	—
„ Ordnance Department ...	74	2	2	74	—	74	74	74
„ Pay Department	74	2	2	74	—	74	74	74
„ Veterinary Department ...	74	2	2	74	—	74	74	74
Inspectors of Army Schools ...	76	69	—	—	—	—	—	—
Officers, Royal Military College ...	77	77	—	77	—	—	72	72
Captains and Lieutenants of Invalids	77	77	—	77	—	—	72	72

~ The Royal Arms. ~

as settled and approved by Order of Council,
on Her Majesty's accession, and as now used
for the United Kingdom of Great Britain
~ and Ireland ~

(In Military Badges the Royal Helmet and
Mantling are omitted)

EMBROIDERY.　　　　MESS JACKET—GENERAL OFFICER.　　　　METAL.

Plate 1.

**The Royal Arms.
Badges of Rank.**

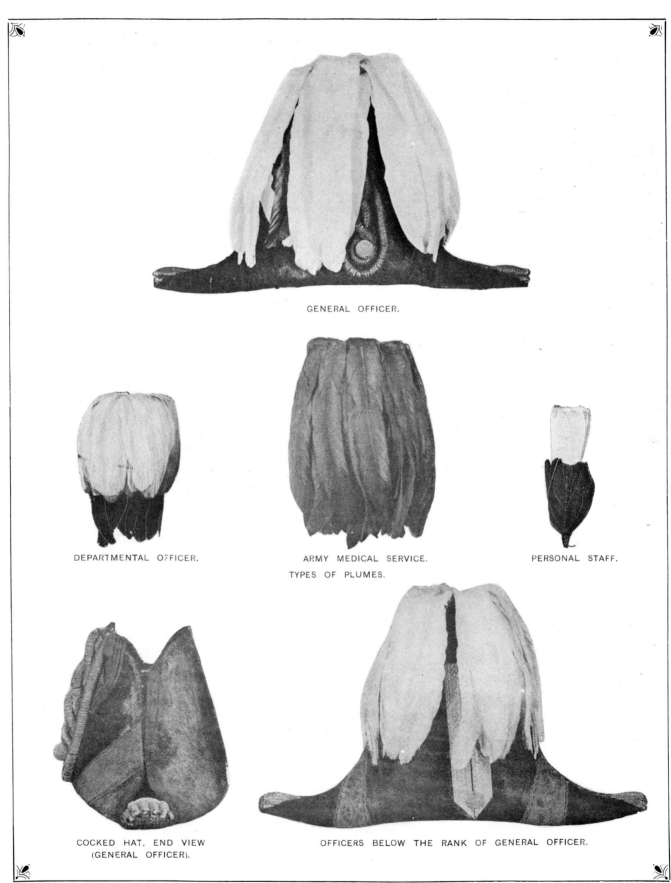

GENERAL OFFICER.

DEPARTMENTAL OFFICER.   ARMY MEDICAL SERVICE.   PERSONAL STAFF.

TYPES OF PLUMES.

COCKED HAT, END VIEW
(GENERAL OFFICER).   OFFICERS BELOW THE RANK OF GENERAL OFFICER.

Plate 2.   **Head-dresses. Cocked Hats and Plumes.**

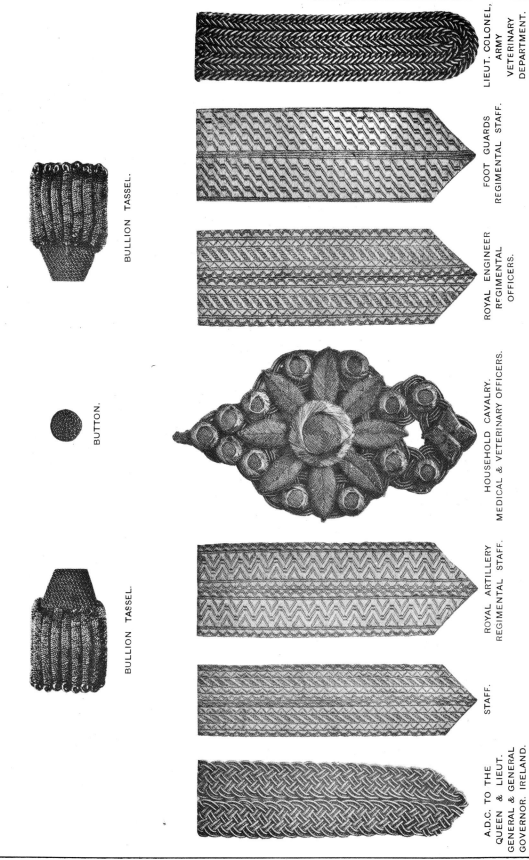

LIEUT. COLONEL, ARMY VETERINARY DEPARTMENT.

FOOT GUARDS REGIMENTAL STAFF.

ROYAL ENGINEER REGIMENTAL OFFICERS.

BULLION TASSEL.

BUTTON.

HOUSEHOLD CAVALRY. MEDICAL & VETERINARY OFFICERS.

BULLION TASSEL.

ROYAL ARTILLERY REGIMENTAL STAFF.

STAFF.

A.D.C. TO THE QUEEN & LIEUT. GENERAL & GENERAL GOVERNOR. IRELAND.

Plate 3.   Head-dresses.—*Continued.*   Trimmings for Cocked Hats.

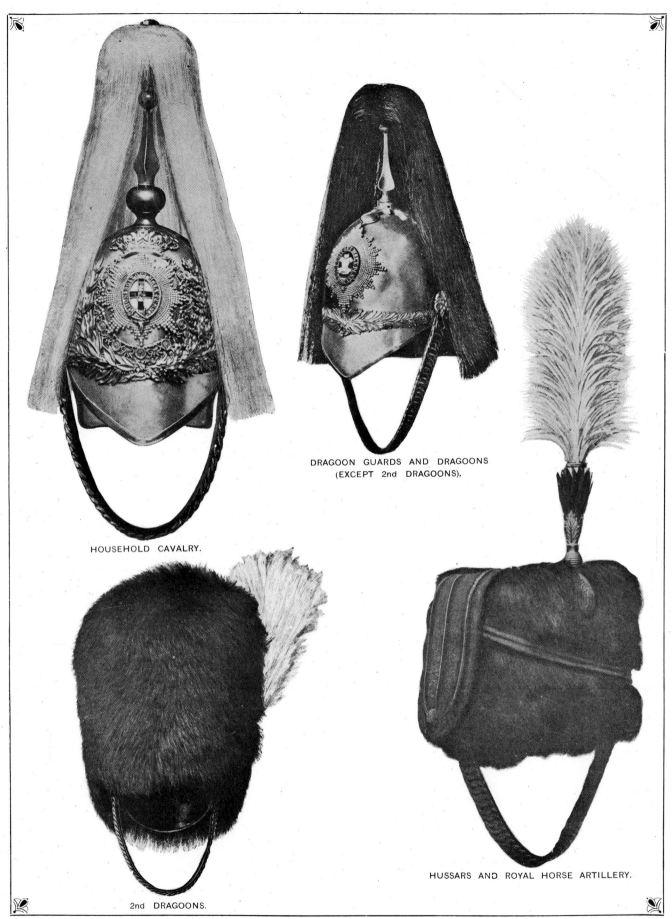

HOUSEHOLD CAVALRY.

DRAGOON GUARDS AND DRAGOONS
(EXCEPT 2nd DRAGOONS).

2nd DRAGOONS.

HUSSARS AND ROYAL HORSE ARTILLERY.

Plate 4. **Head-dresses.**—*Continued.*

LANCERS.

BALL—ROYAL ARTILLERY.

HELMET, UNIVERSAL HOME PATTERN.

Plate 5. **Head-dresses.**—*Continued.*

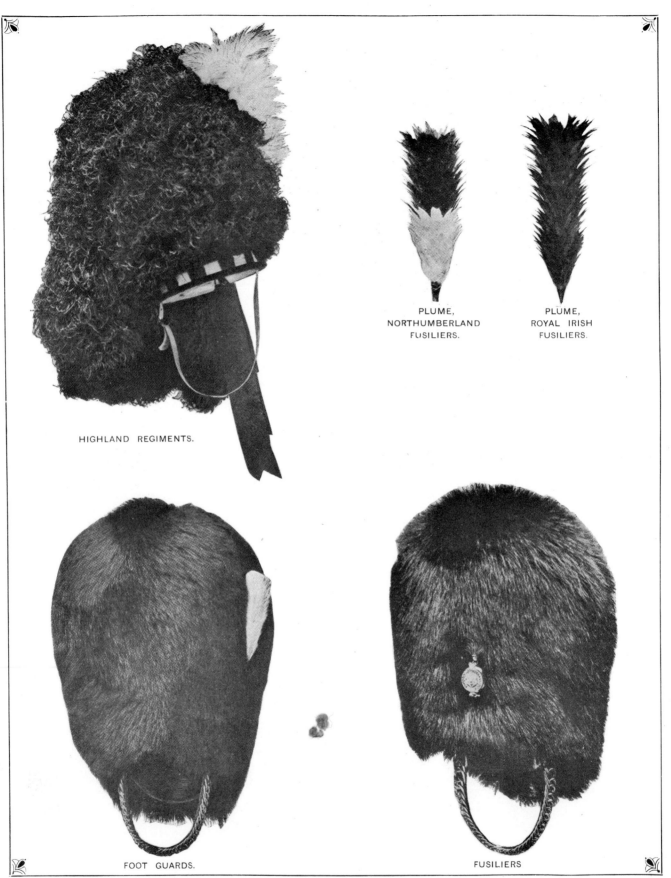

HIGHLAND REGIMENTS.

PLUME,
NORTHUMBERLAND
FUSILIERS.

PLUME,
ROYAL IRISH
FUSILIERS.

FOOT GUARDS.

FUSILIERS

Plate 6. **Head-dresses.**—*Continued.*

HIGHLAND LIGHT INFANTRY.

SCOTTISH RIFLES.

OTHER RIFLE REGIMENTS.

Plate 7.

Head-dresses.—*Continued.*

STAFF.

HOUSEHOLD CAVALRY.

DRAGOON GUARDS.
(1st AND 6th DRAGOONS).

2nd DRAGOONS.

HUSSARS.

LANCERS.

ROYAL ARTILLERY.

ROYAL ENGINEERS.

Plate 8.   **Head-dresses—Undress.   Forage Caps.**

RIFLES.

FOOT GUARDS.

INFANTRY OF THE LINE.

GLENGARRY
(TYPE OF)

FIELD CAP,
SHOWING BADGE AND
CHIN STRAP.

FIELD CAP, UNFOLDED.

PROVOST MARSHAL.

Plate 9.

Head-dresses.—*Continued.*

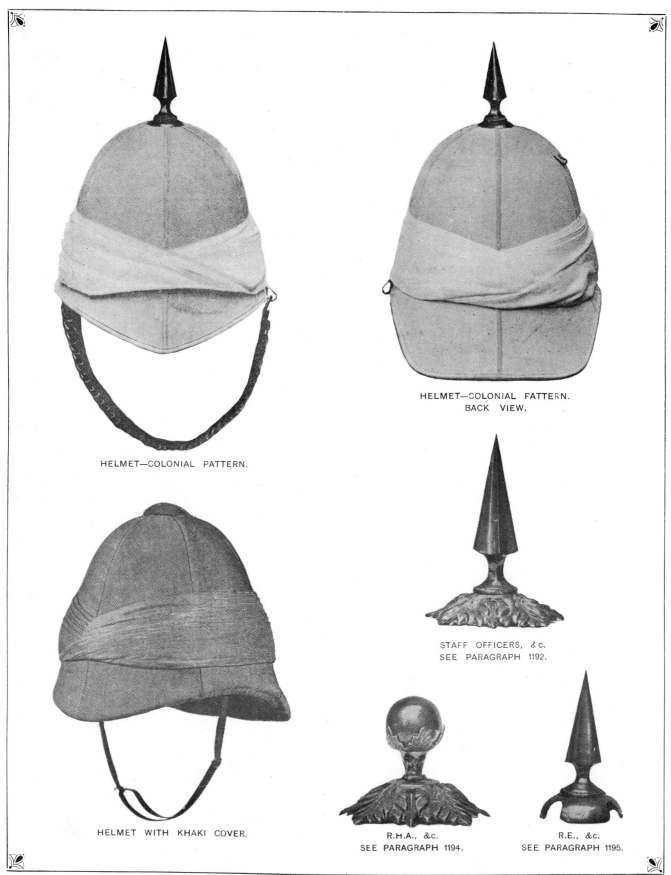

HELMET—COLONIAL PATTERN.

HELMET—COLONIAL PATTERN.
BACK VIEW.

HELMET WITH KHAKI COVER.

STAFF OFFICERS, &c.
SEE PARAGRAPH 1192.

R.H.A., &c.
SEE PARAGRAPH 1194.

R.E., &c.
SEE PARAGRAPH 1195.

Plate 10.

Head-dresses. Foreign Service.
Foreign Service Helmet Furniture. Half size.

HELMET—WEST AFRICAN REGIMENT.
CHINESE REGIMENT.

PITH HAT.

TERAI HAT.

FUR CAPS.—DOMINION OF CANADA.

Plate 11.   **Head=dresses. Foreign Service.**—*Continued.*

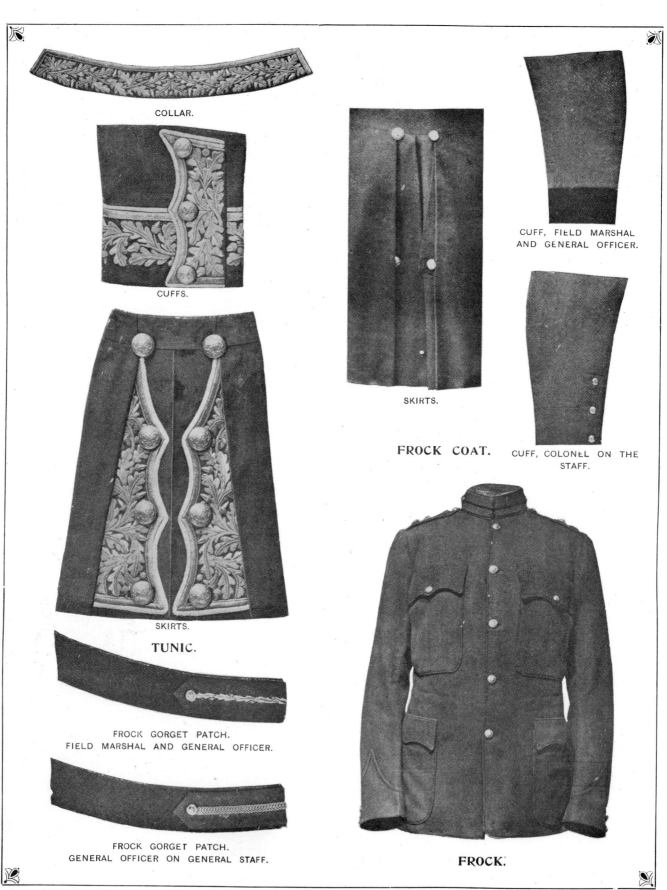

COLLAR.

CUFFS.

SKIRTS.

TUNIC.

CUFF, FIELD MARSHAL
AND GENERAL OFFICER.

SKIRTS.

FROCK COAT.

CUFF, COLONEL ON THE
STAFF.

FROCK GORGET PATCH.
FIELD MARSHAL AND GENERAL OFFICER.

FROCK GORGET PATCH.
GENERAL OFFICER ON GENERAL STAFF.

FROCK.

Plate 12.   Tunic, Field Marshal and General Officer.
Frock Coat and Frock, Field Marshal and General Officer; Colonel on the Staff.

TUNIC WITH AIGUILLETTE OF THE HEAD QUARTERS, GENERAL AND PERSONAL STAFF.
FOR SHOULDER ON WHICH WORN, SEE PARAGRAPH 162.

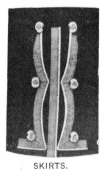

SKIRTS.

FROCK GORGET PATCH.
OFFICERS BELOW RANK OF GENERAL,
ON HEAD-QUARTERS, GENERAL OR
PERSONAL STAFF.

FROCK GORGET PATCH.
COLONEL ON THE STAFF.

RANKS BELOW COLONEL.

COLONEL ON THE STAFF.

Plate 13.

Tunic—Colonel on the Staff, &c.
Collars for Frock—Colonel on the Staff, &c.

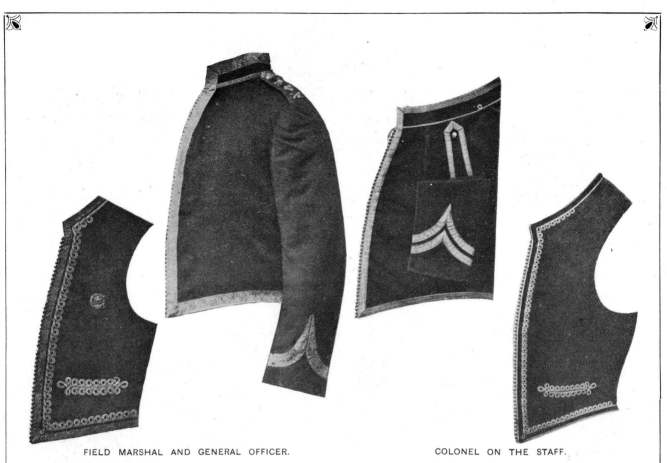

FIELD MARSHAL AND GENERAL OFFICER.   COLONEL ON THE STAFF.

MESS DRESS.

TUNIC COLLAR.

TUNIC SKIRT.

TUNIC.

Plate 14.

**Mess Dress, Staff Officers.
Tunic, A.D.C. to the Queen.**

CUFF.—OFFICER BELOW FIELD RANK.

TUNIC SKIRTS.

CUFF—FIELD OFFICER.

Plate 15.   Tunic & Frock Coat Household Cavalry.

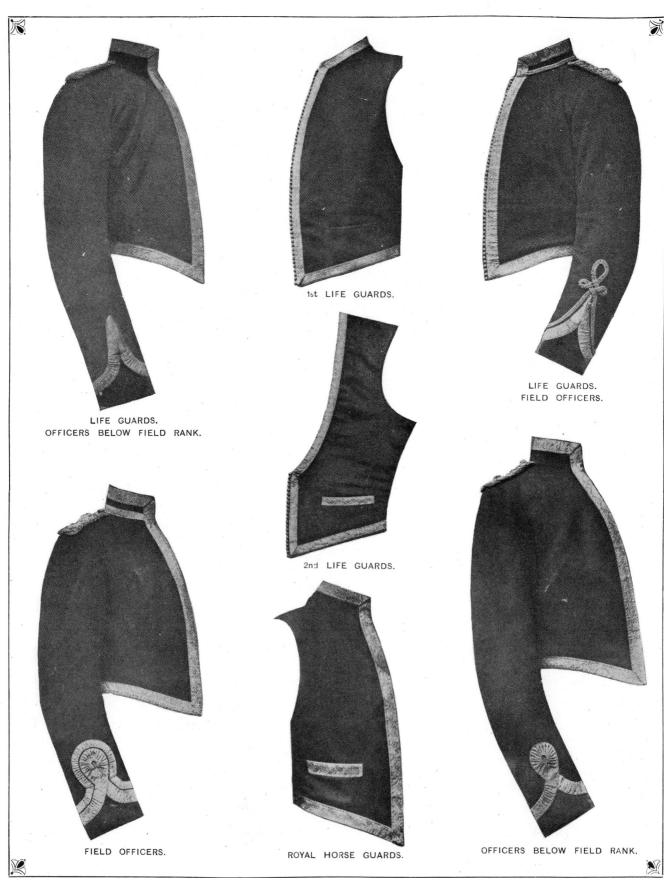

1st LIFE GUARDS.

LIFE GUARDS.
OFFICERS BELOW FIELD RANK.

LIFE GUARDS.
FIELD OFFICERS.

2nd LIFE GUARDS.

FIELD OFFICERS.

ROYAL HORSE GUARDS.

OFFICERS BELOW FIELD RANK.

Plate 16.   **Mess Dress, Household Cavalry.**

LIEUTENANT.

FIELD OFFICER.

TUNIC SKIRTS.

COLLAR.—FIELD OFFICER.
CUFF.—CAPTAIN.

DRAGOON GUARDS & DRAGOONS (EXCEPT 6th DRAGOON GUARDS).

6th DRAGOON GUARDS.—FIELD OFFICERS.

CAPTAIN

LIEUTENANT.

TUNIC SKIRTS.

Plate 17.   **Tunics.—Dragoon Guards and Dragoons.**

FIELD OFFICER.

LIEUTENANT.

FIELD OFFICER.

LIEUTENANT.

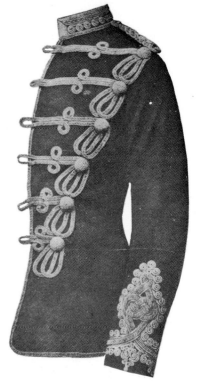

CAPTAIN.

HUSSARS.

FIELD OFFICER.

CUFF.—OFFICERS BELOW
FIELD RANK.

TUNIC SKIRTS.

LANCERS.

Plate 18.   Tunics, Hussars and Lancers.

Plate 19.

Frock, Cavalry of the Line.
Frock Coat, Dragoon Guards and Dragoons.

3rd HUSSARS.

4th HUSSARS.

Plate 20. Patrol Jackets, Hussars.

7th HUSSARS.

8th HUSSARS.

Plate 21.   **Patrol Jackets, Hussars.**

10th HUSSARS.

11th HUSSARS.

Plate 22.   **Patrol Jackets, Hussars.**

13th HUSSARS.

14th HUSSARS.

Plate 23. Patrol Jackets, Hussars.

15th HUSSARS.

18th HUSSARS.

Plate 24.   **Patrol Jackets, Hussars.**

19th HUSSARS.

20th HUSSARS.

Plate 25.
Patrol Jackets, Hussars.

PATTERN NOT YET APPROVED.

5th LANCERS.

ALL LANCERS EXCEPT 5th.

Plate 26.   Patrol Jackets, Lancers.

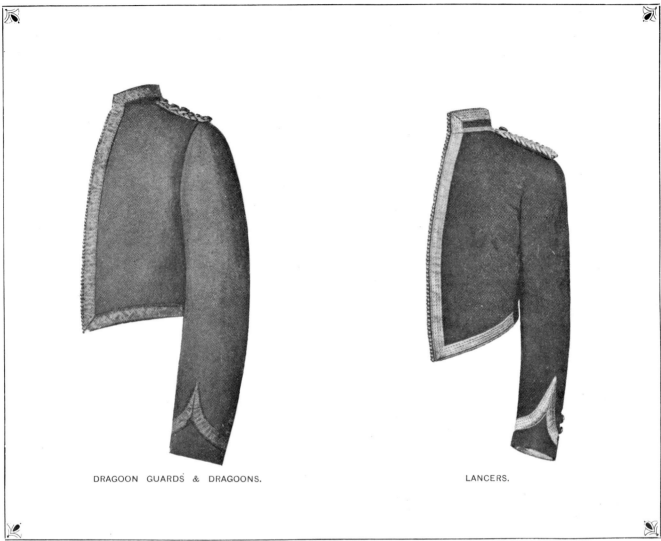

DRAGOON GUARDS & DRAGOONS.   LANCERS.

Plate 27.   **Mess Jackets.**

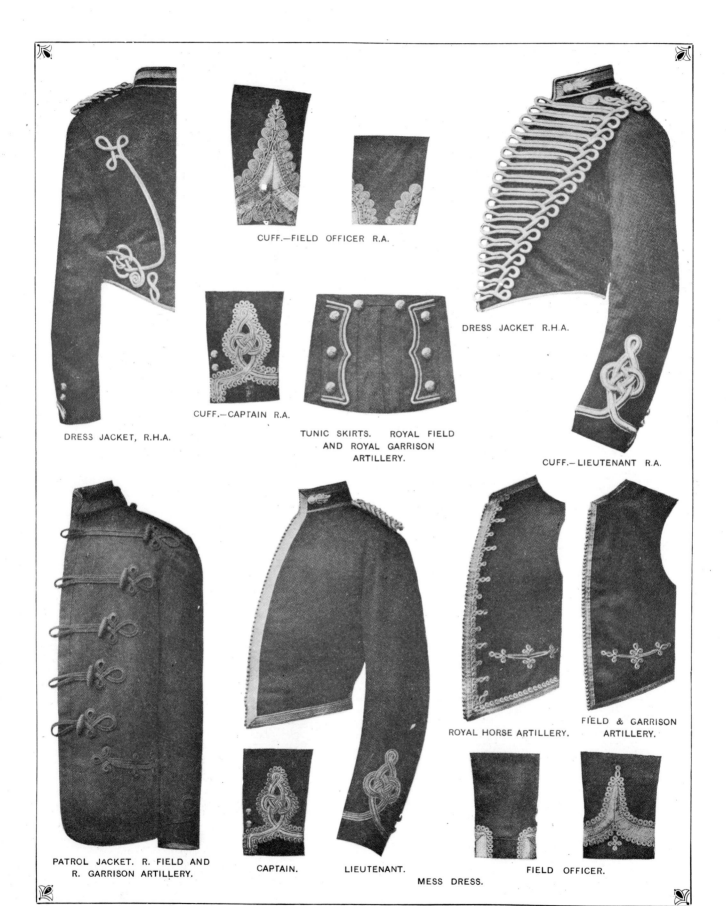

CUFF.—FIELD OFFICER R.A.

DRESS JACKET R.H.A.

CUFF.—CAPTAIN R.A.

DRESS JACKET, R.H.A.

TUNIC SKIRTS. ROYAL FIELD
AND ROYAL GARRISON
ARTILLERY.

CUFF.—LIEUTENANT R.A.

ROYAL HORSE ARTILLERY.

FIELD & GARRISON
ARTILLERY.

PATROL JACKET. R. FIELD AND
R. GARRISON ARTILLERY.

CAPTAIN.

LIEUTENANT.

MESS DRESS.

FIELD OFFICER.

Plate 28.

Royal Artillery.

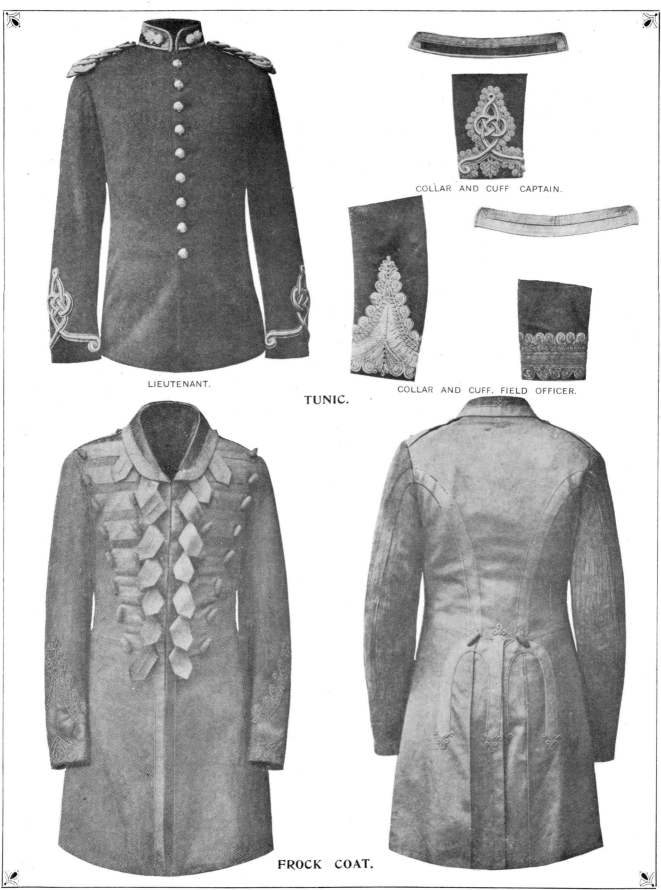

LIEUTENANT.

COLLAR AND CUFF CAPTAIN.

TUNIC.

COLLAR AND CUFF. FIELD OFFICER.

FROCK COAT.

Plate 29.   Royal Engineers.

FROCK.

FIELD OFFICER.

CAPTAIN.

LIEUTENANT.

MESS DRESS.

Plate 30.   Royal Engineers.

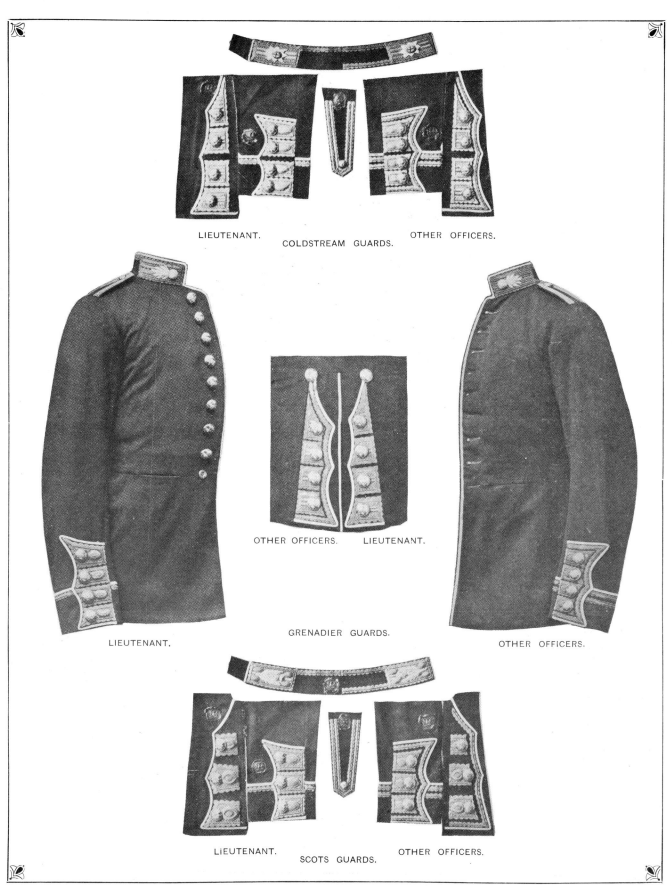

LIEUTENANT.   COLDSTREAM GUARDS.   OTHER OFFICERS.

OTHER OFFICERS.   LIEUTENANT.

LIEUTENANT.   GRENADIER GUARDS.   OTHER OFFICERS.

LIEUTENANT.   SCOTS GUARDS.   OTHER OFFICERS.

Plate 31.   Foot Guards. Tunic, Embroidery, Collars, Cuffs, Skirts, and Shoulder Straps.

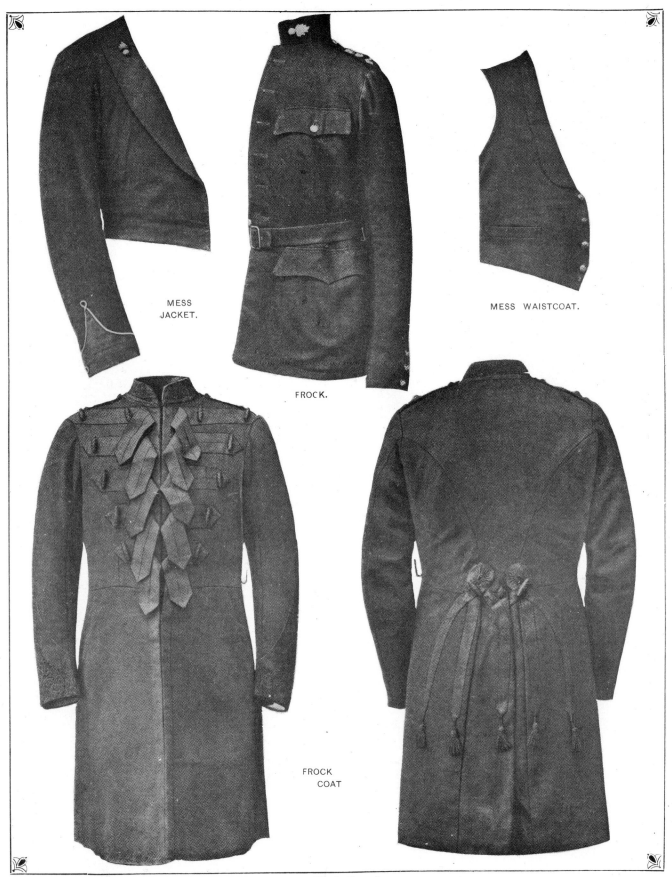

MESS
JACKET.

FROCK.

MESS WAISTCOAT.

FROCK
COAT

Plate 32

Foot Guards

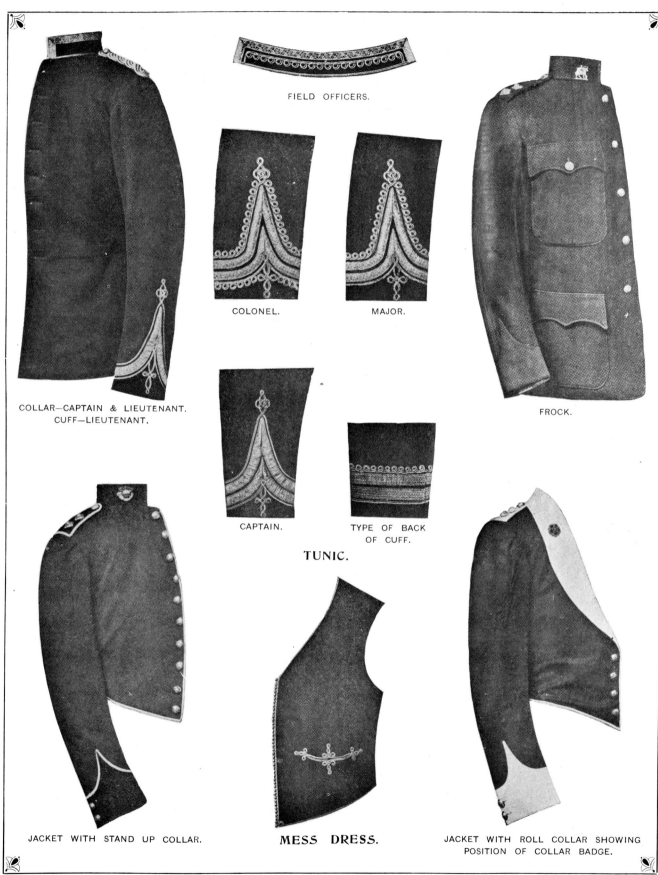

FIELD OFFICERS.

COLONEL.　　　MAJOR.

COLLAR—CAPTAIN & LIEUTENANT.
CUFF—LIEUTENANT.

FROCK.

CAPTAIN.　　TYPE OF BACK
OF CUFF.

TUNIC.

JACKET WITH STAND UP COLLAR.　　MESS DRESS.　　JACKET WITH ROLL COLLAR SHOWING
POSITION OF COLLAR BADGE.

Plate 33.　　　　Infantry of the Line.

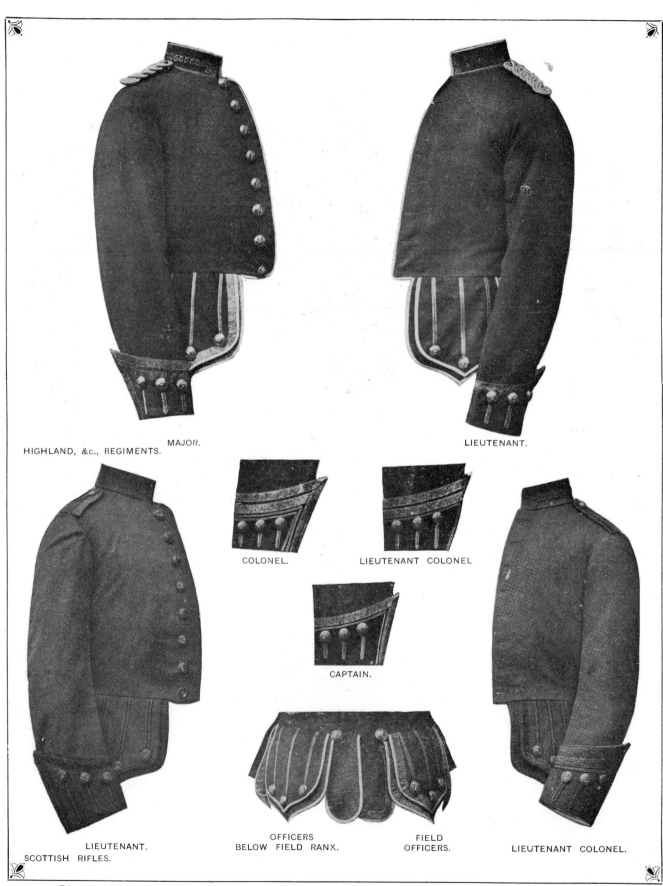

HIGHLAND, &c., REGIMENTS.   MAJOR.

LIEUTENANT.

COLONEL.   LIEUTENANT COLONEL

CAPTAIN.

LIEUTENANT.

SCOTTISH RIFLES.

OFFICERS
BELOW FIELD RANK.

FIELD
OFFICERS.

LIEUTENANT COLONEL.

Plate 34.

Doublet. { **Highland and Scottish Regiments, including Highland Light Infantry, Scottish Rifles.**

See also Plate 36.

HIGHLAND AND SCOTTISH
REGIMENTS.

HIGHLAND LIGHT INFANTRY.

SCOTTISH RIFLES

Plate 35.

Mess Dress.

FIELD OFFICER.

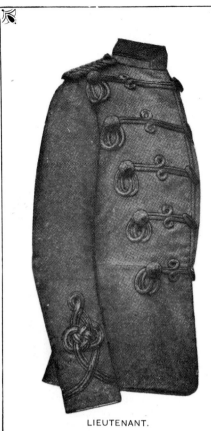

CUFF.—FIELD OFFICER,
ROYAL IRISH RIFLES AND
RIFLE BRIGADE.

CUFF.—FIELD OFFICER,
KING'S ROYAL
RIFLE CORPS.

LIEUTENANT.

TUNIC.

CAPTAIN.

SCOTTISH RIFLES.

RIFLE BRIGADE.

FROCK.
ROYAL SCOTS FUSILIERS.

KING'S ROYAL RIFLE CORPS.
ROYAL IRISH RIFLES.

PATROL JACKET.

Plate 36   Rifle Regiments.

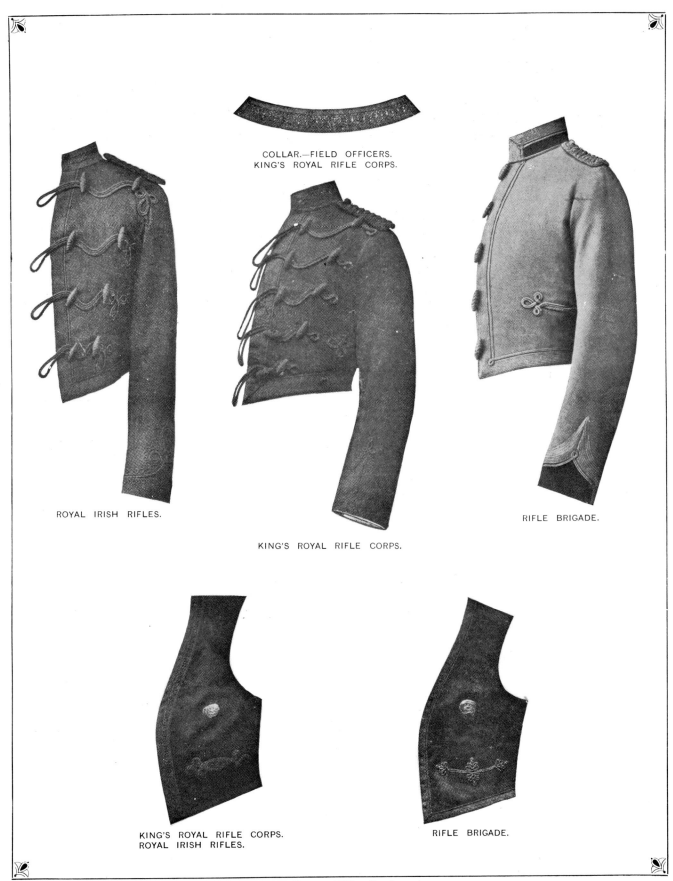

COLLAR.—FIELD OFFICERS.
KING'S ROYAL RIFLE CORPS.

ROYAL IRISH RIFLES.

KING'S ROYAL RIFLE CORPS.

RIFLE BRIGADE.

KING'S ROYAL RIFLE CORPS.
ROYAL IRISH RIFLES.

RIFLE BRIGADE.

Plate 37.   **Mess Dress—Rifle Regiments.**

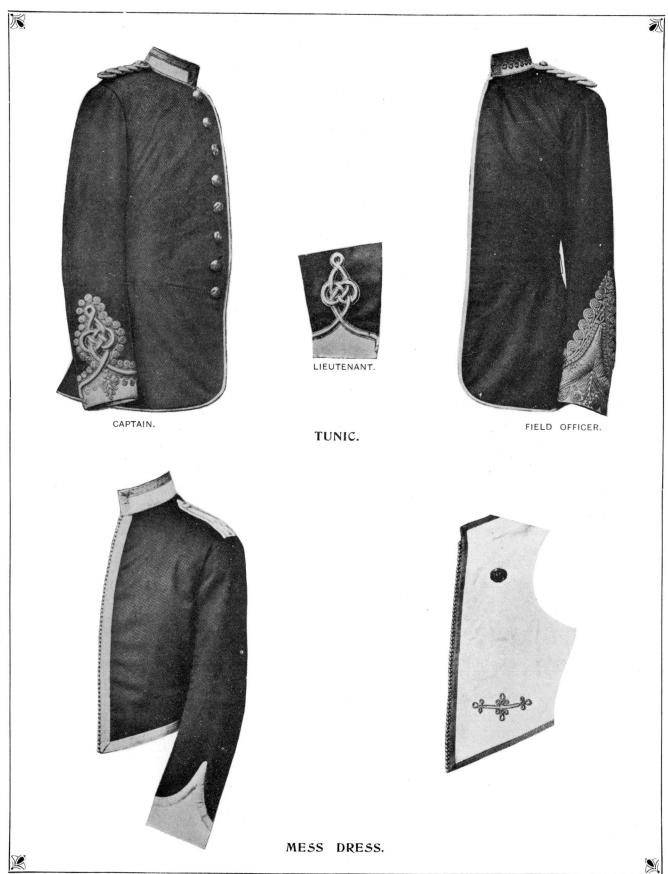

CAPTAIN.

LIEUTENANT.

TUNIC.

FIELD OFFICER.

MESS DRESS.

Plate 38.

Army Service Corps.

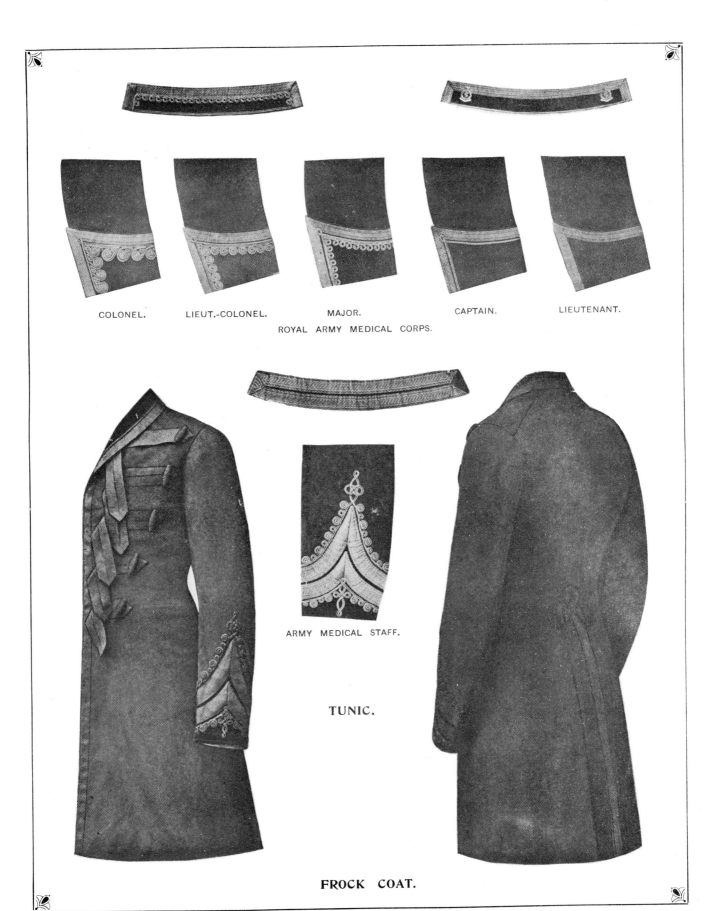

COLONEL.   LIEUT.-COLONEL.   MAJOR.   CAPTAIN.   LIEUTENANT.

ROYAL ARMY MEDICAL CORPS.

ARMY MEDICAL STAFF.

TUNIC.

FROCK COAT.

Plate 39.   Army Medical Service.

PATROL JACKET.

MESS DRESS.

ARMY MEDICAL STAFF.

ROYAL ARMY MEDICAL CORPS.

Plate 40.   **Mess Dress, Army Medical Staff.**
Patrol Jacket & Mess Dress, Royal Army Medical Corps.

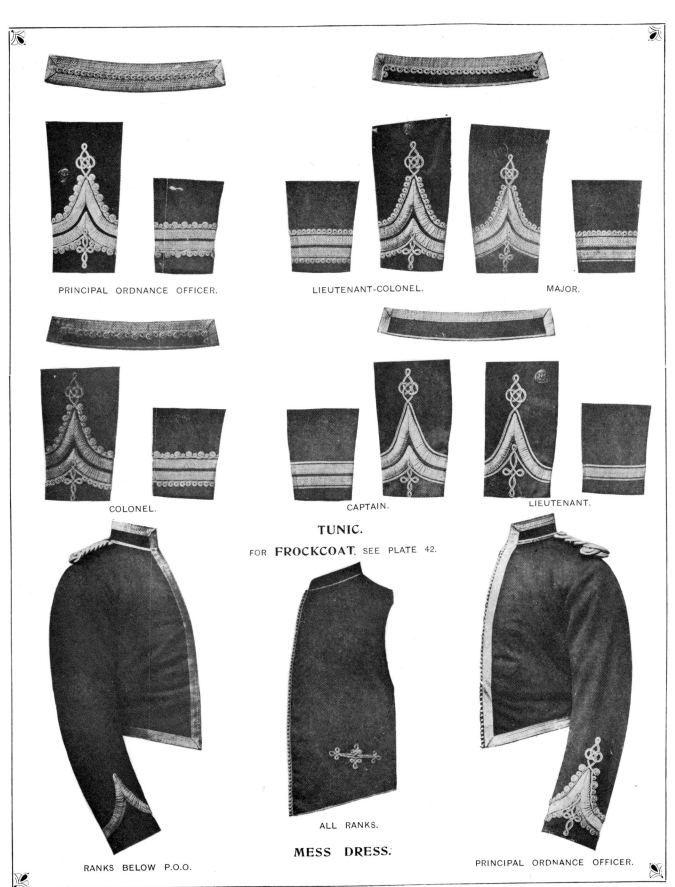

PRINCIPAL ORDNANCE OFFICER.

LIEUTENANT-COLONEL.

MAJOR.

COLONEL.

CAPTAIN.

LIEUTENANT.

TUNIC.

FOR **FROCKCOAT**, SEE PLATE 42.

ALL RANKS.

MESS DRESS.

RANKS BELOW P.O.O.

PRINCIPAL ORDNANCE OFFICER.

Plate 41.   Army Ordnance Corps.

COLONEL
AND LIEUTENANT-COLONEL.

MAJOR.

CAPTAIN.

THE COLLARS & BACKS OF CUFFS ARE AS FOR INFANTRY OF THE LINE.
SEE PLATE 33.

ARMY PAY DEPARTMENT.   **TUNIC.**

ARMY ORDNANCE DEPARTMENT
ARMY PAY DEPARTMENT } **FROCK COAT.**

ARMY PAY DEPARTMENT.

MESS DRESS.

Plate 42.

Army Ordnance Department.
Army Pay Department.

DIRECTOR
GENERAL.   LIEUTENANT
     MAJOR.   COLONEL.   CAPTAIN.   LIEUTENANT.

TUNIC.

FROCK COAT.

MESS DRESS.

PATROL JACKET. ARMY VETERINARY DEPARTMENT.

MAJOR.

TUNIC. PROVOST MARSHAL.

CAPTAIN.

Plate 44.   Patrol Jacket.   Army Veterinary Department.
Tunic.   Provost Marshal.

GREAT COAT—DOMINION OF CANADA.

HIGHLAND REGIMENTS.

TYPE OF
GORGET PATCH.

KHAKI FROCK.

OTHER SERVICES.

Since the above illustrations were prepared, the pockets have been lowered an inch to agree with the Indian patterns.

Plate 45.   **Foreign Service Uniform.**

STAFF OFFICERS.

FORAGE CAP BADGE,
GENERAL OFFICERS.

GARRISON STAFF.

Plate 46.   **Staff.**

2nd LIFE GUARDS.

1st LIFE GUARDS.

ROYAL HORSE GUARDS.

1st (KING'S) DRAGOON
GUARDS.

2nd DRAGOON GUARDS
(QUEEN'S BAYS).

3rd (PRINCE OF WALES'S)
DRAGOON GUARDS.

Cavalry.

Plate 47   BADGES.—FIELD CAP, GLENGARRY and PUGGAREE.

4th (ROYAL IRISH)
DRAGOON GUARDS.

5th (PRINCESS CHARLOTTE OF WALES'S)
DRAGOON GUARDS.

6th DRAGOON GUARDS
(CARABINIERS).

7th (PRINCESS ROYAL'S)
DRAGOON GUARDS.

1st (ROYAL) DRAGOONS

2nd DRAGOONS
(ROYAL SCOTS GREYS).

3rd (KING'S OWN) HUSSARS.

4th (QUEEN'S OWN) HUSSARS.

PUGGAREE BADGE.
5th (ROYAL IRISH) LANCERS.
FOR THE FIELD CAP BADGE
THE CIRCLE IS OMITTED.

Plate 48.   **Badges.**—*Continued.*   **Cavalry of the Line.**

6th (INNISKILLING) DRAGOONS.

PUGGAREE.
7th (QUEEN'S OWN) HUSSARS.

FIELD CAP.

8th (KING'S ROYAL IRISH)
HUSSARS.

9th (QUEEN'S ROYAL) LANCERS.

10th (PRINCE OF WALES'S OWN ROYAL)
HUSSARS.

11th (PRINCE ALBERT'S OWN)
HUSSARS.

12th (PRINCE OF WALES'S ROYAL)
LANCERS.

PUGGAREE BADGE.

13th HUSSARS.

FIELD CAP BADGE.

Plate 49.   Badges.—*Continued*.   Cavalry of the Line.

PUGGAREE BADGE.

FIELD CAP BADGE,

14th (KING'S) HUSSARS.

15th (KING'S) HUSSARS.

16th (QUEEN'S) LANCERS.

17th (DUKE OF CAMBRIDGE'S OWN) LANCERS.

18th HUSSARS.

19th (PRINCE OF WALES'S OWN) HUSSARS.

20th HUSSARS.

21st (EMPRESS OF INDIA'S) LANCERS.

Plate 50. **Badges.**—*Continued.* **Cavalry of the Line.**

ROYAL ARTILLERY FIELD CAP BADGE,

ROYAL ENGINEERS.

PUGGAREE BADGE,
ROYAL ARTILLERY.

FIELD CAP AND PUGGAREE BADGE,
ROYAL MALTA ARTILLERY.

PUGGAREE BADGE.
ROYAL ENGINEERS.

Plate 51. Royal Artillery, Royal Engineers.

PUGGAREE BADGE (½ SIZE),
GRENADIER GUARDS.

PUGGAREE BADGE (½ SIZE),
COLDSTREAM GUARDS.

FIELD CAP BADGE,
GRENADIER GUARDS.

FIELD CAP AND
PUGGAREE BADGE,
IRISH GUARDS.

FIELD CAP BADGE,
COLDSTREAM GUARDS.

FIELD CAP AND PUGGAREE BADGE,
SCOTS GUARDS.

Plate 52. Badges.—Continued. Foot Guards.

THE ROYAL SCOTS
(LOTHIAN REGIMENT).

THE QUEEN'S
(ROYAL WEST SURREY REGIMENT).

THE BUFFS
(EAST KENT REGIMENT).

THE KING'S OWN
(ROYAL LANCASTER REGIMENT).

THE NORTHUMBERLAND
FUSILIERS.

THE ROYAL WARWICKSHIRE
REGIMENT.

PUGGAREE.   FIELD CAP.
THE ROYAL FUSILIERS
(CITY OF LONDON REGIMENT).

THE KING'S
(LIVERPOOL REGIMENT).

THE NORFOLK REGIMENT.

Plate 53.   Badges.—*Continued.*   **Infantry of the Line.**

THE LINCOLNSHIRE REGIMENT.

THE DEVONSHIRE REGIMENT.

THE SUFFOLK REGIMENT.

THE PRINCE ALBERTS'
(SOMERSETSHIRE LIGHT INFANTRY).

(THE PRINCE OF WALES'S OWN).
WEST YORKSHIRE REGIMENT.

THE EAST YORKSHIRE REGIMENT.

THE BEDFORDSHIRE REGIMENT.

THE LEICESTERSHIRE REGIMENT.

THE ROYAL IRISH REGIMENT

Plate 54   **Badges.**—*Continued.*   **Infantry of the Line.**

THE PRINCESS OF WALES'S OWN
(YORKSHIRE REGIMENT).

THE LANCASHIRE FUSILIERS.

ROYAL SCOTS FUSILIERS.

THE KING'S OWN SCOTTISH BORDERERS.

THE CHESHIRE REGIMENT.

THE SOUTH WALES BORDERERS

THE ROYAL WELSH
FUSILIERS.

PUGGAREE BADGE.

GLENGARRY BADGE.

THE CAMERONIANS (SCOTTISH RIFLES).

Plate 55.   **Badges.**—*Continued.*   **Infantry of the Line.**

THE ROYAL INNISKILLING FUSILIERS.

BACK BADGE.

THE GLOUCESTERSHIRE REGIMENT.

THE WORCESTERSHIRE REGIMENT.

THE EAST LANCASHIRE REGIMENT.

THE EAST SURREY REGIMENT

THE DUKE OF CORNWALL'S
LIGHT INFANTRY.

THE DUKE OF WELLINGTON'S
(WEST RIDING REGIMENT).

THE BORDER REGIMENT,

Plate 56.   Badges.—*Continued*.   Infantry of the Line.

THE ROYAL SUSSEX
REGIMENT.

THE HAMPSHIRE REGIMENT.

THE SOUTH STAFFORDSHIRE REGIMENT.

THE DORSETSHIRE REGIMENT.

THE PRINCE OF WALES'S VOLUNTEERS
(SOUTH LANCASHIRE REGIMENT).

THE WELSH REGIMENT.

THE BLACK WATCH
(ROYAL HIGHLANDERS).

THE OXFORDSHIRE LIGHT
INFANTRY.

THE ESSEX REGIMENT.

Plate 57.   **Badges.**—*Continued.*   **Infantry of the Line.**

THE SHERWOOD FORESTERS.
(DERBYSHIRE REGIMENT).

THE LOYAL NORTH
LANCASHIRE REGIMENT.

THE NORTHAMPTONSHIRE
REGIMENT.

PRINCESS CHARLOTTE
OF WALES'S.
(ROYAL BERKSHIRE REGIMENT).

THE QUEEN'S OWN.
(ROYAL WEST KENT REGIMENT).

PUGGAREE BADGE.
FOR THE FIELD CAP, THE BADGE IS
½ THIS SIZE.
THE KING'S OWN.
(YORKSHIRE LIGHT INFANTRY).

THE KING'S.
(SHROPSHIRE LIGHT INFANTRY).

THE DUKE OF CAMBRIDGE'S OWN.
(MIDDLESEX REGIMENT).

PUGGAREE BADGE.

FIELD CAP
BADGE.

THE KING'S ROYAL RIFLE CORPS.

Plate 58.   Badges.—Continued.   Infantry of the Line.

THE DUKE OF EDINBURGH'S
(WILTSHIRE REGIMENT).

THE MANCHESTER
REGIMENT.

THE PRINCE OF WALES'S
(NORTH STAFFORDSHIRE REGIMENT).

THE YORK AND LANCASTER
REGIMENT.

THE DURHAM LIGHT
INFANTRY.

THE HIGHLAND LIGHT
INFANTRY.

SEAFORTH HIGHLANDERS
(ROSS-SHIRE BUFFS,
THE DUKE OF ALBANY'S).

THE GORDON HIGHLANDERS.
(RIGHT FRONT OF BADGE)

THE QUEEN'S OWN
CAMERON HIGHLANDERS.

Plate 59.   Badges.—*Continued.*   Infantry of the Line.

FIELD CAP BADGE.

PRINCESS VICTORIA'S.
(ROYAL
IRISH FUSILIERS).

THE CONNAUGHT
RANGERS.

PUGGAREE BADGE.
THE ROYAL IRISH RIFLES.

PRINCESS LOUISE'S.
(ARGYLL AND SUTHERLAND HIGHLANDERS).

THE PRINCE OF WALES,S
LEINSTER REGIMENT.
(ROYAL CANADIANS).

THE ROYAL
MUNSTER FUSILIERS

THE ROYAL DUBLIN FUSILIERS.

PUGGAREE BADGE.
THE RIFLE BRIGADE.
(THE PRINCE CONSORT'S OWN).

FIELD CAP
BADGE.

WEST INDIA REGIMENT.

Plate 60.   Badges.—*Continued.*   **Infantry of the Line.**

THE ROYAL JERSEY
MILITIA.

THE ROYAL GUERNSEY
MILITIA.

Channel Islands Militia.

ROYAL MALTA REGIMENT
OF MILITIA.

THE ARMY SERVICE CORPS.

ROYAL ARMY MEDICAL CORPS.

ARMY CHAPLAINS.

ARMY ORDNANCE DEPARTMENT.

ARMY PAY DEPARTMENT.
ARMY VETERINARY DEPARTMENT.

INSPECTORS OF ARMY SCHOOLS.

ROYAL MILITARY COLLEGE.

Plate 61.   **Badges.**—*Continued.*   **Departmental Corps, &c.**

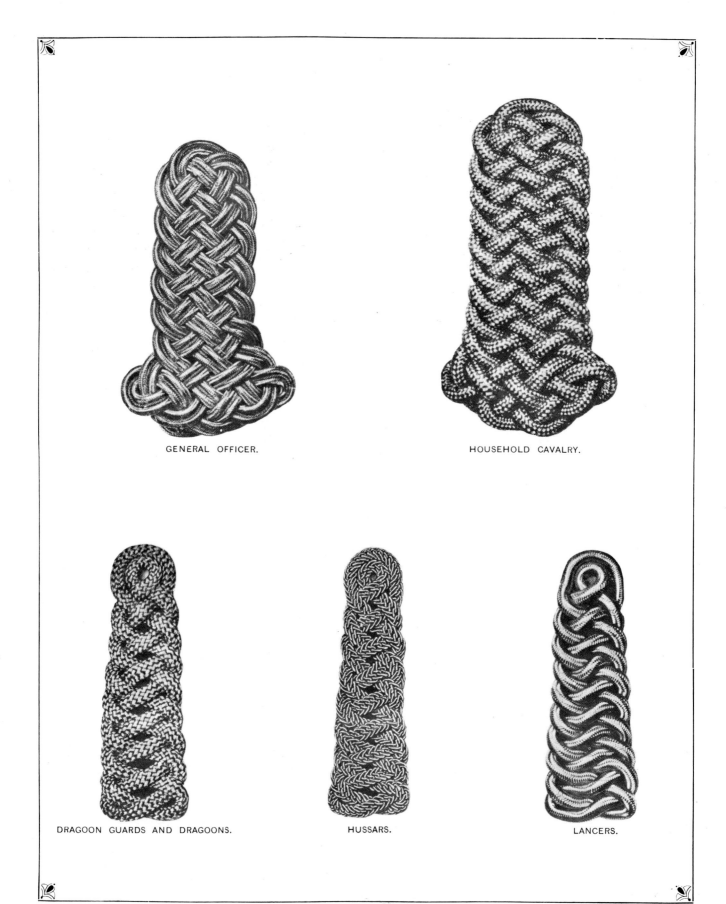

GENERAL OFFICER.

HOUSEHOLD CAVALRY.

DRAGOON GUARDS AND DRAGOONS.

HUSSARS.

LANCERS.

Plate 62.

Shoulder Cords.

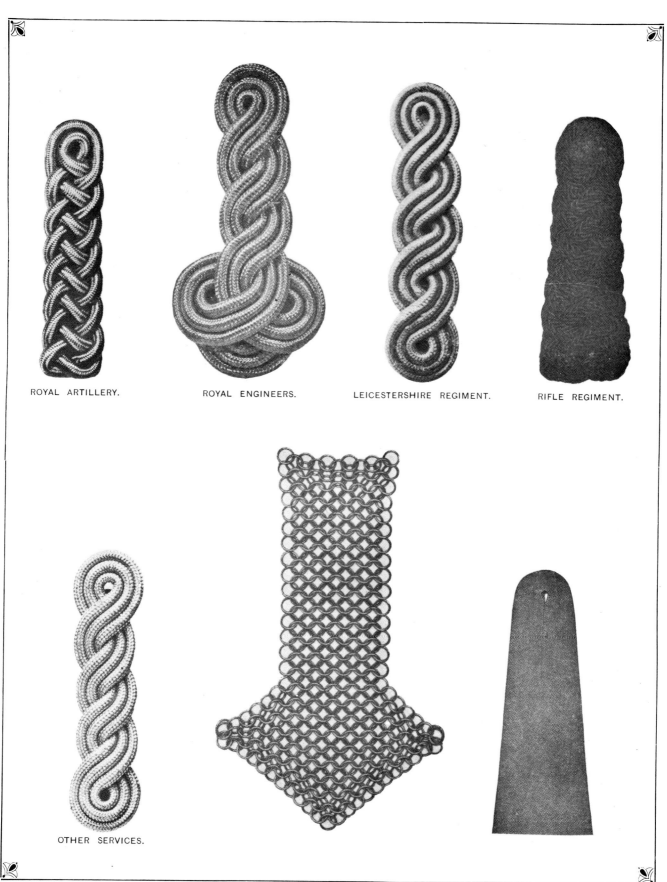

ROYAL ARTILLERY.   ROYAL ENGINEERS.   LEICESTERSHIRE REGIMENT.   RIFLE REGIMENT.

OTHER SERVICES.

Plate 63.   Shoulder Cords, Shoulder Chain, and Shoulder Strap.

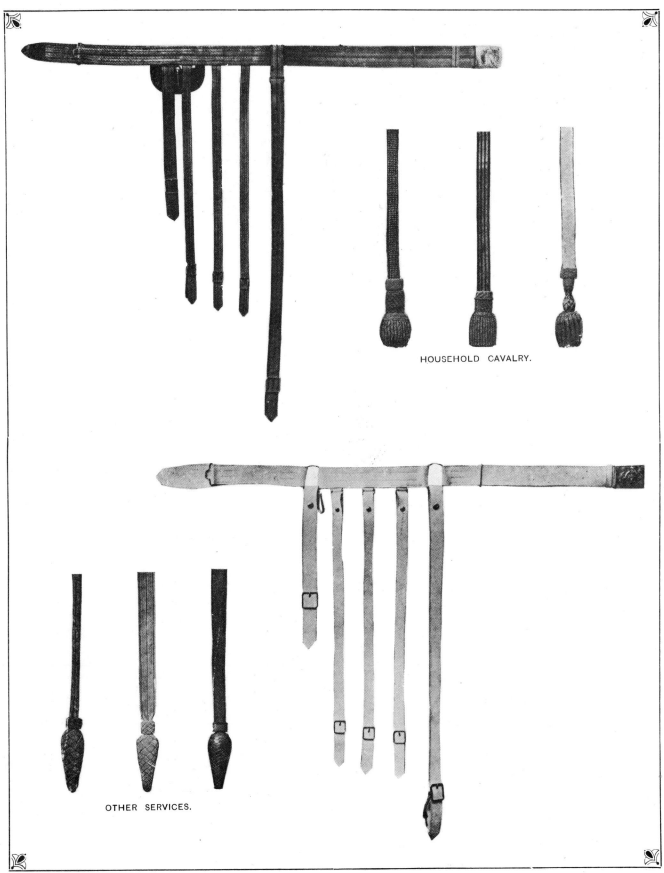

HOUSEHOLD CAVALRY.

OTHER SERVICES.

Plate 64.   Types of Sword Belts—Full-dress and Undress.
Types of Sword Knots.

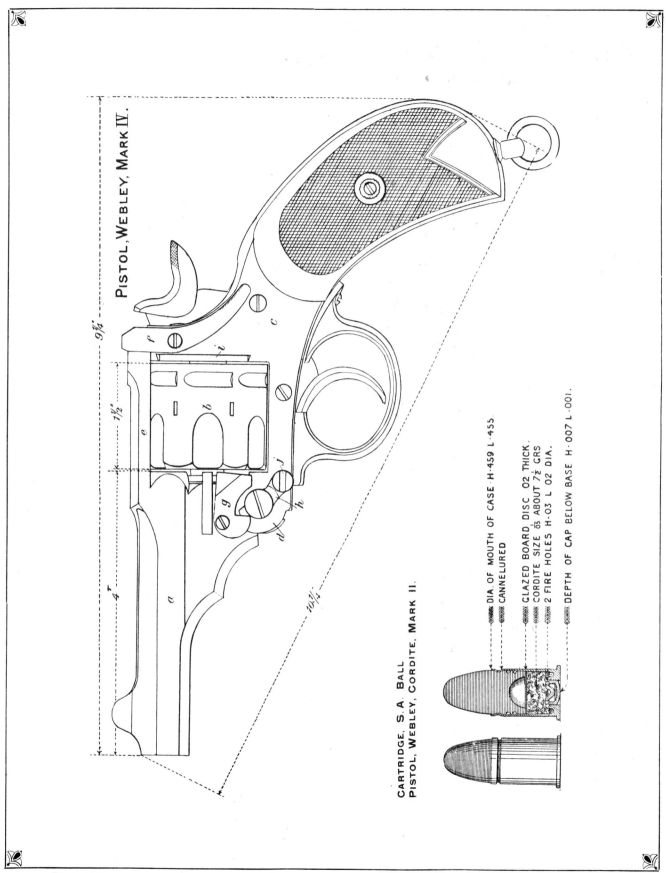

PISTOL, WEBLEY, MARK IV.

9¾"

7½"

4"

10¾"

CARTRIDGE, S. A. BALL
PISTOL, WEBLEY, CORDITE, MARK II.

DIA. OF MOUTH OF CASE. H·459 L·455.
CANNELURED
GLAZED BOARD DISC ·02 THICK.
CORDITE SIZE 65 ABOUT 7½ GRS
2 FIRE HOLES H·03 L ·02 DIA.
DEPTH OF CAP BELOW BASE H·007 L·001.

Plate 65.   Webley Pistol. Mark IV. ¾-size.

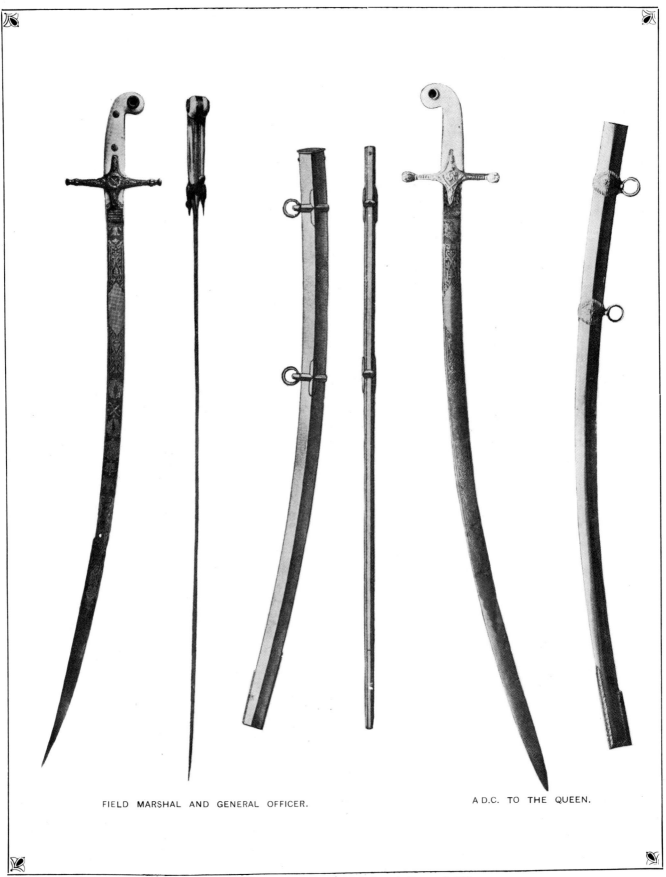

FIELD MARSHAL AND GENERAL OFFICER.   A.D.C. TO THE QUEEN.

Plate 66.   *Sword and Scabbard.* **Field Marshal and General Officer.**
        ,,   ,,   **A.D.C. to the Queen.** $\frac{1}{5}$ **Size.**

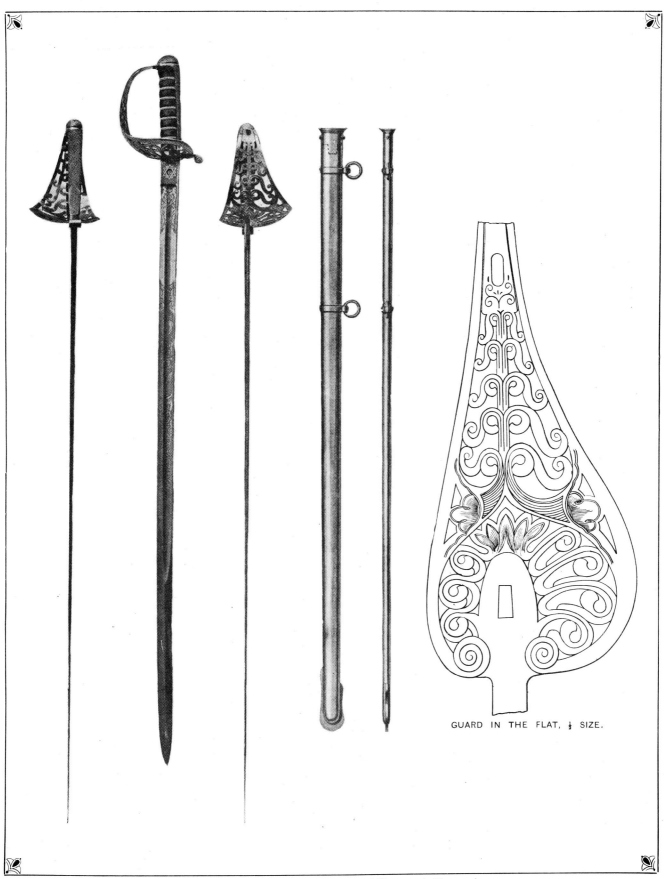

GUARD IN THE FLAT, ⅓ SIZE.

Plate 67.   Sword and Scabbard. Cavalry Officers. ⅕ Size.

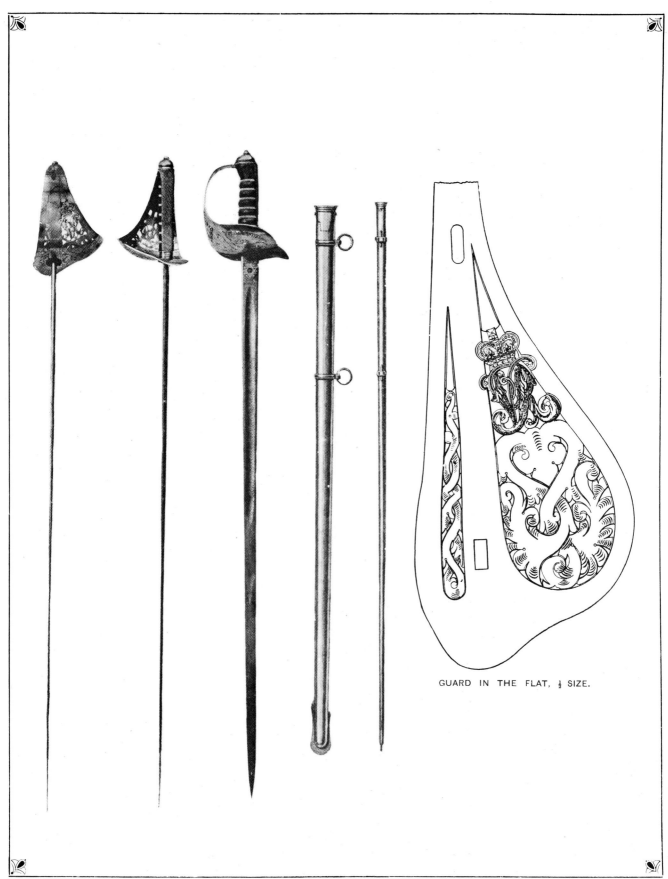

GUARD IN THE FLAT, ½ SIZE.

Plate 68.   Sword and Scabbard.   Infantry Officers.   ⅛ Size.

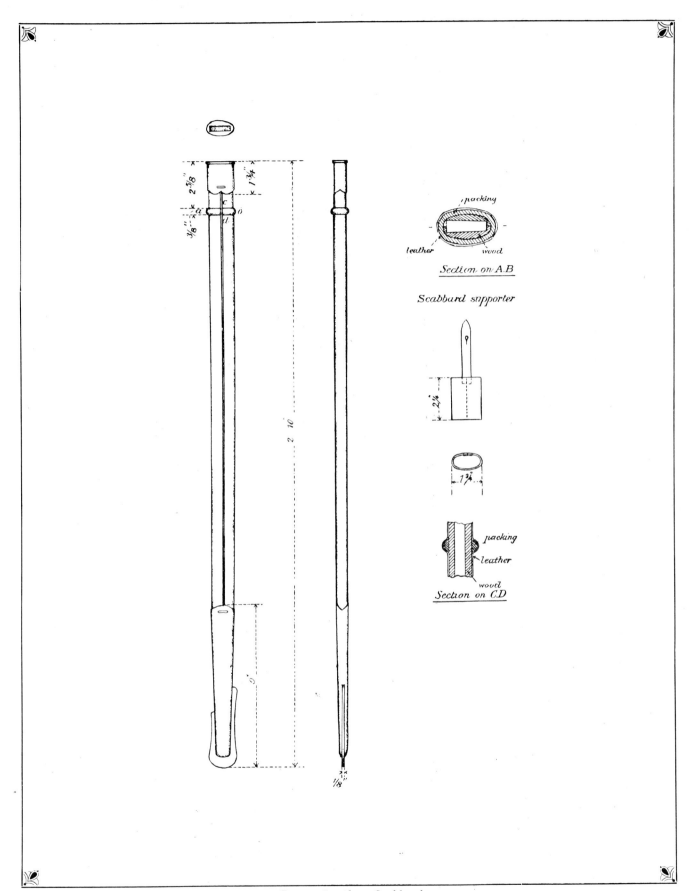

packing

leather wood

Section on A.B

Scabbard supporter

1¾"

packing

leather

wood

Section on CD

Plate 69.   **Brown Leather Scabbard.**

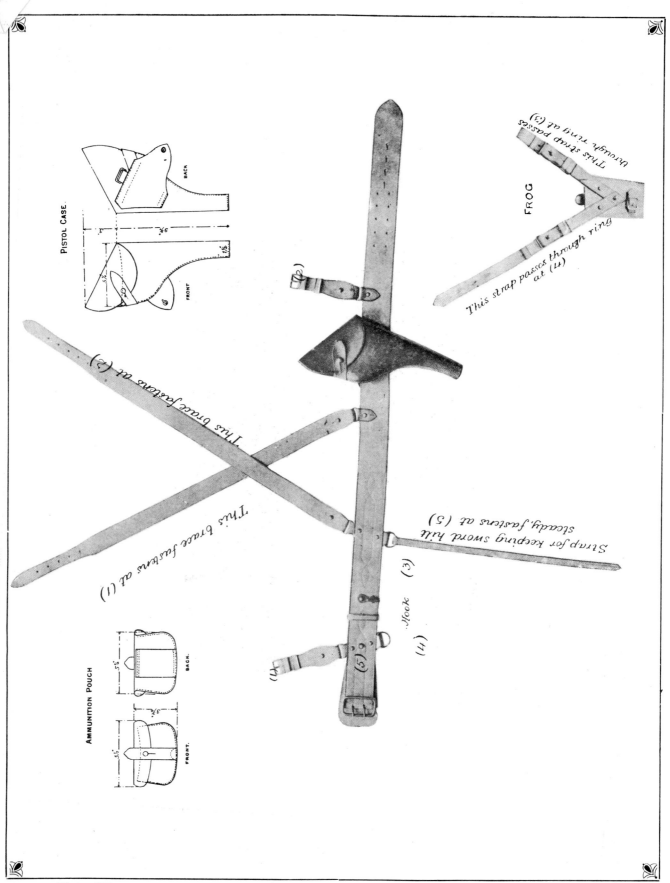

PISTOL CASE.

BACK.

FRONT.

FROG

This strap passes through ring at (3)

This strap passes through ring at (4)

This brace fastens at (2)

This brace fastens at (1)

Strap for keeping sword hilt steady, fastens at (5)

Hook (3)

(4)

(5)

AMMUNITION POUCH

BACK.

FRONT.

Plate 70.   " Sam Browne " Belt.

Plate 71.   15th Hussars.   Leopard Skin and Device.

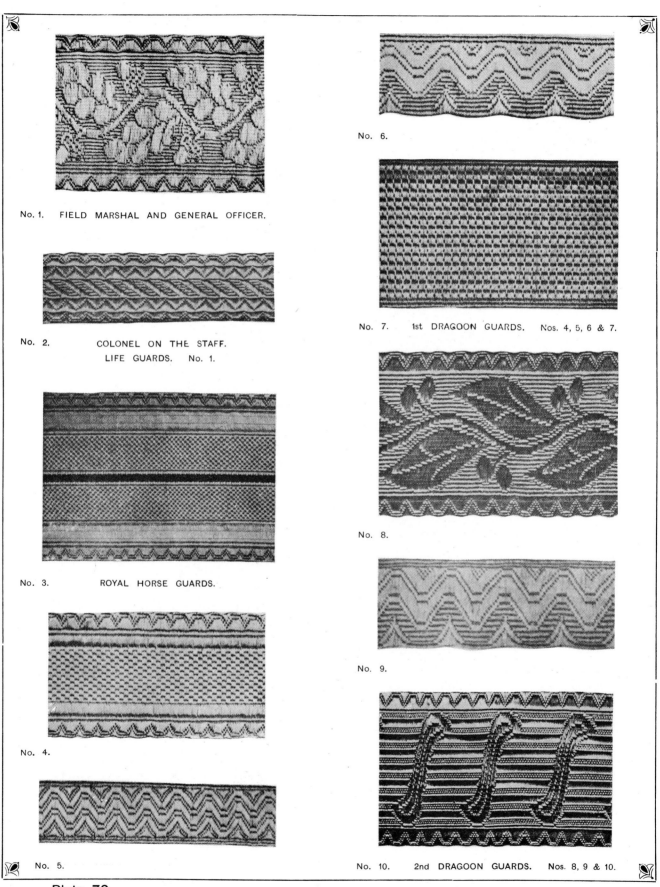

No. 1.   FIELD MARSHAL AND GENERAL OFFICER.

No. 2.   COLONEL ON THE STAFF.
LIFE GUARDS.   No. 1.

No. 3.   ROYAL HORSE GUARDS.

No. 4.

No. 5.

No. 6.

No. 7.   1st DRAGOON GUARDS.   Nos. 4, 5, 6 & 7.

No. 8.

No. 9.

No. 10.   2nd DRAGOON GUARDS.   Nos. 8, 9 & 10.

Plate 72.

DESIGNS FOR LACE.

For width of lace see description of article on which it is worn.

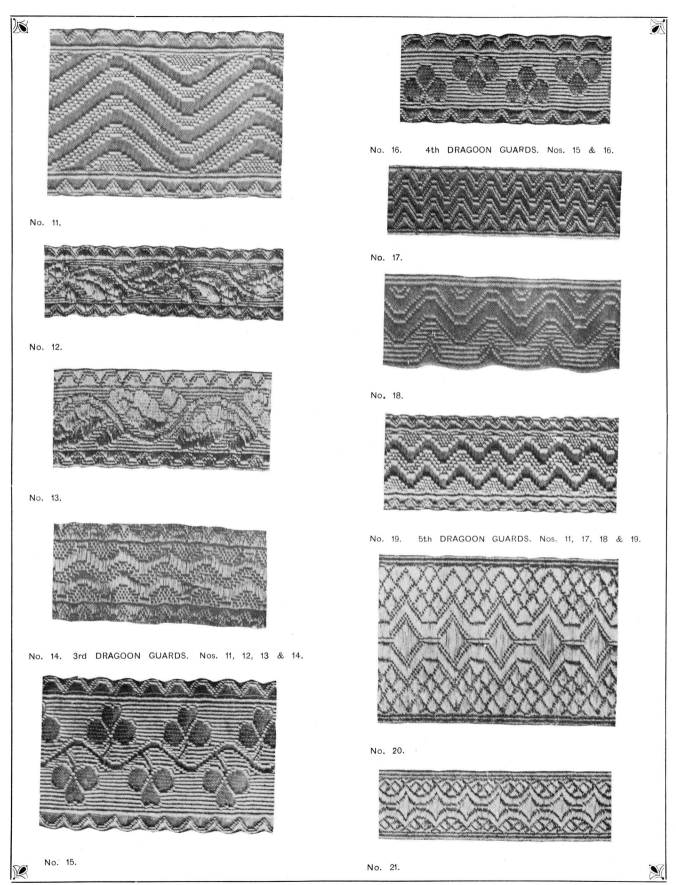

No. 11.

No. 12.

No. 13.

No. 14. 3rd DRAGOON GUARDS. Nos. 11, 12, 13 & 14.

No. 15.

No. 16. 4th DRAGOON GUARDS. Nos. 15 & 16.

No. 17.

No. 18.

No. 19. 5th DRAGOON GUARDS. Nos. 11, 17, 18 & 19.

No. 20.

No. 21.

Plate 73.   **Designs for Lace.**—*Continued.*

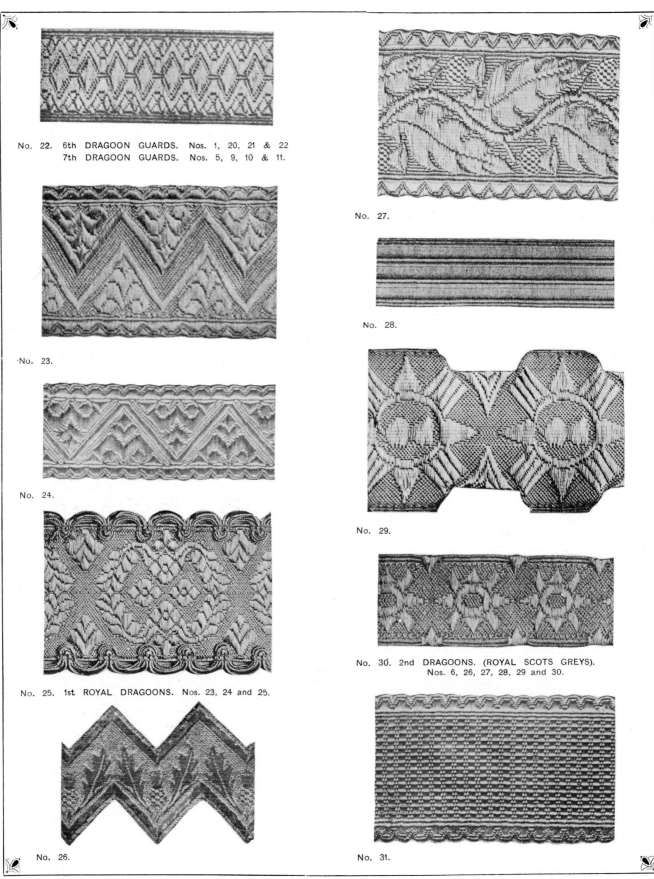

No. 22. 6th DRAGOON GUARDS. Nos. 1, 20, 21 & 22
7th DRAGOON GUARDS. Nos. 5, 9, 10 & 11.

No. 23.

No. 24.

No. 25. 1st ROYAL DRAGOONS. Nos. 23, 24 and 25.

No. 26.

No. 27.

No. 28.

No. 29.

No. 30. 2nd DRAGOONS. (ROYAL SCOTS GREYS).
Nos. 6, 26, 27, 28, 29 and 30.

No. 31.

Plate 74.   **Designs for Lace.**—*Continued.*

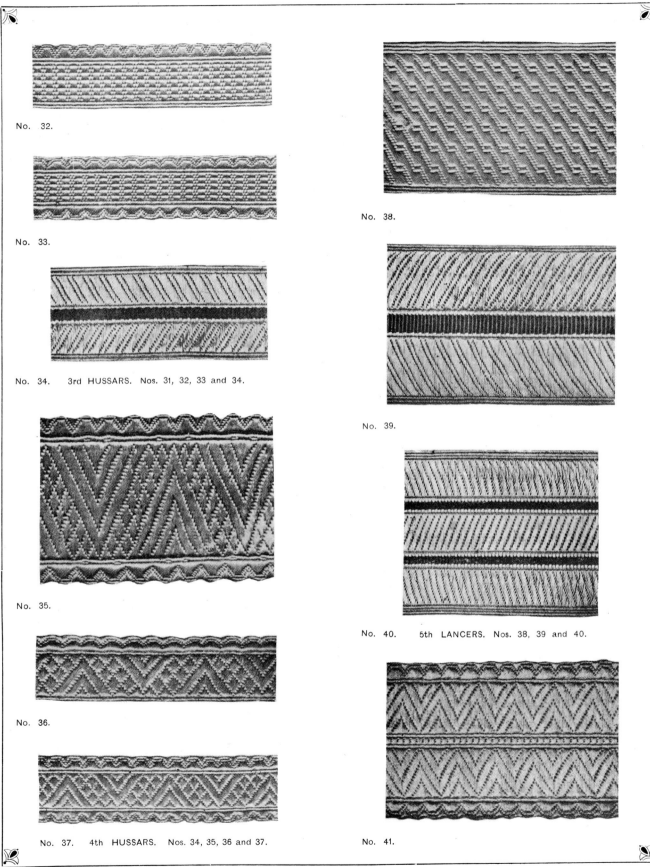

No. 32.

No. 33.

No. 34.   3rd HUSSARS. Nos. 31, 32, 33 and 34.

No. 35.

No. 36.

No. 37.   4th HUSSARS.   Nos. 34, 35, 36 and 37.

No. 38.

No. 39.

No. 40.   5th LANCERS. Nos. 38, 39 and 40.

No. 41.

Plate 75.   Designs for Lace.—*Continued*

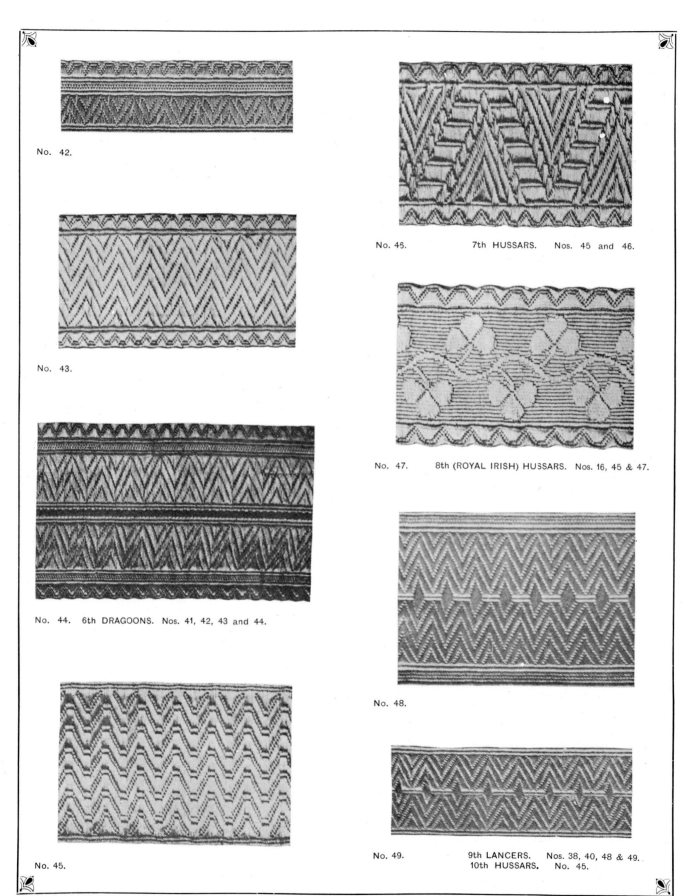

No. 42.

No. 43.

No. 44.   6th DRAGOONS.   Nos. 41, 42, 43 and 44.

No. 45.

No. 46.   7th HUSSARS.   Nos. 45 and 46.

No. 47.   8th (ROYAL IRISH) HUSSARS.   Nos. 16, 45 & 47.

No. 48.

No. 49.   9th LANCERS.   Nos. 38, 40, 48 & 49.
                10th HUSSARS.   No. 45.

Plate 76.   Designs for Lace.—*Continued*.

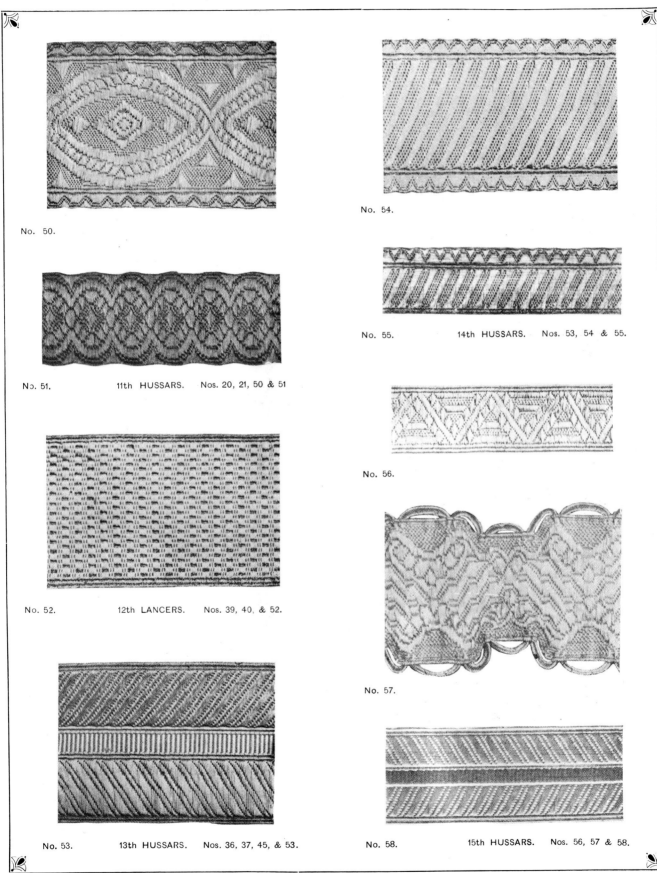

No. 50.

No. 51.　　　11th HUSSARS.　　Nos. 20, 21, 50 & 51

No. 52.　　　12th LANCERS.　　Nos. 39, 40, & 52.

No. 53.　　　13th HUSSARS.　　Nos. 36, 37, 45, & 53.

No. 54.

No. 55.　　　14th HUSSARS.　　Nos. 53, 54 & 55.

No. 56.

No. 57.

No. 58.　　　15th HUSSARS.　　Nos. 56, 57 & 58.

Plate 77.　　　Designs for Lace.—*Continued.*

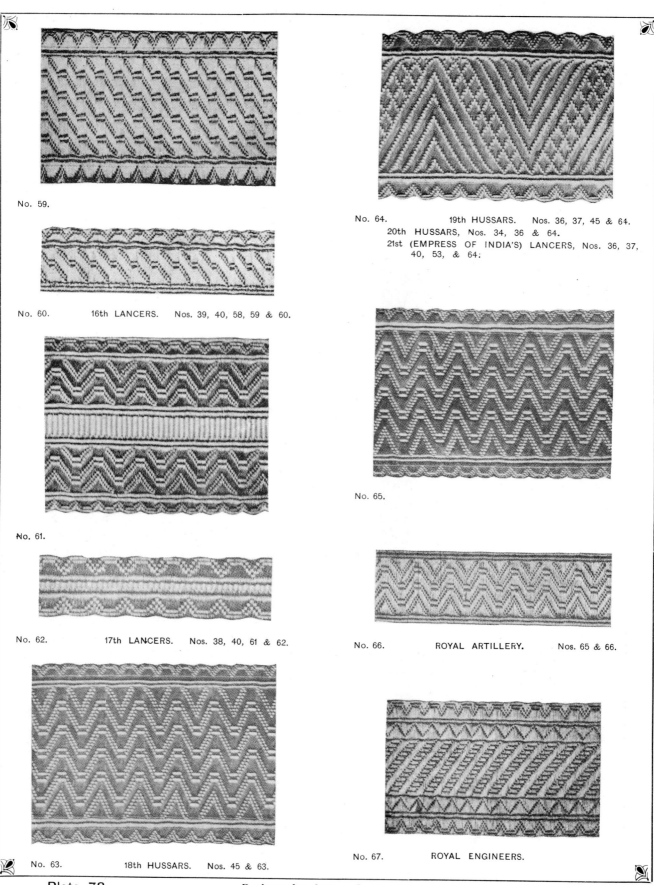

No. 59.

No. 60.　　16th LANCERS.　Nos. 39, 40, 58, 59 & 60.

No. 61.

No. 62.　　17th LANCERS.　Nos. 38, 40, 61 & 62.

No. 63.　　18th HUSSARS.　Nos. 45 & 63.

No. 64.　　　　19th HUSSARS.　Nos. 36, 37, 45 & 64.
20th HUSSARS, Nos. 34, 36 & 64.
21st (EMPRESS OF INDIA'S) LANCERS, Nos. 36, 37, 40, 53, & 64:

No. 65.

No. 66.　　ROYAL ARTILLERY.　Nos. 65 & 66.

No. 67.　　　ROYAL ENGINEERS.

Plate 78.　　Designs for Lace.—*Continued.*

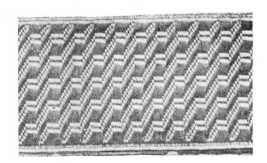

No. 68.   BRIGADE OF FOOT GUARDS.

No. 69.   ENGLISH REGIMENTS.

No. 70.   SCOTCH REGIMENTS.

No. 71.   IRISH REGIMENTS.

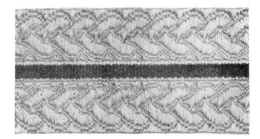

No. 72.   INFANTRY, Nos. 69, 70, 71 & 72.

No. 73.   WEST INDIA REGIMENT, Nos. 72 & 73.

No. 74.   ARMY SERVICE CORPS, Nos. 2 & 74.
ARMY ORDNANCE CORPS.
  ,,   PAY DEPARTMENT.   } Nos. 2 & 74.
  ,,   VETERINARY DEPARTMENT.   }

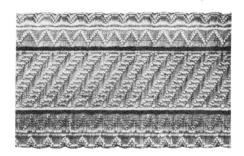

No. 75.   ARMY MEDICAL STAFF AND
    ROYAL ARMY MEDICAL CORPS, Nos. 2 & 75.

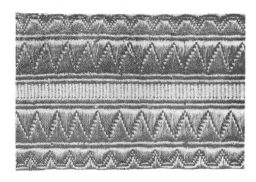

No. 76.
    INSPECTORS OF ARMY SCHOOLS; Nos. 69 & 76.

No. 77.
        OFFICERS, ROYAL MILITARY COLLEGE.
CAPTAINS AND LIEUTENANTS OF INVALIDS, Nos. 72 & 77.

Plate 79   Designs for Lace.—*Continued.*